Scorn

SCORN

Matthew Parris

Published in the United Kingdom in 2009 by Max Press,
Little Books Limited, London W11 3QP

10 9 8 7 6 5 4 3 2 1

A CIP catalogue record for this book is available from the British Library.

ISBN: 978 1 906251 28 4

Printed in the UK by CPI Bookmarque, Croydon, CR0 4TD

CONTENTS

Contents

INTRODUCTION

For the greatly enlarged twenty-first-century edition of this anthology my assistant editor, Tom Mitchelson, and I have stuck to the guiding principle of including quotations quite capriciously – because we like them or are struck by the novelty or originality – and occasionally excluding what we're bored with or consider too well known already.

The world remembers well enough what Churchill said to Bessie Braddock when she accused him of being drunk. Churchill is well represented here, of course – as are Dorothy Parker, Oscar Wilde, and all those others upon whom the journalist too pushed to check may fall back by writing "Was it Dorothy Parker who said ...?" and comfort himself that the answer may well be 'No', but readers can always write to tell him so.

Beside the great and famous swords of malice, however, there are some marvellous and little-recorded daggers from the last decade. There are remarks, too – by, for instance, or about, our current crop of political leaders – which may not be particularly clever but are satisfying for their topicality. Tony Blair's (alleged) 'fucking Welsh' wins no award for elegance, but somehow sticks in the mind – as does his 'big, clunking fist' description of Gordon Brown.

The book is not therefore a comprehensive dictionary, nor is it a roll-call of rhetorical merit, but a whimsical collection. Our new index tries to include the butts of others' scorn as well as the authors of the scorn itself. Look yourself up, Piers Morgan – you're there on both counts.

So, this is not a textbook. I have not strung out the entries in a dry, chronological list. Nor have I attempted to divide them into neat sections – 'attacks on honour', 'attacks on appearance', 'attacks on ability', etc. – or where would you put the remark that a man's an incompetent, warty scoundrel? Instead, I have tried to order these quotations in a way that allows them to speak, one to another.

Scanning my chosen remarks, many struck me as voices answering, echoing or rebuking each other down the ages. Often there seemed to be a dialogue going on, sometimes between people who had never heard of each other, sometimes between people who had. So I have tried to arrange my quotations as a sort of conversation, a 'rally'. Often – not always – this works well. Sometimes the thread linking the dialogue is tenuous. Occasionally it may break. Rallies are not continuous. More than once a new voice will take the ball and run with it to a different court. But the feelings and ideas which link human expressions of scorn have enough in common to bounce these quotations off each other in a verbal sport which, at least sometimes, finds meaning and momentum.

The direction of the conversation has been signposted, by topic, very broadly in the headings at the top of each page, and there is an index of authors and victims at the end. But I hope that this dialogue of voices has enough shape to invite its being read as a play, rather than consulted as a directory.

A play or directory of what? There are many excellent anthologies of insult, which I have consulted freely, some of which are credited in the Acknowledgements. But they leave so much out. 'Insult' is too restrictive. 'Scorn' became my chosen title, for language can be used to express anger, hatred or disapprobation in a range of ways of which simple insult is only a part. When Job curses the day he was conceived, he scorns life itself, but this is not really an insult. When Hobbes describes human society as 'nasty, brutish, and short', that is scorn, not insult. Neither is 'witty'. Neither are 'put-downs'. Wit and put-down – taking a verbal dig at others – are part of scorn, but not the whole of it. What I have tried to explore has been the dark side of language: humorous or serious, the use of the spoken and written word to hurt, wound or ridicule – to decry not just other persons but things too: and art, and life, and God himself.

The language of scorn, though vast, finds itself pursuing one or more of only four purposes. The first purpose is part factual, part polemical: the *indictment* – the conveying of hurtful facts or a hurtful argument. The literature is enormous and a little outside my theme; it finds a handful of examples in this book, such as Burke's indictment of Warren Hastings and Geoffrey Howe's of Margaret Thatcher.

The second is not to persuade or inform but to discomfort by a reference to existing, agreed knowledge: *mockery* – words which allude to something already known or suspected but whose mention, precisely because it is known, is hurtful. It could be, for example, a reference to someone's big nose or humble parentage, or a physical or moral defect, a failing.

A third purpose of scorn comprises the very simplest form of abuse: the nose-thumb or *snarl*. This is the use of language in circumstances where the alternative might be to spit, an expression of pure hatred: 'I loathe you' or 'ya-boo-sucks'. Such abuse conveys neither reason nor justification for the scorn; it conveys the scorn alone.

And finally the most curious of the four: the *curse* – a verbal formula used to invoke some malign external power to hurt one's victim. This uses words as we might use a pin to stick in a voodoo doll.

It is fascinating to observe the decline in the potency and

frequency of real cursing between ancient times and our own. God and the prophets do a great deal of it in the Old (and to some extent the New) Testament. Judaism and Islam use the curse. So did the ancient Egyptians – we include here a desecrator's curse. In early times, in primitive cultures now, and very strongly in Eastern European cultures today, the use of language to curse is rich and lively, while the use of wit, indictment and other verbal abuse is often disappointingly crude.

As faith in the supernatural declines, so does the living curse. It degenerates into a notional curse ('damn you', 'a plague on both your houses') which neither alludes to any actual failing nor conveys real information. It takes the form of a curse but is not a true curse: it is just a snarl. Modern cursing, though common, is uninteresting and routine because its soul is dead. We have lost our link with the supernatural. Correspondingly, other forms of scorn have been getting cleverer and wittier since the ancients. Words, stripped of the innate magical powers invoked by the simple act of pronouncing them, are obliged to carry interest and meaning in their own right.

As I gathered material for this book it became clear that the curse is really a subject on its own, and needs an anthology of its own; it cannot be properly integrated into other forms of verbal abuse. But it is too interesting to ignore. I have therefore included, along with ancient, primitive, and ethnic abuse, a short section in which a sampler of curses, from ancient to modern times, is assembled more as a list than a dialogue.

Scorn has not been difficult to collect. The British Library, the Cambridge University Library, and appeals for suggestions to some 500 people in public or academic life have brought in a wealth of material. The problem, as ever, has been what to leave out. For a short book one must leave out most. This collection is therefore utterly and unapologetically idiosyncratic.

I have had a problem with Shakespeare. His work alone yields a treasury of insult, and such a collection has already been published. But, though he provides both wit and argument in his scorning, Shakespeare is really outstanding for his simple, schoolboyish, but verbally dazzling *mockery*. A glance at his vocabulary of insult gives the impression of relentless verbal heavy-shelling of a gloriously crude kind: 'Thou drone, thou snail, thou slug, thou sot', 'breath of garlic-eaters!', 'you mad mustachio purple-hued maltworns!', 'leathern-jerkin, crystal-button, not-pated, agate-ring, puke-stocking, caddis-garter, smooth-tongue, Spanish pouch!', 'Whoreson, obscene, greasy tallow-catch', 'oh polished perturbation!', 'you Banbury cheese!', 'show your sheep-biting face', 'stale old mouse-eaten dry cheese', 'I will smite his noddles!', 'you whoreson upright rabbit!', 'you fustilarian! I'll tickle your catastrophe!'. You could fill a book with this; I have decided to let others do so. Fascinating – to me – has been what, in Shakespeare's case, the insults reveal about the insulter. Scorn tells us much – unwittingly – about the tastes and prejudices of the scorner. Shakespeare's real horror was of grossness. He hated urine, foul odours and uncleanness. Unlike many others, he rarely attacks women, but can be coldly, horribly dismissive of them. I have become convinced that Shakespeare was a fastidious gay man.

Scorn also reveals much about the offensive-defensive divide. Its literature is crammed full – starting spectacularly with the Romans – of anti-homosexual invective, the key image being that of the effeminate, passive gay man who is buggered by others. Now, though, we begin to find confident answering invective from the gay camp. There is much anti-Semitic insult, less insult returned. Anti-black invective is prodigious and rich; anti-white invective is edgy, defensive and scarce.

Eschewing political correctness, we've included much. Finally, attribution has often been a problem. A handful of individuals in political and literary history – Dr Johnson, Disraeli, Churchill, Dorothy Parker, for instance – have become so famous for their wit and scorn that the world has begun to attribute to them sayings which more careful research reveals were not theirs. Further, famous scorners begin to attract their Boswells, and find their conversation recorded and remembered, where ours would be forgotten, or unattributed. It seems that if you acquire a sufficiently powerful reputation for insult, the reputation will begin to grow by its own momentum, as everything you say is noted, and extra sayings of unknown authorship are attributed, speculatively, to you.

Gathering this collection has been fun. But more than a year of staring at unremitting lists of unpleasant remarks does, eventually, lower the spirits. We are looking forward to raising our eyes at last from the bucketful of misery and spite which follows.

Matthew Parris
Derbyshire

ACKNOWLEDGMENTS

Nothing in this book is new. To my assistant editor, Tom Mitchelson, and my helpers for earlier editions, David Prosser and Simon Christmas, has fallen the task of gathering the mountain from which I have assembled this personal molehill of an anthology. They have worked hard for many months, and I am grateful. I have relied not only on their industry, but on their judgment.

My thanks to those hundreds of friends and long-shot acquaintances whom we contacted for suggestions, many of which have found their way into the book. Thanks too to Dr Richard Parkinson at the British Museum and to the editors of dozens of dictionaries, anthologies and works of reference in this field, on whose research we have drawn. These are too numerous to list in full, but the following have been particularly useful.

An Anthology of Invective and Abuse, ed. Hugh Kingsmill (London, 1930); *A Dictionary of Contemporary Quotations*, ed. Jonathan Green (London, 1982); *A Dictionary of International Slurs*, ed. A.A. Roback (Wisconsin, 1979); *A Dictionary of Sexist Quotations*, ed. Selma James (Hemel Hempstead, 1984); *The Garden of Priapus: Sexuality and Aggression in Roman Humour* by Amy Richlin (London, 1983); *The Guinness Dictionary of Poisonous Quotes*, ed. Colin Jarman (London, 1991); *Lexicon of Musical Invective* by Nicholas Slonimsky (Washington, DC, 1965); *Maledicta: The International Journal of Verbal Aggression*, ed. Rheinhold Aman (1977-86); *Picking on Men* by Judy Allen (London, 1985); *Shakespeare's Insults*, ed. Wayne Hill and Cynthia J. Ottchen (Cambridge, 1992); *Far Too Noisy, My Dear*

Mozart, ed. Jennifer Higgie (Michael O'Mara Books, 1997).

Acknowledgement is also due to HarperCollins Publishers Limited and Germaine Greer for *The Female Eunuch*; to William Heinemann Limited for *Cakes and Ale* by W.Somerset Maugham; to Guy Lee for *The Poems of Catullus* (OUP, 1990) by permission of Oxford University Press; to The Society of Authors on behalf of the Bernard Shaw Estate; to John Murray (Publishers) Limited for *Slough* by John Betjeman; to Laurence Pollinger Limited and the Estate of Frieda Lawrence Ravagli for *How Beastly the Bourgeois Is* by D.H.Lawrence; to David Higham Associates and Osbert Sitwell for *A Certain Statesman*; to Channel 4 and Open Media Limited for the Dennis Potter; and to Faber and Faber Limited for the following extracts: Phillip Larkin's 'This be the Verse' from *High Windows*; W.H. Auden's *Six Odes IV (To John Warner, Son of Rex and Frances Warner)*; and John Osborne's *Look Back in Anger*, and to Matthew d'Ancona, Editor of The Spectator, for permission to quote from the magazine's attack on Liverpool. For more than a decade *The Week* has offered us a discerning pick.

The illustrations on pages xv and 118 are reprinted courtesy of the British Museum Department of Egyptian Antiquities and the British Library respectively.

Every effort has been made to trace copyright holders. The author and publishers apologise for any errors or omissions, and would be grateful to be notified of any corrections that should appear in any reprint.

Finally, a word of thanks to my dear secretary, Eileen Wright, who would never sanction language such as may be found on the next page – to which, please now turn.

Come'ere, you fucker.

This, the earliest recorded insult I have found, dates from around 2300 BC. It is from the tomb of Ti at Saqqara, Egypt. The hieroglyph (circled) is fairly self-explanatory. Academics have rendered the insult, which one fisherman is hurling at another, as "Come here, you copulator".

Woman was God's *second* mistake.
  Friedrich Nietzsche

When God made man, she was only testing.
  Graffiti in ladies' lavatory, London W1 1

They are crabbed as constant companions
haughty when visited,
lewd when neglected...
stubborn in a quarrel,
not to be trusted with a secret...
boisterous in their jealousy...
lustful in bed...
Better to whip than to humour them...
better to scourge than to gladden them...
They are waves that drown you,
they are fires that burn you...
they are moths for sticking to one,
they are serpents for cunning...
  The Instructions of King Cormac MacAirt

'O Grandson of Conn, O Cormac,' said Carbre,
'how do you distinguish women?'
'Not hard to tell,' said Cormac. 'I distinguish them,
but I make no difference among them.'

God created Adam, lord of all living creatures,
but Eve spoiled it all.
  Martin Luther

To what purpose is it for women to make vows, when men have so many millions of ways to make them break them? And when sweet words, fair promises, tempting, flattering, swearing, lying will not serve to beguile the poor soul, then with rough handling, violence and plain strength of arms they are, or have been heretofore, rather made prisoners to lust's thieves than wives and companions to faithful honest lovers.

The Law's Resolutions of Woman's Rights, *published anonymously 1632 but probably written in the 1580s*

All men are rapists and that's all they are. They rape us with their eyes, their laws and their cocks.

Marilyn French

The male is by nature superior, and the female inferior: the one rules and the other is ruled.

Aristotle, Politics, I.5

The difference between rape and seduction is salesmanship.

Bill Carpenter, mayor of Independence, Missouri

A good part – and definitely the most fun part – of being a feminist is about frightening men… Of course, there's a lot more to feminism… but scaring the shit out of the scumbags is an amusing and necessary part because, sadly, a good many men still respect nothing but strength.

Julie Burchill, in Time Out

The male function is to produce sperm. We now have sperm banks.

Valerie Solanas, in S C.U.M. Manifesto

Nature intended women to be our slaves... they are our property; we are not theirs. They belong to us, just as a tree that bears fruit belongs to a gardener. What a mad idea to demand equality for women! ...Women are nothing but machines for producing children.

Napoleon Bonaparte

Marie Stopes was living with him, an arrangement which I would have thought would satisfy any woman's craving for birth control.

Muriel Spark on Lord Douglas and the campaigner for contraception, Marie Stopes

It's a pity it was not her parents, rather than her, who thought of birth control.

Muriel Spark on Marie Stopes

I myself have never been able to find out precisely what feminism is: I only know that people call me a feminist whenever I express sentiments that differentiate me from a doormat.

Rebecca West

I consider that women who are authors, lawyers and politicians are monsters.

Auguste Renoir

When a woman inclines to learning there is usually something wrong with her sex apparatus.

Friedrich Nietzsche

I would venture to guess that Anon, who wrote so many poems without signing them, was often a woman.

Virginia Woolf, A Room of One's Own

Woman who can, do. Those who cannot, become feminists.
Anonymous

A very little wit is valued in a woman; as we are pleased with a few words spoken plain by a parrot.
Jonathan Swift, Thoughts on Various Subjects

Sir, a woman's preaching is like a dog's walking upon his hinder legs. It is not done well; but you are surprised to find it done at all.
Samuel Johnson

I have always been amazed that women are allowed to enter churches. What sort of conversations can they have with God?
Charles Baudelaire

It is clearly absurd that it should be possible for a woman to qualify as a saint with direct access to the Almighty while she may not qualify as a curate.
Mary Stocks

We have no desire to say anything that might tend to encourage women to embark on accountancy, for although women might make excellent book-keepers, there is much in accountancy proper that is, we think, unsuitable for them.
English Institute of Chartered Accountants, in the Accountant, *1912*

All women are little balls of fluff in the eyes of the Creator.
Donald Pomerleau, Baltimore Police Commissioner, testifying in a sex discrimination case

Then their itch can't bear delay, then woman acts her true
self, and from all equally the shout is repeated from the
whole apse, 'Now it's right, let in the men.' The adulterer is
asleep, she orders a boy to grab his cloak and hurry over; if
there is none, she runs to the slaves; if you take away the
hope of slaves, the milkman comes, for a fee; if he is sought
and there are no men, there's no delay, for her part, in
putting her butt under a donkey.

Juvenal on women, VI. 327-34, tr. Amy Richlin

What a mighty man he turns out to be! He raped ten women
– I would never have expected this from him. He surprised us
all. We all envy him.

*Vladimir Putin, Russian President, to visiting Israeli Prime Minister Ehud
Olmert, on Israeli President Moshe Katsav*

Among some people in this country, for a man to express his
love for his wife he must beat her sometimes.

*George Mashamba, South African senator, addressing a parliamentary
committee on Education*

Do you know why God withheld the sense of humour from
women? That we may love you instead of laugh at you.

Mrs Patrick Campbell, an actress, to a man

An ego like a raging tooth.

W.B. Yeats on Mrs Patrick Campbell

A man is in general better pleased when he has a good dinner
upon his table, than when his wife talks Greek.

Samuel Johnson

These are rare attainments for a damsel, but pray tell me, can she spin?
> *James I, when introduced to a young girl proficient in Latin, Greek and Hebrew. Attrib.*

That woman can speak eighteen languages and she can't say 'no' in one of them.
> *Dorothy Parker of a guest surrounded by men at one of her parties*

One tongue is sufficient for a woman.
> *John Milton, asked if he would allow his daughters to learn foreign languages. Attrib.*

The only place men want depth in a woman is in her cleavage.
> *Zsa Zsa Gabor*

As men do walk a mile, women should talk an hour, after supper. 'Tis their exercise.
> *Francis Beaumont*

Most women have no Characters at all.
> *Alexander Pope,* Epistles to Several Persons, 'To a Lady'

Beneath this stone, a lump of clay
Lies Arabella Young
Who on the 21st of May
Began to hold her tongue.
  Epitaph, Hatfield, Massachusetts

It has been said in the praise of some men, that they could talk for hours together upon anything; but it must be owned to the honour of the other sex, that there are many among them who can talk whole hours together upon nothing ... I have often been puzzled to assign a cause why women should have this talent of ready utterance in so much greater perfection than men. I have sometimes fancied that they have not a retentive power, or the faculty of suppressing their thoughts, as men have, but that they are necessitated to speak every thing they think ... A friend of mine, who is an excellent anatomist, had promised me by the first opportunity to dissect a woman's tongue, and to examine whether there may not be in it certain juices which render it so wonderfully voluble or flippant, or whether the fibres of it may not be made up of a finer or more pliant thread; or whether there are not in it some particular muscles which dart it up and down by such sudden glances and vibrations; or whether, in the last place, there may not be certain undiscovered channels running from the head and the heart to this little instrument of loquacity, and conveying into it a perpetual affluency of animal spirits.
  Joseph Addison, in the Spectator, *1711*

[Men's] slanderous tongues are so short, and the time
wherein they have lavished out their words freely hath been
so long, that they know we cannot catch hold of them to pull
them out, and they think we will not write to reprove their
lying lips.

Jane Anger, Her Protection for Women, *1589*

A Preface.
To all women in general,
and gentle Reader whatsoever

Fie on the falsehood of men, whose minds go oft a-madding
and whose tongues cannot so soon be wagging, but straight
they fall a-tattling! Was there ever any so abused, so
slandered, so railed upon, or so wickedly handled unde-
servedly, as are we women?

Jane Anger, Her Protection for Women, *1589*

The only difference between men is the colour of their
neckties.

Helen Broderick in Top Hat

A man's mind, what there is of it – has always the advantage
of being masculine – as the smallest birch tree is of a higher
kind than the most soaring palm – and even his ignorance is
of a sounder quality.

George Eliot, Middlemarch

George Eliot had the heart of Sappho; but the face, with the
long proboscis, the protruding teeth of the Apocalyptic horse,
betrayed animality.

George Meredith on George Eliot

Woman the fountain of all human frailty!
What mighty ills have not been done by woman?
Who was't betrayed the Capitol? A woman.
Who lost Mark Anthony the world? A woman.
Who was the cause of a long ten year war,
And laid at last Old-Troy in ashes? Woman.
Destructive, damnable, deceitful woman.
Woman to man first as blessing giv'n,
When innocence and love were in their prime,
Happy a while in Paradise they lay,
But quickly woman long'd to go astray,
Some foolish new adventure needs must prove,
And the first Devil she saw she chang'd her love,
To his temptations lewdly she inclin'd
Her soul, and for an apple damn'd mankind.
Thomas Otway, The Orphan, *1680*

A man wrapped up in himself makes a very small parcel.
John Ruskin

He has the heart of a cucumber fried in snow.
Ninon de Lenclos, French courtesan, on the Marquis de Sévigné

The more I see of men, the more I admire dogs.
Marie de Rabutin-Chantal, Marquise de Sévigné

You will find that the woman who is really kind to dogs is always one who has failed to inspire sympathy in men.
Max Beerbohm, Zuleika Dobson

When a man's best friend is his dog, that dog has a problem.
Edward Abbey

...So when she's spreading all that mess on her face is another good time – do not be shy – to visit and inspect her. You will find a thousand pots of make-up colours and grease, that have melted and run down into her sweaty cleavage.

Ovid, Cures for Love

I have ... observed, that in all ages [women] have been more careful than the men to adorn that part of the head which we generally call the outside.

Joseph Addison, in the Spectator, 1712

Sure, deck your lower limbs in pants;
Yours are the limbs, my sweeting.
You look divine as you advance –
Have you seen yourself retreating?

Ogden Nash

A woman which is fair in show is foul in condition, she is like unto a glow-worm which is bright in the hedge and black in the hand; in the greenest grass lieth hid the greatest serpents; painted pots commonly hold deadly poison; and in the clearest water the ugliest toad: and the fairest woman hath some filthiness in her.

Joseph Swetnam, Arraignment of Lewd, idle, forward and unconstant women. This pamphlet led to a play being written about Swetnam in 1619 called Swetnam the Woman-Hater Arraigned by Women, in which he is beaten up by women

English women are elegant until they are ten years old, and perfect on grand occasions.

Nancy Mitford

Take a close-up of a woman past sixty? You might as well use a picture of a relief map of Ireland!

Nancy Astor, asked for a close-up photograph. Attrib.

I hate those short skirts, for women's knees are like badly risen rock-cakes.

Sir Norman Hartnell, dress-designer to Queen Elizabeth II

I wonder why men can get serious at all. They have this delicate long thing hanging outside their bodies, which goes up and down by its own will. First of all, having it outside your body is terribly dangerous. If I were a man I would have a fantastic castration complex to the point that I wouldn't be able to do a thing. Second, the inconsistency of it, like carrying a chance time alarm or something. If I were a man I would always be laughing at myself.

Yoko Ono, On Film No.4

The female body, even at its best, is very defective in form. Below the neck at the bow, and below the waist astern, there are two masses that simply refuse to fit into a balanced composition. Viewed from the side, a woman presents an exaggerated S bisected by an imperfectly straight line, and so she inevitably suggests a drunken dollar-mark.

H.L. Mencken

My mother used to say it was a great relief to her being an old woman because men left her alone.

Jill Nicholls, in Spare Rib

Men are creatures with two legs and eight hands.

Jayne Mansfield

Give a man a free hand and he'll run it all over you.
Mae West

If, sir, I possessed the power of conveying unlimited sexual attraction through the potency of my voice, I would not be reduced to accepting a miserable pittance from the BBC for interviewing a faded female in a damp basement.
Gilbert Harding to Mae West's manager, who suggested he should be more 'sexy' when interviewing her

Let us love dogs; let us love only dogs! Men and cats are unworthy creatures.
Maria Bashkirtseff

There is but one thing in the world worse than a shameless woman, and that's another woman.
Aristophanes, Thesmophoriazusae

I used to be Snow White ... but I drifted.
Mae West

She's the original good time that was had by all.
Bette Davis on a starlet of her day

If I ever get hold of that hag, I'll tear every hair out of her moustache.
Tallulah Bankhead on Bette Davis

Mme de Genlis, in order to avoid the scandal of coquetry, always yielded easily.
Charles Maurice Talleyrand

Lady Capricorn, he understood, was still keeping open bed.
Aldous Huxley, Antic Hay

She's the sort of woman who lives for others – you can always tell the others by their hunted expression.
C.S. Lewis, The Screwtape Letters

He's the kind of man who will end up dying in his own arms.
Mamie Van Doren on Warren Beatty

Madame, you must really be more careful. Suppose it had been someone else who found you like this.
Armand-Emmanuel du Plessis, Duc de Richelieu, when he discovered his wife with her lover

She's like the old line about justice – not only must be done but must be seen to be done.
John Osborne, Time Present

You were born with your legs apart. They'll send you to the grave in a Y-shaped coffin.
Joe Orton, What the Butler Saw

If the girls at a Yale weekend were laid end to end I wouldn't be a bit surprised.
Dorothy Parker

Prostitution gives her an opportunity to meet people. It provides fresh air and wholesome exercise, and it keeps her out of trouble.
Joseph Heller, Catch–22

Women might be able to fake orgasms, but men can fake whole relationships.
Sharon Stone

She is chaste whom nobody has asked.
Ovid, Amores, *I.8*

A homely face and no figure have aided many women heavenward.
Minna Antrim, Naked Truth and Veiled Allusions

Ladies, just a little more virginity, if you don't mind.
Herbert Beerbohm Tree, directing a group of actresses

Age cannot wither her, nor custom stale her infinite virginity.
Daniel Webster, on hearing of an exchange of views about his friend Peggy Eaton's scandalous reputation

... Your virginity, your old virginity, is like one of our French wither'd pears: it looks ill, it eats drily ...
William Shakespeare, All's Well That Ends Well

Sara could commit adultery at one end and weep for her sins at the other, and enjoy both operations at once.
Joyce Cary, The Horse's Mouth

You can lead a whore to culture but you can't make her think.
Dorothy Parker, in a speech to the American Horticultural Society

Masculinity and stupidity are often indistinguishable.
H.L. Mencken, In Defence of Women

Mrs Balinger is one of those ladies who pursue Culture in bands, as though it were dangerous to meet it alone.
Edith Wharton

A woman is only a woman,
But a good cigar is a smoke.
Rudyard Kipling; later used by Groucho Marx

Kipling is a jingo imperialist, he is morally insensitive and aesthetically disgusting.
George Orwell

Women have many faults, men have only two:
Everything they say, and everything they do.
Anonymous

A woman's place is in the wrong.
James Thurber

Men are nicotine-stained, beer-besmirched, whisky-greased, red-eyed devils.
Carry Nation

Men's men: be they gentle or simple, they're very much of a muchness.
George Eliot, Daniel Deronda

I will rather trust a Fleming with my butter, Parson Hugh the Welshman with my cheese, an Irishman with my aqua-vitae bottle, or a thief to walk my ambling gelding, than my wife with herself.
William Shakespeare, The Merry Wives of Windsor

Macho isn't mucho.
Zsa Zsa Gabor

I've never found brawn appealing. If I went out with Macho
Man I think I'd have a permanent headache. Kind of 'You
Tarzan – Mi-graine'.
Overheard on a bus. Quoted in Picking on Men *by Judy Allen*

Whatever women do they must do twice as well as men to be
thought half as good. Luckily, this is not difficult.
Charlotte Whitton

The five worst infirmities that afflict the female are indocility,
discontent, slander, jealousy, and silliness.
Confucian Marriage Manual

Women want mediocre men, and men are working to be as
mediocre as possible.
Margaret Mead

Twenty million young women rose to their feet with the cry
'we will not be dictated to' – and promptly became stenogra-
phers.
G.K. Chesterton

Why are women ... so much more interesting to men than
men are to women?
Virginia Woolf, A Room of One's Own

The only thing that can make a woman feel lonelier than a
vibrator can make her feel is a man.
Isha Elafi

Once you know what women are like, men get kind of boring. I'm not trying to put them down, I mean I like some of them sometimes as people, but sexually they're dull.
Rita Mae Brown

To call man an animal is to flatter him; he's a machine, a walking dildo.
Valerie Solanas, in S.C.U.M. Manifesto

The male is a biological accident: the Y (male) chromosome is an incomplete X (female) chromosome, that is, has an incomplete set of genes. In other words, the male is an incomplete female, a walking abortion, aborted at the chromosome stage.
Valerie Solanas, in S.C.U.M. Manifesto

I think of a man and I take away reason and accountability.
Answer to 'How do you Write Women So Well?' Put to novellist Melvyn Udall in As Good As It Gets *(Scriptwriters Mark Andrus and James L Brooks)*

A woman without a man is like a fish without a bicycle.
Florynce Kennedy and Gloria Steinem

Love may arise from a generous sentiment – namely, the liking for prostitution; but it soon becomes corrupted by the liking for ownership.
Charles Baudelaire

Because women can do nothing except love, they've given it a ridiculous importance.
W. Somerset Maugham, The Moon and Sixpence

Bachelors begin at thirty-six. Up till this time they are regarded as single men. Most of them are very tidy, smell of mothballs, and have an obsessional old maid's fix about one of their ashtrays being moved an inch to the right.

Jilly Cooper, Men and Super Men

Love is the affection of a mind that has nothing better to engage it.

Theophrastus, Greek philosopher

Just the exchange of two momentary desires and the contact of two skins.

Nicholas Chamfort on love, 1805

By the time you swear you're his,
Shivering and sighing,
And he vows his passion is Infinite, undying –
Lady, make a note of this:
One of you is lying.

Dorothy Parker, Enough Rope, 'Unfortunate Coincidence'

How alike are the groans of love to those of the dying.

Malcolm Lowry, Under the Volcano

Love is the universal migraine. A bright stain on the vision blotting out reason.

Robert Graves

Love is a gross exaggeration of the difference between one person and everybody else.

George Bernard Shaw

The cure for love is to be loved back.
> *Friedrich Nietzsche*

Girls bored me – they still do. I love Mickey Mouse more than any woman I've ever known.
> *Walt Disney*

Madame: I was told that you took the trouble to come here to see me three times last evening. I was not in. And, fearing lest persistence expose you to humiliation, I am bound by the rules of politeness to warn you that I shall never be in.
> *Gustave Flaubert in a letter to Louise Colet, his former mistress. Colet scribbled on the note 'lache, couard et canaille'*

A great cow of ink.
> *Gustave Flaubert on George Sand*

There is no such thing as an ugly woman, but there is such a thing as too little vodka.
> *Russian saying*

O, she is the antidote to desire.
> *William Congreve,* The Way of the World

Now I know the meaning of grotesque.
> *Sydney Smith on seeing the wife of Dr Grote, Regius Professor of Greek, wearing a turban*

When I first saw Moore I at last understood why Yanks call a woman a broad.
> *Paul Johnson on Guardian columnist Suzanne Moore*

Fuck-me shoes and a bird's-nest hairdo.

Germaine Greer on her fellow Guardian *writer Suzanne Moore's dress and appearance*

No longer from head to foot than from hip to hip, she is spherical like a globe; I could find out countries in her.

In what part of her body stands for Ireland?

Marry, sir, in her buttocks; I found it out by the bogs.

Where Scotland?

I found it by the barrenness, hard in the palm of the hand.

Where France?

In her forehead, armed and reverted, making war against her heir.

Where England?

I looked for the chalky cliffs, but I could find no whiteness in them. But I guess it stood in her chin, by the salt rheum that ran between France and it.

Where Spain?

Faith, I saw it not; but I felt it hot in her breath.

Where America, the Indies?

O, sir, upon her nose, all o'er embellished with rubies, carbuncles, sapphires, declining their rich aspect to the hot breath of Spain, who sent whole armadas of carracks to be ballast at her nose.

Where stood Belgia, the Netherlands?

O, sir, I did not look so low.

William Shakespeare, The Comedy of Errors

... our English gentle-women are now growne so farre past shame, past modesty, grace and nature, as to clip their haire like men with lockes and foretops, and to make this whorish cut the very guise and fashion of the times, to the eternal infamy of their sex, their Nation, and the great scandal of religion.

William Prynne on the seventeenth-century fashion of short hair

Armies of men, herds really, with cameras at the ready, stampeded ... to observe sweet-natured, patient women whose bodies are shaped in a manner that you hardly ever see in the course of normal life. Fat, balding, ugly, drunken, uncouth and deeply unattractive men with flashlights tell these exquisite women what to do and the women do it.

Stephen Pile on topless models promoting motor bikes in the Sunday Times

A woman with a heavily-lived face poised unceremoniously on top of a torso like a dressmaker's dummy.

Paul Johnson on Lynn Barber, in the Spectator

Probably the only place where a man can feel really secure is in a maximum security prison, except for the imminent threat of release.

Germaine Greer, The Female Eunuch

The flashers, grabbers, bottom-pinchers, purse-snatchers, kerb-crawlers, verbal abusers, peeping Toms and the ultimate cowards, the ones who roam in packs, have left an indelible impression on woman's minds and – more in anger than in fear – women are determined to evade, forestall and undermine these invaders of our freedom.

Valerie Grove, in the Evening Standard

The Queen is most anxious to enlist every one who can speak or write to join in checking this mad, wicked folly of 'Woman's Rights', with all its attendant horrors, on which her poor feeble sex is bent, forgetting every sense of womanly feeling and propriety.

Queen Victoria

A red-haired, red-faced man of 65 seemingly in transit
between Dr Jekyll and Mr Hyde.
>   *Peter McKay on Paul Johnson in the* Sunday Times

No man, not even a doctor, ever gives any other definition of
what a nurse should be than this – 'devoted and obedient'.
This definition would do just as well for a porter. It might
even do for a horse. It would not do for a policeman.
>   *Florence Nightingale*

The legend of the jungle heritage and the evolution of man as
a hunting carnivore has taken root in man's mind ... He may
even believe that equal pay will do something terrible to his
gonads.
>   *Elaine Morgan,* The Descent of Woman

An open invitation to any feminist, any harridan or any rattle-
headed female with a chip on her bra strap to take action
against her employers.
>   *Tony Marlow MP on equal-pay law*

How do you know that an advance was unwanted until you've
made it?
>   *Alan Clark MP, responding to accusations of sexual harrassment*

A gentleman is a patient wolf.
>   *Henrietta Tiarks*

Certain women should be struck regularly, like gongs.
>   *Noel Coward,* Private Lives

Homosexuality is a sickness, just as are baby-rape or wanting to become the head of General Motors.

Eldridge Cleaver, black Muslim, Soul on Ice, 'Notes on a Native Son'

He is the summit of sex, the pinnacle of masculine, feminine and neuter. Everything that he, she and it can ever want. I spoke to sad but kindly men on this newspaper who have met every celebrity coming from America for the past thirty years. They say that this deadly, winking, sniggering, snuggling, chromium-plated, scent-impregnated, luminous, quivering, giggling, fruit-flavoured, mincing, ice-covered, heap of mother love has had the biggest reception and impact on London since Charlie Chaplin arrived at the same station, Waterloo, on September 12th 1921. This appalling man, and I use the word appalling in no other than its true sense of terrifying, has hit this country in a way that is as violent as Churchill receiving the cheers on VE Day. He reeks of emetic language that can only make grown men long for a quiet corner, an aspidistra, a handkerchief and the old heave-ho. Without doubt he is the biggest sentimental vomit of all time. Slobbering over his Mother, winking at his brother, and counting the cash at every second, this superb piece of calculating candyfloss has an answer for every situation.

William Connor ('Cassandra') on Liberace, in the Daily Mirror. *The column became the subject of a famous libel case won by the entertainer*

I became one of the stately homos of England.

Quentin Crisp, The Naked Civil Servant

A bull who would copulate only with other bulls would be sent to the knackers.

Piers Paul Read, in The Times, *1994*

This sort of thing may be tolerated by the French, but we are British – thank God.

> Viscount Montgomery of Alamein on the proposed relaxation of laws against homosexuality in 1965

I was too polite to ask.

> Gore Vidal, asked whether his first sexual experience was homosexual or heterosexual

If Michelangelo had been a heterosexual, the Sistine Chapel would have been painted basic white and with a roller.

> Rita Mae Brown

The middle age of a bugger is not to be contemplated without horror.

> Virginia Woolf

She looked like Lady Chatterley above the waist and the gamekeeper below.

> Cyril Connolly on Vita Sackville-West

When his cock wouldn't stand up he blew his head off. He sold himself a line of bullshit, and bought it.

> Germaine Greer on Ernest Hemingway

The trouble with Ian is that he gets off with women because he can't get on with them.

> Rosamond Lehmann on Ian Fleming

Except in streetcars one should never be unnecessarily rude to a lady.

> O. Henry, Strictly Business, 'The Gold That Glittered'

They are comforted by our means, they are nourished by the meats we dress; their bodies freed from diseases by our cleanliness, which otherwise would surfeit unreasonably through their own noisomeness. Without our care they lie in their beds as dogs in litter and go like lousy mackerel swimming in the heat of summer.
Jane Anger, Her Protection for Women, 1589

The fastest way to a man's heart is through his chest.
Roseanne Barr

Gout is very much in my line, gentlemen are not.
Dr Elizabeth Garrett Anderson, letter to a man hoping to be treated for gout

It makes me feel masculine to tell you that I do not answer questions like this without being paid for answering them.
Lillian Hellman, when asked by Harper's Magazine *when she felt most masculine*

Many a man has been a wonder to the world, whose wife and valet have seen nothing in him that was even remarkable. Few men have been admired by their servants.
Michel de Montaigne, Essais, III

No man is a hero to his valet.
Anne-Marie Bigot de Cornuel

But that is not because the hero is no hero, but because the valet is a valet.
Friedrich Nietzsche

A fly, Sir, may sting a stately horse and make him wince; but one is but an insect, and the other is still a horse.
Samuel Johnson

Brigands demand your money or your life; women require both.
Samuel Butler. Attrib.

The tyranny of the weak over the strong. It is the only tyranny that ever lasts.
Oscar Wilde on the history of women

A woman will always sacrifice herself if you give her the opportunity. It is her favourite form of self-indulgence.
W. Somerset Maugham, The Circle

Damn the North! And damn the South! And damn Wellington! The question is, how am I going to get rid of this damned Princess of Wales?
Prince of Wales, later George IV, on a political marriage for him despite his private marriage to Mrs Fitzherbert

A sort of friendship recognized by the police.
Robert Louis Stevenson on matrimony

Nothing is to me more distasteful than that entire complacency and satisfaction which beam in the countenances of a new-married couple.
Charles Lamb, Essays of Elia, 'A Bachelor's Complaint of Married People'

'We stay together, but we distrust one another.'
'Ah, yes…but isn't that a definition of marriage?'
Malcolm Bradbury, The History Man

My first wife drove me to drink. It is the only thing I'm indebted to her for.
W.C. Fields

If you want to sacrifice the admiration of many men for the criticism of one, go ahead, get married.
Katherine Hepburn

After a certain age marriage is mostly, its bitter and tender moments both, a mental game of thrust and parry played on the edge of the grave.
John Updike

It was very good of God to let Carlyle and Mrs Carlyle marry one another and so make two people miserable instead of four.
Samuel Butler on the Carlyles

To marry a man out of pity is folly; and, if you think you are going to influence the kind of fellow who has 'never had a chance, poor devil,' you are profoundly mistaken. One can only influence the strong characters in life, not the weak; and it is the height of vanity to suppose that you can make an honest man of anyone.
Margot Asquith

Marriage is like a cage: one sees the birds outside desperate to get in, and those inside equally desperate to get out.
Michel de Montaigne, Essais, *III*

There follows a pre-nuptial negotiation between Millamant and Mirabell (contemplating marriage) in William Congreve's Way of the World ...

MILLAMANT

... Oh, I hate a lover that can dare to think he draws a moment's air independent on the bounty of his mistress. There is not so impudent a thing in nature as the saucy look of an assured man confident of success: the pedantic arrogance of a very husband has not so pragmatical an air. Ah, I'll never marry, unless I am first made sure of my will and pleasure.

MIRABELL

Would you have 'em both before marriage? Or will you be contented with the first now, and stay for the other till after grace?

MILLAMANT

Ah, don't be impertinent. My dear liberty, shall I leave thee? My faithful solitude, my darling contemplation, must I bid you then adieu? Ay-h, adieu. My morning thoughts, agreeable wakings, indolent slumbers, all ye *douceurs*, ye *sommeils du matin*, adieu. I can't do't, 'tis more than impossible – positively, Mirabell, I'll lie a-bed in a morning as long as I please.

MIRABELL

Then I'll get up in a morning as early as I please.

MILLAMANT

Ah! Idle creature, get up when you will. And d'ye hear, I won't be called names after I'm married; positively I won't be called names.

MIRABELL

Names?

MILLAMANT

Ay, as wife, spouse, my dear, joy, jewel, love, sweet-
heart, and the rest of that nauseous cant, in which men
and their wives are so fulsomely familiar – I shall never
bear that. Good Mirabell, don't let us be familiar or
fond, nor kiss before folks, like my Lady Fadler and Sir
Francis; nor go to Hyde Park together the first Sunday in
a new chariot, to provoke eyes and whispers, and then
never be seen there together again, as if we were proud
of one another the first week, and ashamed of one
another ever after. Let us never visit together, nor go to
a play together, but let us be very strange and well-bred.
Let us be as strange as if we had been married a great
while, and as well-bred as if we were not married at all.

MIRABELL

Have you any more conditions to offer? Hitherto your
demands are pretty reasonable.

MILLAMANT

Trifles; as liberty to pay and receive visits to and from
whom I please; to write and receive letters, without
interrogatories or wry faces on your part; to wear what I
please, and choose conversation with regard only to my
own taste; to have no obligation upon me to converse
with wits that I don't like, because they are your acquaintance, or to be intimate with fools, because they may be
your relations. Come to dinner when I please, dine in my
dressing-room when I'm out of humour, without giving a
reason. To have my closet inviolate; to be sole empress of
my tea-table, which you must never presume to approach
without first asking leave. And lastly, wherever I am, you
shall always knock at the door before you come in. These
articles subscribed, if I continue to endure you a little

longer, I may by degrees dwindle into a wife.

MIRABELL

Your bill of fare is something advanced in this latter account. Well, have I liberty to offer conditions:- that when you are dwindled into a wife, I may not be beyond measure enlarged into a husband?

MILLAMANT

You have free leave: propose your utmost, speak and spare not.

MIRABELL

I thank you. *Imprimis*, then, I covenant that your acquaintance be general; that you admit no sworn confidant or intimate of your own sex; no she-friend to screen her affairs under your countenance, and tempt you to make trial of a mutual secrecy. No decoy-duck to wheedle you a *fop-scrambling* to the play in a mask, then bring you home in a pretended fright, when you think you shall be found out, and rail at me for missing the play, and disappointing the frolic which you had to pick me up and prove my constancy.

MILLAMANT

Detestable *imprimis*! I go to the play in a mask!

MIRABELL

Item, I article, that you continue to like your own face as long as I shall, and while it passes current with me, that you endeavour not to new coin it. To which end, together with all vizards for the day, I prohibit all masks for the night, made of oiled skins and I know not what – hog's bones, hare's gall, pig water, and the marrow of a roasted cat. In short, I forbid all commerce with the gentlewomen in what-d'ye-call-it court. *Item*, I shut my doors against all bawds with baskets, and pennyworths of muslin, china, fans, atlases, etc. *Item*, when you shall be breeding –

MILLAMANT

Ah, name it not!

MIRABELL

Which may be presumed, with a blessing on our
endeavours –

MILLAMANT

Odious endeavours!

MIRABELL

I denounce against all strait lacing, squeezing for a shape,
till you mould my boy's head like a sugar-loaf, and instead
of a man-child, make me father to a crooked billet.
Lastly, to the dominion of the tea-table I submit; but with
proviso, that you exceed not in your province, but
restrain yourself to native and simple tea-table drinks, as
tea, chocolate, and coffee. As likewise to genuine and
authorised tea-table talk, such as mending of fashions,
spoiling reputations, railing at absent friends, and so
forth. But that on no account you encroach upon the
men's prerogative, and presume to drink healths, or toast
fellows; for prevention of which, I banish all foreign
forces, all auxiliaries to the tea-table, as orange-brandy,
all aniseed, cinnamon, citron, and Barbadoes waters,
together with ratafia and the most noble spirit of clary.
But for cowslip-wine, poppy-water, and all dormitives,
those I allow. These provisos admitted, in other things I
may prove a tractable and complying husband.

MILLAMANT

Oh, horrid provisos! Filthy strong waters! I toast
fellows, odious men! I hate your odious provisos.

MIRABELL

Then we're agreed. Shall I kiss your hand upon the contract?
William Congreve, The Way of the World

I am unwell. Bring me a glass of brandy.
> George, Prince of Wales, in 1795, on having kissed for the first time his
> bride-to-be Princess Caroline of Brunswick

She's been married so many times she has rice marks on her face.
> Henry Youngman on Zsa Zsa Gabor

There are two tragedies in life. One is to lose your heart's
desire. The other is to gain it.
> George Bernard Shaw

Marriage is the assassin of love.
> Aristotle Onassis

Marriages are like tornadoes. There's all this blowing and
sucking at the beginning; and at the end you lose your house.
> James Caan

Courtship to marriage, as a very witty prologue to a very dull
play.
> William Congreve, The Old Bachelor

Beat yourself up . . . save the old man time.
> Tyneside wedding anniversary card

A man in love is incomplete until he has married. Then he's
finished.
> Zsa Zsa Gabor

The most happy marriage I can picture or imagine to myself
would be the union of a deaf man to a blind woman.
> Samuel Taylor Coleridge

All tragedies are finish'd by death, All comedies are ended by
a marriage.
> Lord Byron, Don Juan, III

A women's silly, never staid,
By many longings stirred and swayed.
If husband can't her needs supply,
Adultery's the way she'll try...
Her lustful loins are never stilled:
By just one man she's unfulfilled.
She'll spread her legs to all the men
But, ever hungry, won't say 'When'.
Thus married women love to stray
And wish their husbands' lives away.
Since none a woman's lust can sate
I don't commend the marriage state.
> De Coniuge non Ducenda, *anonymous poem on marriage, c.1225-50.*
> *One of the most popular anti-matrimonial satires of the late Middle Ages,*
> *surviving in over fifty manuscripts*

As I roll back from you,
From your flabby breasts and breath,
A faint froth is our only link.

How many beaches are you?
Must I comb them all?

I'm not a wave to roll again forever,
And unlike the sea, I don't come
Every fifteen seconds.
> *Jim Lindsey,* 'Blank Verse for a Fat Demanding Wife'

The majority of husbands remind me of an orangutan trying to play the violin.

Honoré de Balzac

Mrs Hall of Sherbourne was brought to bed yesterday of a dead child, some weeks before she expected, owing to a fright. I suppose she happened to look unawares at her husband.

Jane Austen, letter

In a television interview to be broadcast today, William Hague reveals that he and Ffion have no immediate plans for a baby. His conviction is wise. For most men there's a thrill in being told the baby looks the spitting image of its father. But hearing this from cooing relatives in the maternity hospital is one thing, being paid the compliment in the foetal monitoring unit by the technician doing the 12-week scan is quite another. Mr Hague has enough to depress him already without that.

Matthew Norman, journalist

Going to marry her! Going to marry her! Impossible! You mean, a part of her; he could not marry her all himself. It would be a case, not of bigamy, but of trigamy; the neighbourhood or the magistrates should interfere. There is enough of her to furnish wives for a whole parish. One man marry her! – it is monstrous. You might people a colony with her ; or give an assembly with her; or perhaps take your morning walks around her, always providing there were frequent resting places, and you are in rude health. I once was rash enough to try walking round her before breakfast, but only got half-way and gave it up exhausted. Or you might read the Riot Act and disperse her; in short, you might do anything with her but marry her.

Sydney Smith on hearing that a young man planned to marry a fat widow

Smug Sydney.
> Lord Byron on Sydney Smith

What a hideous, odd-looking man Sydney Smith is. With a mouth like an oyster and three double chins.
> Mrs Brookfield, on Sydney Smith

A man...is so in the way in the house.
> Elizabeth Gaskell, Cranford

The cloy of all pleasure, the luggage of life,
Is the best that can be said for a very good wife.
> John Wilmot, Earl of Rochester

To lose a lover or even a husband or two during the course of one's life can be vexing. But to lose one's teeth is a catastrophe.
> Hugh Wheeler

Here lies my wife; here let her lie!
Now she's at rest, and so am I.
> John Dryden, 'Epitaph Intended for Dryden's Wife'

Bigamy is having one husband too many. Monogamy is the same.
> Anonymous, quoted in Erica Jong, Fear of Flying

Mine, or other people's?
> Peggy Guggenheim on being asked how many husbands she had had.

With all my heart. Whose wife shall it be?
> John Horne Tooke, replying to the suggestion that he take a wife

I give to Elizabeth Parker the sum of £50, whom, through my foolish fondness, I made my wife; and who in return has not spared, most unjustly, to accuse me of every crime regarding human nature, save highway-robbery.
Charles Parker, excerpt from will, 1785

I bequeath all my property to my wife on the condition that she remarry immediately. Then there will be at least one man to regret my death.
Heinrich Heine

I do give and bequeath to Mary Davis the sum of five shillings, which is sufficient to enable her to get drunk for the last time at my expense.
David Davis, excerpt from will, 1788

Now at least I know where he is.
Queen Alexandra, to Lord Esher, shortly after the death of her husband Edward VII, noted for his string of mistresses

There are few who would not rather be taken in adultery than in provincialism.
Aldous Huxley, Antic Hay

It should be a very happy marriage – they are both so much in love with him.
Irene Thomas

I have very little of Mr Blake's company. He is always in paradise.
Mrs Blake of her husband William

You have sent me a Flanders mare.
> *Henry VIII when he saw Anne of Cleves, his fourth wife, for the first time.*
> *Quoted by Tobias Smollett*

I like him and his wife. He is so ladylike, and she is such a perfect gentleman.
> *Sydney Smith*

All my wife has ever taken from the Mediterranean – from that whole vast intuitive culture – are four bottles of Chianti to make into lamps, and two china condiment donkeys labelled Sally and Peppy.
> *Peter Shaffer*

I've been married six months. She looks like a million dollars, but she only knows a hundred and twenty words and she's only got two ideas in her head. The other one's hats.
> *Eric Linklater,* Juan in America

She is an excellent creature, but never can remember which came first, the Greeks or the Romans.
> *Benjamin Disraeli on his wife. Attrib.*

...fools are like husbands as pilchards are to herrings; the husband's the bigger.
> *William Shakespeare,* Twelfth Night

Twenty years of romance makes a woman look like a ruin; but twenty years of marriage makes her something like a public building.
> *Oscar Wilde*

When I don't look like a tragic muse, I look like the smoky relic of the great Boston Fire.
   Louisa May Alcott on herself

A wedding is just a funeral where you can smell your own flowers.
   Victor Lewis-Smith

I married beneath me – all women do.
   Nancy Astor

I could do without your face, Chloe, and without your neck, and your hands, and your limbs, and to save myself the trouble of mentioning the points in detail, I could do without you altogether.
   Martial, Roman poet

There are only about 20 murders a year in London and not all are serious – some are just husbands killing their wives.
   Commander G.H. Hatherhill of Scotland Yard, 1954

Divorce! Never. But murder often!
   Dame Sybil Thorndike, asked when she had ever considered divorcing during her marriage to Lewis Casson

It's going to be very, very expensive, but it will be worth every penny.
   John Cleese referring to his divorce

The three great lies of modern divorce: it was pressure of work, it's an amicable break, and there's no one else involved.
   Julie Burchill

If you are afraid of loneliness, don't marry.
>   *Anton Chekhov*

They fuck you up, your mum and dad.
They may not mean to, but they do.
They fill you with the faults they had
And add some extra, just for you.
>   *Philip Larkin, 'This Be The Verse'*

As a child I thought I hated everybody, but when I grew up I realised it was just children that I didn't like.
>   *Philip Larkin*

No one is such a determinist that he fails to blame his parents.
>   *Dr Anthony Daniels*

A loud noise at one end and no sense of responsibility at the other.
>   *Ronald Knox on babies*

Do not leave your mother alone with your dog. The unruliness of mothers is great.
>   *Dabi'Ibn al-harith al-Burjumi on some people who had refused to return a borrowed dog. For this piece of hija, or Arabic invective poetry, he was imprisoned*

I haven't spoken to my mother-in-law for eighteen months. I don't like to interrupt her.
>   *Ken Dodd*

Who has not watched a mother stroke her child's cheek or kiss *in a certain way* and felt a nervous shudder at the possessive outrage done to free solitary human soul?
John Cowper Powys, The Meaning of Culture

His mother should have thrown him away and kept the stork.
Mae West

The first half of our lives is ruined by our parents, and the second half by our children.
Clarence Darrow, US lawyer

They make pederasty an incomprehensible vice.
Brian Sewell, asked by the head of St Paul's Boys school what he thought of the pupils

I wonder who thought of the innocence of children. It must have been a person of great originality.
Ivy Compton-Burnett

Money – the one thing that keeps us in touch with our children.
Giles Brandreth

Men are generally more careful of the breed of their horses and dogs than of their children.
William Penn

It is no wonder that people are so horrible when they start their life as children.
Kingsley Amis

It is no use telling me that there are bad aunts and good aunts. At the core they are all alike. Sooner or later, out pops the cloven hoof.
  P.G.Wodehouse, The Code of the Woosters

Happy families are all alike; each unhappy family is unhappy in its own way.
  Leo Tolstoy

A man who, beyond the age of 26, finds himself on a bus can count himself a failure in life.
  Sometimes attrib. to Margaret Thatcher. Possibly Virginia Woolf

From the earliest times the old have rubbed it into the young that they are wiser than they, and before the young had discovered what nonsense this was they were too old, and it profited them to carry on the imposture.
  W. Somerset Maugham, Cakes and Ale

I have lived some thirty years on this planet, and I have yet to hear the first syllable of valuable or even earnest advice from my seniors.
  Henry David Thoreau

At sixteen I was stupid, confused, insecure and indecisive. At twenty-five I was wise, self-confident, prepossessing and assertive. At forty-five I am stupid, confused, insecure and indecisive. Who would have supposed that maturity is only a short break in adolescence?
  Jules Feiffer

Whenever a man's friends begin to compliment him about looking young, he may be sure that they think he is growing old.

> *Washington Irving,* Bracebridge Hall, 'Bachelors'

The three ages of man: youth, middle age, and 'You're looking well, Enoch!'

> *The late Enoch Powell MP on being told by the Editor of this book that he looked well*

The young always have the same problem – how to rebel and conform at the same time. They have now solved this by defying their parents and copying one another.

> *Quentin Crisp,* The Naked Civil Servant

Look, the intellects of our lazy youth are asleep, nor do they wake up for the exercise of a single respectable occupation; slumber and languor and, what is more disgusting than slumber and languor, the pursuit of wicked things, has invaded their spirit: the obscene pursuit of singing and dancing keeps them effeminate, and curling the hair and shrilling the voice into womanish cajoleries, competing with women in the softness of the body and cultivating themselves with the foulest elegances, that is the pattern of our young men. Who of your agemates is what I might call intellectual enough, diligent enough, rather, who is enough of a man? Softened up and emasculated as they were born, they remain all their lives, laying siege to other people's chastity, careless of their own.

> *Seneca, first century BC,* Controversiae, I, Introduction, *on the youth of his day. Tr. Amy Richlin*

Old Cary Grant fine. How you?
> *Cary Grant replying to a telegram to his agent, asking: 'How old Cary Grant?'*

I am just turning forty and taking my time about it.
> *Harold Lloyd at seventy-seven, when asked his age, in* The Times

Middle age is when you've met so many people that every new person you meet reminds you of someone else.
> *Ogden Nash*

Do you think my mind is maturing late, or simply rotted early?
> *Ogden Nash*

Education is the brief interval between ignorance and arrogance.
> *Old adage*

The misery of a child is interesting to a mother, the misery of a young man is interesting to a young woman, the misery of an old man is interesting to no one.
> *Victor Hugo,* Les Misérables, *'Saint Denis'*

Life, as it is called, is for the most of us one long postponement.
> *Henry Miller*

Poor old Daddy – just one of those sturdy old plants left over from the Edwardian Wilderness, that can't understand why the sun isn't shining any more.
> *John Osborne,* Look Back in Anger

When it is said of a man that he didn't suffer fools gladly, it means he was an intolerant old brute. When it is said of an old lady that she was lively and vivacious, it means she was usually plastered.

Anthony Howard on the obituarist's code

There are one hundred and ninety-three living species of monkeys and apes. One hundred and ninety-two of them are covered with hair. The exception is a naked ape self-named Homo sapiens.

Desmond Morris, The Naked Ape

I have no patience whatever with these Gorilla damnifications of humanity.

Thomas Carlyle on Charles Darwin

Only two things are infinite, the universe and human stupidity, and I'm not sure about the forme

Albert Einstein

Capacity, competition, desperation, death to other living things; the forces that make the world go round.

John Updike

Drinking when we are not thirsty and making love all year round, madam; that is all there is to distinguish us from other animals.

Pierre-Augustin Caron de Beaumarchais, Le Mariage de Figaro

The human race, to which so many of my readers belong.

G.K. Chesterton

He grew up from manhood into boyhood.
Ronald Knox on G.K. Chesterton

Society is now one polish'd horde,
Form'd of two mighty tribes, the *Bores* and *Bored*.
Lord Byron, Don Juan, *XIII*

All charming people have something to conceal, usually their
total dependence on the appreciation of others.
Cyril Connolly

Style, like sheer silk, too often hides eczema.
Albert Camus, The Fall

To succeed in the world it is not enough to be stupid – you
must also be well-mannered.
Voltaire

I sometimes think that God, in creating man, somewhat over-
estimated his ability.
OscarWilde

A certain type of man is only stirred to the heights of passion
by administrative inconvenience.
Anthony Powell

There is no over-estimating the shallowness of the human heart.
Theodore Dalrymple

Man is a sick fly, taking a dizzy ride on a small dot in space
revolving at ridiculous speeds.
H.L. Mencken

No one ever lacks a good reason for suicide.
Cesare Pavese who committed suicide in 1950

Millions long for immortality who do not know what to do with themselves on a rainy Sunday afternoon.
Susan Ertz

No arts; no letters; no society; and which is worst of all, continual fear and danger of violent death; and the life of man, solitary, poor, nasty, brutish, and short.
Thomas Hobbes, Leviathan

Have I not reason to hate and to despise myself? Indeed I do; and chiefly for not having hated and despised the world enough.
William Hazlitt, On the Pleasure of Hating

Extreme hopes are born of extreme misery.
Bertrand Russell

All of man's unhappiness stems from his inability to stay in a room alone.
Pascal

Hell is other people.
Jean-Paul Sartre

Hull is other people.
Jonathan Cecil, British actor

For what do we live but to make sport of our neighbours, and laugh at them in our turn?
Jane Austen, Pride and Prejudice

The belief in the supernatural source of evil is not necessary; men alone are quite capable of every wickedness.
Joseph Conrad, Under Western Eyes

A desperate man never forgives a favour.
Dominic Lawson

If you pick up a starving dog and make him prosperous, he will not bite you. That is the principle difference between a dog and a man.
Mark Twain

He has all the characteristics of a dog except loyalty.
Sam Houston, American politician, on fellow-politician Thomas Jefferson Green

Man is the only animal that blushes. Or needs to.
Mark Twain

If a dog whines it does it because it's in pain or is hungry. But if a human being whines, nine times out of ten it's doing it because it enjoys it.
Julie Burchill

Depend upon it that if a man talks of his misfortunes there is something in them that is not disagreeable to him.
Dr Johnson

I like animals. It's people who like animals I don't like.
Jean Genet

Shyness is just egotism out of its depth.
Penelope Keith

A sentimentalist is one who desires the luxury of an emotion without paying for it.
Oscar Wilde

You take somebody that cries their goddam eyes out over phoney stuff in the cinema and nine times out of ten they're mean bastards at heart.
J. D. Salinger, The Catcher in the Rye

It is not enough to succeed. Friends must fail.
Gore Vidal

A friend in need is an acquaintance.
Mariella Frostrup

Every time a friend succeeds, a little part of me dies.
Gore Vidal

If friendship were cars, then women would constantly be out there tinkering with them, polishing them, servicing them – whereas men would just let them rust away in the front garden.
Christopher Middleton

Man is the only animal that can remain on friendly terms with the victims he intends to eat until he eats them.
Samuel Butler

In most mankind gratitude is merely a secret hope for greater favours.
Duc de la Rochefoucauld

I wish I loved the human Race;
I wish I loved its silly face;
I wish I liked the way it walks;
I wish I liked the way it talks;
And when I'm introduced to one
I wish I thought What Jolly Fun!
> *Sir Walter Alexander Raleigh,* Laughter from a Cloud, 'Wishes of an
> Elderly Man'

There is nothing so ill-bred as audible laughter, with its disagreeable noise and shocking distortion of the face.
> *Lord Chesterfield*

The world itself is but a large prison, out of which some are
daily led to execution.
> *Sir Walter Ralegh, after his trial for treason. Attrib.*

I am told I am a true cosmopolitan. I am unhappy
everywhere.
> *Stephen Vizinczey, in the* Guardian

Man originates in muck, wades a while in muck, makes muck
and in the end returns to muck.
> *Johann Christoff Friedrich von Schiller in* The Robbers

Man is a noble animal, splendid in ashes, and pompous in the
grave.
> *Sir Thomas Browne*

Often it seems a pity Noah and his party didn't miss the boat.
> *Mark Twain*

Because half-a-dozen grasshoppers under a fern make the field ring with their importunate chink, whilst thousands of great cattle, reposed beneath the shadow of the British oak, chew the cud and are silent, pray do not imagine that those who make the noise are the only inhabitants of the field; that of course they are many in number; or that, after all, they are other than the little shrivelled, meagre, hopping, though loud and troublesome insects of the hour.
Edmund Burke

So hard to teach but so easy to deceive.
Greek Stoic philosopher, on mankind

Those who can, do. Those who can't, teach. Those who can't teach, teach gym.
Woody Allen

One has often wondered whether upon the whole earth there is anything so unintelligent, so unapt to perceive how the world is really going, as an ordinary young Englishman of our upper classes.
Matthew Arnold, Culture and Anarchy

The king blew his nose twice, and wiped the royal perspiration repeatedly from a face which is probably the largest uncivilized spot in England.
Oliver Wendell Holmes on William IV

Good-morning, gentlemen both.
Elizabeth I, addressing a group of eighteen tailors

To promote a Woman to beare rule, superioritie, dominion, or empire above any Realme, nation, or Citie, is repugnant to nature; contumelie to God, a thing most contrarious to his reveled will and approved ordinance; and finallie, it is the subversion of good Order, of all equitie and justice...For who can denie but it is repugneth to nature, that the blind shall be appointed to leade and conduct such as do see? That the weake, the sicke, and impotent persons shall norishe and kepe the hole and the strong? And finallie, that the foolishe, madde, and phrenetike shall governe the discrete, and give counsel to such as be of sober mind? Of such be all women, compared unto man in bearing of authoritie. For their sight in civile regiment is but blindness; their strength, weakness; their counsel, foolishness; and judgement, phrensie, if it be rightlie considered ...

John Knox, First Blast of the Trumpet against the Monstrous Regiment of Women. *Knox attacks various women rulers hostile to the Reformation: Catherine de Medici, Mary of Guise, and above all Mary Tudor. But by generalizing about all women, he offended Elizabeth I, a potentially powerful pro-Reformation figure, when she ascended to the throne. Knox tried to apologise in a letter to Sir William Cecil ('I had no suspicion of the book, and for a whole year was ignorant of its publication') but Elizabeth remained implacable.*

The most notorious whore in all the world.

Peter Wentworth on Mary, Queen of Scots

She was happy as the Dey was long.

Chief Justice Lord Norbury, on Queen Caroline's affair with the Muslim Dey of Algiers, 1820

Most gracious Queen we thee implore
To Go Away and sin no more
But if that effort be too great
To go away, at any rate.
Anonymous epigram on Queen Caroline, wife of George IV

The bloom of her ugliness is going off.
Colonel Disbrowe on the ageing looks of Queen Charlotte

Beauty is only skin deep, but ugliness goes clean to the bone.
Dorothy Parker

Anne . . . when in good humour, was meekly stupid, and
when in bad humour, was sulkily stupid.
Thomas Babington Macaulay on Queen Anne

The Church's wet nurse, Goody Anne.
Horace Walpole on Queen Anne

One of the smallest people ever set in a great place.
Walter Bagehot on Queen Anne

The wisest fool in Christendom.
Henri IV of France on James I of England. Attrib.

One of the moral monsters of history.
Samuel Taylor Coleridge on Charles II

Henry VIII perhaps approached as nearly to the ideal standard
of perfect wickedness as the infirmities of human nature will
allow.
Sir James Mackintosh

A blot of blood and grease upon the History of England.
  Charles Dickens on Henry VIII

An old, mad, blind, despised, and dying king –
Princes, the dregs of their dull race, who flow
Through public scorn – mud from a muddy spring;
Rulers who neither see, nor feel, nor know,
But leechlike to their fainting country cling,
Till they drop, blind in blood, without a blow…
  Percy Bysshe Shelley on George III, his family and government, England in
  1819. Written after troops attacked a crowd of unarmed protesters, killing
  several, who were demonstrating in favour of parliamentary reform

Throughout the greater part of his life, George III was a kind of consecrated obstruction.
  Walter Bagehot

'Since I had the pleasure of your Royal Highness's acquaintance.'
  John Wilkes on the Prince of Wales, later George IV, when the Prince asked
  (because he had proposed a toast to the King's health) him how long he had
  shown such concern for his father's wellbeing

No danger. For no man would take away my life to make you king.
  Charles II to his brother James, the Duke of York, on the risk of the King
  going about without protection

After you have seen 150 Lord Mayors, they all begin to look the same.
  George IV

A tree's a tree. How many do you need to look at?
Ronald Reagan on plans to expand California's Redwood National Park 1967

Never was a person less mourned by his fellow men than the late King ... if ever George IV had a friend, a true friend, in any social class, so we may claim that his or her name never reached our ears.
The Times, commentary

A more contemptible, cowardly, selfish, unfeeling dog does not exist than this King ... with vices and weaknesses of the lowest and most contemptible order.
Charles Greville, diarist, on George IV

Who's your fat friend?
George 'Beau' Brummell to Beau Nash who had introduced the Prince Regent

Queen Victoria was like a great paperweight that for half a century sat upon men's minds, and when she was removed their ideas began to blow all over the place haphazardly.
H.G.Wells

Strip your Louis Quatorze of his king gear and there is left nothing but a poor forked radish with a head fantastically carved.
Thomas Carlyle on Louis XIV

Nowadays, a parlour maid as ignorant as Queen Victoria was when she came to the throne, would be classed as mentally defective.
George Bernard Shaw on Queen Victoria

Sir, I am loth to interrupt the rapture of mourning in which the nation is now enjoying its favourite festival – a funeral. But in a country like ours the total suspension of common sense and sincere human feeling for a whole fortnight is an impossibility.

A letter from George Bernard Shaw to the Morning Leader *after the death of Queen Victoria. The Editor declined to publish the letter*

Very sorry can't come. Lie follows by post.

Telegram from Charles Beresford to the Prince of Wales, later Edward VIII, following a dinner invitation at short notice

I don't mind your being killed, but I object to your being taken prisoner.

Lord Kitchener to the Prince of Wales, when he asked to go to the Western Front in the First World War

No thank you; I only smoke on special occasions.

Anonymous commoner, confused and overawed, on being asked by George VI at a banquet whether he cared for a cigar

A Corpulent voluptuary.

Rudyard Kipling on Edward VII

Born into the ranks of the working class, the new King's most likely fate would have been that of a street-corner loafer.

James Keir Hardie, Labour leader, on George V

For seventeen years he did nothing at all but kill animals and stick in stamps.

Harold Nicolson, biographer of George V, on his subject

He will go from resort to resort getting more tanned and more tired.

> Westbrook Pegler on the abdication of Edward VIII, quoted by Alistair Cooke, Six Men

God grant him peace and happiness but never understanding of what he has lost.

> Stanley Baldwin on the abdication of Edward VIII

[A] wife capable of behaving in this way: tantrums and suicide charades – anyone trying to do it with paracetamol isn't trying – is a witless little girl unfit for marriage to anyone. And the wife capable of exploiting her position to get revenge through mass publicity is a destructive little chancer emotionally located in the foothills of adolescence. The footling story of Diana Spencer makes a bitter republican point, the liability of fairy tales to have been written by the Brothers Grimm!...

Charles has claims to be a victim of the Asiatic fixing of his family. No wife brought from Karachi to Southall by imperious parents-in-law could better respect an arranged marriage than the English rose heavily urged for the Crown Prince. She was English (after much public scorn of the former Teutonic norm), a virgin and thus free from all tattle, and she looked good. The facts: that she is virtuoso of on-camera tears, that her delight in life is the nightclub and that she seems to have no mind at all, were disregarded. An intelligent man has been fettered in 'a suitable marriage' to a frothball and has sought to live his life apart from her. What sharper intimation of the shabbiness of monarchy could there be?

There are many reasons for dispensing with monarchy, but two will suffice. The job could be done better; and monarchy, just by existing, induces pathetic impulses in other people. There has to be something wrong with an institution which assembles, in various degrees of competitive abjectness, Lord St John of Fawsley, in whom I have real difficulty believing, Sir Alastair Burnet and Lord Rees-Mogg.

These Firbankian grotesques, prime fruit of the trees of deference, can be relied upon to squelch noisily under royal foot. Happy calling someone twenty years younger 'Sir' or 'Maa-am' they proclaim a social pyramid in which their own status is secured by guileful proximity to the apex. They fawn and teach us to fawn. Unlike the late Richard Dimbleby, grand under-butler to the nation, they do not tell us that the Queen looks radiant, but they are lit by all the royal refection into which they can creep.

Such courtiers only echo the sick adoration of part of the nation. Royalty has done a roaring trade since the war in glossy iconic tosh, books about royal lives, houses, tours, weddings, ancestry and interior décor, books, God help us, about royal dogs. The appetite of silly people for living vicarious, reverential lives through this assembly of low-octane duds in jodhpurs is tragic.

Edward Pearce, Guardian, 'The Aspirin of the People'

Prince Charles is an insensitive, hypocritical oaf and Princess Diana is a selfish, empty-headed bimbo. They should never have got married in the first place. I blame the parents.

Richard Littlejohn, in the Sun

Harlot and trollop.
> *Alleged remarks by Prince Philip in a letter to Diana. Officially denied.*

So thick and yet so thin.
> *Comedian Linda Smith on Princess Diana*

A sort of social hand-grenade, ready to explode, leaving unsuspecting playboys legless and broken.
> *Trevor Phillips on the Princess of Wales, shortly before her death*

Michael Shea, the Queen's former press secretary, claims he hasn't read the *Sun* since he left Buck House in 1987 ... that hasn't prevented him passing judgement on the 'gutter press'. From his new, exalted position £120,000 up Lord Hanson's backside, Shea pours bile and contempt on the tabloids, the people who work for them and the people who read them ... We stand accused of lack of deference, prurience and downright spiteful invention ...

Lack of deference? Rather that than a forelock-tugging flunkey.

Prurience? No more so than readers of the Observer who queued round the block for a full-frontal gander at Madonna's naughty bits.

Spiteful invention? No one is trying to pretend that the papers don't get it wrong from time to time ... Reporters would get things wrong less often if people like Shea told the truth.

'The intention was always to be helpful and forthcoming to all concerned,' Shea writes in *The Times*...

Shea was a master of evasion, more slippery than a Jacuzzi full of KY jelly. You might say he was the first Sensitol-lubricated PR man – particularly appropriate when you consider where he has spent most of his life.

Royal reporters say meeting Shea was like shaking hands with a bar of wet soap. Except you come away feeling clean when you shake hands with a bar of wet soap.

Perhaps if Shea had been more open and honest – if he had given Her Majesty better advice – matters would not have come to quite the unpleasant head they have recently. I bear no personal animosity towards the Royals and I suspect few other people do.

It is the Sir Alan Fitztightlys of this world, the bowling and scraping courtiers like Shea, who consider themselves above the common herd by virtue of their employer, that I can't abide...

Richard Littlejohn on Michael Shea, the Queen's former press secretary, in the Sun

I'm prepared to take advice on leisure from Prince Philip. He's a world expert on leisure. He's been practising for most of his adult life.

Neil Kinnock on Prince Philip, in the Western Mail

The Duke of Edinburgh runs the country behind the scenes; he is the actual head of the Royal Family. He's a racist; he grew up with Nazis, and one of his aunts married one of Hitler's generals. Beneath the surface he has a German name – Frankenstein. Well it sounds like Frankenstein.

Mohamed Al-Fayed

She is a lady short on looks, absolutely deprived of any dress sense, has a figure like a Jurassic monster, [seems] very greedy when it comes to loot, no tact and wants to upstage everyone else.

Sir Nicholas Fairbairn MP on Sarah, Duchess of York, in the Independent

Why don't you naff off!
Princess Anne to reporters, in the Daily Mirror

My, you must have fun chasing the soap around the bath.
Diana, Princess of Wales, shaking hands with a one-armed man in
Australia, 1983

Actually I vote Labour, but my butler's a Tory.
Earl Mountbatten to a canvasser during the 1945 election

The difference between us is that my family begins with me,
whereas yours ends with you.
Iphicrates, Athenian general and the son of a cobbler, replying to a
descendant of the Athenian hero Harmodius who mocked his lowly origins ·

Of course they have, or I wouldn't be talking to you.
Barbara Cartland, when asked by BBC reporter Sandra Harris in a radio
interview whether she thought English class barriers had broken down

Miss Cartland makes much of the fact that part of the proceeds
of the book are going to the Mountbatten Memorial Trust, and
indeed insists that Earl Mountbatten helped her with the
writing … she draws conspicuous attention to the connection
on the front of the jacket (twice), in the blurb, on the back
jacket (photographically), on the title-page, on the half-title
and in an Author's Note. All that expert help, however, has still
not managed to correct her apparent belief that Trafalgar came
shortly before Waterloo; perhaps she has confused English
history with the London Underground System.
Bernard Levin, on Barbara Cartland's 240th novel, Love at the Helm

Aristocrats spend their childhood being beaten by fierce nannies and their later years murdering wildlife, so it's hardly surprising their sex lives are a bit cock-eyed.
Jilly Cooper, Men and Super Men

In the British aristocracy the gene pool has always had a shallow end.
Former US ambassador Raymond Seitz

These bloody people. I can't bear that man. I mean, he's so awful, he really is.
Prince Charles on Royal Correspondent, Nicholas Witchell

How do you keep the natives off the booze long enough to get them past the test?
The Duke of Edinburgh to a driving instructor in Scotland

An aristocracy in a republic is like a chicken whose head has been cut off; it may run about in a lively way, but in fact it is dead.
Nancy Mitford, Noblesse Oblige

Sacred to the memory of
Captain Anthony Wedgewood
Accidently shot by his gamekeeper
Whilst out shooting
'Well done thou good and faithful servant'
Epitaph

Poor Matt. He's gone to heaven, no doubt, but he won't like God.
Robert Louis Stevenson on Matthew Arnold

How beastly the bourgeois is
especially the male of the species - ...
Nicely groomed, like a mushroom
standing there so sleek and erect and eyeable –
And a fungus, living on the remains of bygone life
sucking his life out of the dead leaves of greater life than his
own.

And even so, he's stale, he's been there too long.
Touch him, and you'll find he's all gone inside
just like an old mushroom, all wormy inside, and hollow
under a smooth skin and an upright appearance.
Full of seething, wormy, hollow feelings
rather nasty –
How beastly the bourgeois is!

Standing in their thousands, these appearances, in damp
England
what a pity they can't all be kicked over
like sickening toadstools, and left to melt back, swiftly
into the soil of England.

D.H. Lawrence, Pansies, 'How beastly the bourgeois is'

But that vast portion, lastly, of the working-class which, raw
and half-developed, has long lain half-hidden amidst its
poverty and squalor, and is now issuing from its hiding place
to assert an Englishman's heaven-born privilege of doing as he
likes, and is beginning to perplex us by marching where it
likes, meeting where it likes, bawling what it likes, breaking
what it likes – to this vast residuum we may with great
propriety give the name of Populace.

Matthew Arnold, Culture and Anarchy

Walk through her cities, walk with a pal
Through the streets between the power-house and green
canal
And see what they're at – our proletariat.
O my, what peeps
At disheartened sweeps –
Fitters and moulders,
Wielders and welders,
Dyers and bakers
And boiler-tube makers,
Poufs and ponces,
All of them dunces.
Those over thirty,
Ugly and dirty,
What are they doing
Except just stewing?
Content for the year
With foods out of tins and very small beer –
Flaking the rust off obsolete plant
Slacking at the corners thinking 'I can't.'
Sloping up the hill, for they've nowhere else to go –
To the park and the platforms where the windbags blow
Spying on athletes playing on a green,
Spying on kisses as shown on a screen,
Their minds as pathetic as a boxer's face,
Ashamed, uninteresting, and hopeless race.

  W.H. Auden on the English proletariat, from The Orators

Poverty is an anomaly to rich people. It is very difficult to
make out why people who want dinner do not ring the bell.
  Walter Bagehot

Let them eat cake.

Marie-Antoinette repeating an old saying when told the people had no bread to eat

Voting and buying drugs: the two activities that will drag a professional person into a place where people live on land owned by the council.

Giles Coren in The Times

MY LORD,- Now I am recovering from an illness of several months' duration, aggravated no little by your lordship's rude reception of me at the Cascine, in presence of my family and innumerable Florentines. I must remind you in the gentlest terms of the occurrence. We are both of us old men, my lord, and are verging on decrepitude and imbecility. Else my note might be more energetic. I am not unobservant of distinctions. You, by the favour of a minister, are Marquis of Normanby, I by the grace of God am.
WALTER SAVAGE LANDOR

W.S. Landor, letter to Lord Normanby, who had cut him

A louse, sir, is still but a louse though it crawl on the curls of a Queen.

Robert Burns

Someone has said that the King may make a nobleman, but he cannot make a gentleman.

Edmund Burke

As he rose like a rocket, he fell like a stick.

Thomas Paine on Edmund Burke

Lady Jane Seymour, granddaughter of Richard Brinsley Sheridan, had been chosen 'Queen of Beauty' some time before at a pseudo-medieval tournament led by Louis Napoleon. The following is an exchange of correspondence between her and Lady Shuckburgh ...

Lady Seymour presents her compliments to Lady Shuckburgh, and would be obliged to her for the character of Mary Steadman, who states that she lived twelve months, and still is, in Lady Shuckburgh's establishment. Can Mary Steadman cook plain dishes well? make bread? and is she honest, good-tempered, sober, willing and cleanly? Lady Seymour would also like to know the reason why she leaves Lady Shuckburgh's service? Direct, under cover to Lord Seymour, Maiden Bradley.

Lady Shuckburgh presents her compliments to Lady Seymour. Her ladyship's note, dated October 28, only reached her yesterday, November 3. Lady Shuckburgh was unacquainted with the name of the kitchen-maid until mentioned by Lady Seymour, as it is her custom neither to apply for or give characters to any of the under servants, this being always done by the housekeeper, Mrs Couch – and this was well known to the young woman; therefore Lady Shuckburgh is surprised at her referring any lady to her for a character. Lady Shuckburgh having a professed cook, as well as a housekeeper, in her establishment, it is not very likely that she herself should know anything of the abilities or merits of the under servants; therefore she is unable to answer Lady Seymour's note. Lady Shuckburgh cannot imagine Mary Steadman to be capable of cooking for any except the servants'-hall table.

Lady Seymour presents her compliments to Lady Shuckburgh, and begs she will order her housekeeper, Mrs Pouch, to send the girl's character without delay; otherwise another young woman will be sought for elsewhere. As Lady Seymour's children cannot remain without their dinners because Lady Shuckburgh, keeping a 'professed cook and a housekeeper', thinks a knowledge of the details of her establishment beneath her notice. Lady Seymour understands from Steadman that, in addition to her other talents, she was actually capable of dressing food fit for the little Shuckburghs to partake of when hungry. (*Attached to this was a cartoon of the three Shuckburgh children, with large heads and cauliflower wigs, slavering over a chop prepared by a grinning Mary Stedman, while their mother hovered in dismay*)

MADAM,
Lady Shuckburgh has directed me to acquaint you that she declines answering your note, the vulgarity of which is beneath contempt; and although it may be the characteristic of the Sheridans to be vulgar, coarse, and witty, it is not that of a 'lady', unless she happens to have been born in a garret and bred in a kitchen. Mary Steadman informs me that your ladyship does not keep either a cook or a housekeeper, and that you only require a girl who can cook a mutton chop. If so, I apprehend that Mary Steadman, or any other scullion, will be found equal to cook for or manage the establishment of the Queen of Beauty. I am, your ladyship, & c.,
ELIZABETH COUCH (not Pouch).

I've been offered titles, but I think they get one into disreputable company.
George Bernard Shaw

I like the Garter; there is no damned merit in it.
Lord Melbourne

Not really. Experience has taught us that those who matter don't mind and those who mind don't matter.
Ambassador to a dinner guest who had forced her fellow guests to swap seats after discovering precedence ought to accord her a place closer to the Ambassador. She had said to him: 'I expect you find these questions of precedence very troublesome, Your Excellency'

We invite people like that to tea, but we don't marry them.
Lady Chetwode on her future son-in-law, John Betjeman

What you need is a couple of aspirates.
F.E. Smith to Jimmy Thomas, who never pronounced his h's. He had complained of an' eadache

No writer before the middle of the 19th century wrote about the working classes other than as grotesque or as pastoral decoration. Then when they were given the vote certain writers started to suck up to them.
Evelyn Waugh

I never knew the working classes had such white skins.
Lord Curzon, seeing some troops bathing during the First World War

We are all beautiful (except white people, they are full of and made of shit)...

Imamu Amiri Baraka, Black Magic, A school of prayer

One of the things that makes a Negro unpleasant to white folks is the fact that he suffers from their injustice. He is thus a standing rebuke to them.

H.L. Mencken

[A person is] a male Person, including an Indian and excluding a person of Mongolian or Chinese race.

Canada Franchise Act 1885

We have every kind of mixture you can have. I have a black, I have a woman, two Jews and a cripple.

James Watt, US Interior Secretary, on the balanced composition of an advisory board

Porkie

Jamaican term of abuse for white people

What negroes want is tight pussy, loose shoes and a warm place to shit.

Earl Butz, US Secretary for Agriculture in the Nixon administration

When black man thief, him steal half a bit; but when white man thief, him steal a whole sugar plantation.

Black American slave. Attrib.

When the white man is about to leave a garden for good, he wrecks it.

Yoruba proverb

Making love to a white man is like making love to a skinned animal.

Anonymous Nigerian woman

The white man knows how to make everything, but he does not know how to distribute it.

Sitting Bull

The national religion of the Creeks, Cherokees, Chickasaws and all the other Indians, is to torture all their prisoners from morning to night, til at length they roast them to death ... Yea, it is a common thing among them for the son, if he thinks his father lives too long, to knock out his brains.

John Wesley, Works, *V*

White people say to me 'Isn't there anything good about us?' and I reply 'Yes. You sure can ski. You're beautiful skiers.'

Paul Mooney

The Sioux Indians are a set of miserable, dirty, lousy, blanketed, seething, lying, sneaking, murdering, graceless, faceless, dog-eating SKUNKS as the Lord ever permitted to infect the earth, and whose immediate and final extermination all MEN, excepting Indian agents and traders, should pray for.

Topeka Weekly Daily, *1869*

I'm a coloured, one-eyed Jew.

Sammy Davis, Jr., when asked what his handicap was during a game of golf

There is only one race greater than the Jews – and that is the Derby.

Victor Sassoon

All those who are not racially pure are mere chaff.
  Adolf Hitler, Mein Kampf

His 140,000 words were 140,000 offences against the spirit
of the German language.
  Leon Feuchtwanger on Hitler's Mein Kampf

The white race is the cancer of all human history. It is the
white race and it alone, its ideologies and inventions, which
eradicate autonomous civilizations wherever it spreads.
  Susan Sontag, Partisan Review

They are more like animals than human beings. Those of them
who live deep in the north – between the end of the even
climates and the end of the habitable world – have been so
affected by the extreme distance of the sun from the Zenith
above their heads, resulting in cold climate and thick
atmosphere, that their temperatures have become chilly and
their humours rude. Consequently their bodies are huge,
their colour pale and their hair long. For the same reason they
lack keenness in intelligence and perspicacity and are charac-
terized by ignorance and stupidity. Folly and mental blindness
prevail among them.
  Sai'd, eleventh-century Moslem scientist, on Northern Europeans

The gentleman will please remember that when his half-
civilized ancestors were hunting the wild boar in Silesia, mine
were princes of the earth.
  *Judah Benjamin, replying to an anti-Semitic remark by a senator of
  German origin. Attrib.*

...a tendency – from which I suffer myself – to presume that anyone of any eminence at all is Jewish, unless he or she can show definitive proof to the contrary.
Chaim Bermant

It is extremely difficult for a Jew to be converted, for how can he bring himself to believe in the divinity of – another Jew?
Heinrich Heine

If a Jew can have the rope free of charge he will let himself be hanged.
Russian insult

If the Jew is of gold, his testicles are of copper.
Moorish insult

Lord, I ascribe it to Thy grace,
And not to chance, as others do,
That I was born of Christian race,
And not a Heathen, or a Jew.
English hymn by Isaac Watts, from his Divine Songs for Children

No, not really. Except this: We think they're stupid.
Dominic Lawson, when asked at a Spectator lunch whether Jews held any prejudice against Gentiles comparable to anti-Semitism

Few people can be happy unless they hate some other person, nation or creed.
Bertrand Russell

An ambassador is an honest man sent to lie abroad for the good of his country.
Sir Henry Wotton

The great nations have always acted like gangsters, and the small nations like prostitutes.
> *Stanley Kubrick, in the* Guardian

If people behaved in the way nations do, they would all be put in straightjackets.
> *Tennessee Williams*

This going into Europe will not turn out to be the thrilling mutual exchange supposed. It is more like nine middle-aged couples with failing marriages meeting in a darkened bedroom in a Brussels hotel for a Group Grope.
> *E.P. Thompson on the EEC, in the* Sunday Times, *1975*

The majority of those men are homosexuals — perhaps not the majority but in the USA there are already 25 percent of them and in England and Germany it is the same. You cannot imagine it in the history of France.
> *Edith Cresson, French Prime Minister*

The most significant British contribution to the European Community to date is BSE.
> *The German newspaper,* Allgemeine Zeitung

A small acquaintance with history shows that all Governments are selfish and the French Governments more selfish than most.
> *Lord Eccles*

I do not dislike the French from the vulgar antipathy between neighbouring nations, but for their insolent and unfounded airs of superiority.
> *Horace Walpole*

France was a long despotism tempered by epigrams.
Thomas Carlyle, History of the French Revolution

Never doubt the courage of the French. They are the ones who discovered snails are edible.
Doug Larson

In all the four corners of the earth one of these three names is given to him who steals from his neighbours; brigand, robber or Englishman.
Les Triades de l'Anglais

Poltroons, cowards, skullers and dastards.
Eustache Deschamps on the English

France is a dog-hole.
William Shakespeare, All's Well That Ends Well

England is a nation of shopkeepers.
Napoleon Bonaparte

A cold-blooded, calculating, unprincipled usurper, without a virtue; no statesman, knowing nothing of commerce, political economy or civil government, and supplying ignorance by bold presumption.
Thomas Jefferson on Napoleon Bonaparte

The ignorance of French society gives one a rough sense of the infinite.
Joseph E. Renan

What a pity it is that we have no amusements in England but vice and religion.
Reverend Sydney Smith

They are short, blue-vested people who carry their own
onions when cycling abroad, and have a yard which is 3.37
inches longer than other people's.
    Alan Coren on the French

I found there a country with thirty-two religions and only
one sauce.
    Talleyrand on America

He is a silk stocking filled with dung.
    Napoleon Bonaparte on Talleyrand

Nobody can simply bring together a country that has 365
kinds of cheese.
    Charles de Gaulle on France

One cannot trust people whose cuisine is so bad ... The only
thing they have ever done for European agriculture is mad
cow disease. ... After Finland, it is the country with the
worst food.
    Jacques Chirac, French President, on Britain

Cheese-eating surrender monkeys.
    Groundsman Willie in The Simpsons, *on the French*

It was wonderful to find America, but it would have been
more wonderful to miss it.
    Mark Twain

The American people generally do the right thing ... after
first exhausting every available alternative.
    Winston Churchill

Right, your Excellency. But I reckon a Frenchman's got a little standby for a dull time too; he can turn in and see if he can find out who his father was.

Mark Twain, replying to the French novelist Paul Bourget, who had remarked: 'Life can never be entirely dull to an American. When he has nothing else to do he can always spend a few years trying to discover who his grandfather was'

I heard an Englishman, who had been long resident in America, declare that in following, in meeting, or in overtaking, in the street, on the road, or in the field, at the theatre, the coffee-house, or at home, he had never overheard Americans conversing without the word DOLLAR being pronounced between them. Such unity of purpose ... can ... be found nowhere else, except ... in an ants' nest.

Frances Trollope, A Commentary on Travels on a Mississippi Steamer

When an American heiress wants to buy a man, she at once crosses the Atlantic. The only real materialistic people I have ever met are the Europeans.

Mary McCarthy

America is the only nation in history which miraculously has gone from barbarism to degeneration without the usual interval of civilization.

Georges Clemenceau

Be nice to America – or we'll bring you democracy.

Bumper sticker in the USA

America is one long expectoration.

Oscar Wilde

It is absurd to say that there are neither ruins nor curiosities in America when they have their mothers and their manners.
Oscar Wilde

No one can be as calculatedly rude as the British, which amazes Americans, who do not understand studied insult and can only offer abuse as a substitute.
Paul Gallico

The trouble with America is that there are far too many wide open spaces surrounded by teeth.
Charles Luckman

They have wonderful minds. So much is stored inside – all those sports scores and so on.
Jane Seymour on American men, in Time

America is a large, friendly dog in a very small room. Every time it wags its tail it knocks over a chair.
Arnold Toynbee

Americans are people who laugh at African witch doctors and spend 100 million dollars on fake reducing systems.
L.L. Levinson

To Americans English manners are far more frightening than none at all.
Randall Jarrell

The American male doesn't mature until he has exhausted all other possibilities.
Wilfred Sheed, Officer Politics

The national dish of America is menus.
Robert Robertson

Show me a nation whose national beverage is beer, and I'll show you an advanced toilet technology.
Paul Hawkins

As always the British shudder at the latest American vulgarity, and then embrace it with enthusiasm two years later.
Alistair Cooke

There won't be any revolution in America ... the people are too clean. They spend all their time changing their shirts and washing themselves. You can't feel fierce and revolutionary in a bathroom.
Eric Linklater, Juan in America

There is nothing the matter with Americans except their ideals. The real American is all right; it is the ideal American who is all wrong.
G.K. Chesterton

The Americans often appease their enemies, but they always betray their friends.
Anonymous Middle East Ruler

What you do to your enemies today, you will do to your friends tomorrow.
Afghan proverb

Not so much an axis of evil, more an arc of insufferability.
US pundit describing America's European allies

Knavery seems to be so much the striking feature of its inhabitants that it may not in the end be an evil that they will become aliens to this country.

George III on America

Paralytic sycophants, effete betrayers of humanity, carrion-eating servile imitators, arch-cowards and collaborators, gang of women-murderers, degenerate rabble, parasitic traditional-ists, playboy soldiers, conceited dandies.

Approved terms of abuse in 1953 for East German Communist speakers when describing Britain

It is related of an Englishman that he hanged himself to avoid the daily task of dressing and undressing.

Johann Wolfgang von Goethe

The English think soap is civilization.

Heinrich von Treitschke

I know why the sun never sets on the British Empire: God wouldn't trust an Englishman in the dark.

Duncan Spaeth

Like a prostitute who, having sold her body all her life, decides to quit and close her business, and then tells everyone she wants to be chaste and protect her flesh as if it were jade.

He Manzi on Great Britain, in the Shanghi Liberation Daily. *The reference is to Britain's discovery of a passion for democracy in Hong Kong under Chinese Rule, having long denied Hong Kong democracy under British rule*

I wish I could bring Stonehenge to Nyasaland to show there was a time when Britain had a savage culture.
Dr Hastings Banda, President of Malawi, in the Observer

One of the most precious freedoms of the British is the freedom from culture.
Lord Goodman

A demon took a monkey to wife – the result by the Grace of God was the English.
Indian saying

An Englishman, even if he is alone, forms an orderly queue of one.
George Mikes

The Earth contains no race of human beings so totally vile and worthless as the Welsh.
Walter Savage Landor, letter to Robert Southey

'The Welsh,' said the Doctor, 'are the only nation in the world that has produced no graphic or plastic art, no architecture, no drama. They just sing,' he said with disgust, 'sing and blow down wind instruments of plated silver.'
Evelyn Waugh, Decline and Fall

But Lord! to see the absurd nature of Englishmen, that cannot forbear laughing and jeering at everything that looks strange.
Samuel Pepys, Diary

The only good that comes from the east is the sun.
Portuguese saying

Last Sunday I came – a man whom the Lord God made – to the town of Flint, with its great double walls and rounded bastions: may I see it all aflame! An obscure English wedding was there, with but little mead – an English feast! And I meant to earn a shilling solid reward for my harper's art. So I began with ready speed, to sing an ode to the kinsmen; but all I got was mockery, spurning of my song, and grief.

Lewis Glyn Cothi or Tudur Penllyn, tr. From the Welsh by Kenneth Jackson, The English Wedding

Your proper child of Caledonia believes in his rickety bones that he is the salt of the earth. Prompted by a glozing pride, not to say by a black and consuming avarice, he has proclaimed his saltiness from the house tops in and out of season, unblushingly, assiduously, and with results which have no doubt been most satisfactory from his own point of view. There is nothing creditable to the race of men, from filial piety to a pretty taste in claret, which he has not sedulously advertised as a virtue peculiar to himself. This arrogation has served him passing well. It has brought him into unrivalled esteem. He is the one species of human animal that is taken by all the world to be fifty per cent cleverer and pluckier and honester than the facts warrant. He is the draw with a peacock's tail of his own painting. He is the ass who has been at pains to cultivate the convincing roar of a lion. He is the fine gentleman whose father toils with a muck fork. And, to have done with parable, he is the bandy-legged lout from Tullietudlescleugh, who, after a childhood of intimacy with the cesspool and the crablouse, and twelve months at 'the college' on moneys wrung from the diet of his family, drops his threadbare kilt and comes south in a slop suit to instruct the English in the arts of civilization and in the English language. And because he is Scotch and the Scotch superstition is heavy on our Southern lands, England will forthwith give him a chance, for an English chance is his birthright. Soon, forby, shall he be living in 'chambers' and writing idiot books. Or he shall swell and hector and fume in the sub-editor's room of a halfpenny paper. Or a pompous and gravel-blind city house shall grapple him to its soul in the capacity of confidential clerk. Or he shall be cashier in a jam factory, or 'boo and boo' behind a mercer's counter, or 'wait on' in a coffee tavern, or for that matter, soak away his chapped spirit in the four ale bars off Fleet Street.

T.W. H. Crosland on the Scots, in The Unspeakable Scot

England, the heart of a rabbit in the body of a Lion. The jaws of a serpent in an abode of popinjays.

Eustache Deschamps, fourteenth century writer, on England

England is not a bad country – it's just a mean, cold, ugly, divided, tired, clapped-out, post-imperial, post-industrial, slag heap covered in polystyrene hamburger cartons.

Margaret Drabble

The departure of the Wise men from the East seems to have been on a more extensive scale than is generally supposed, for no one of that description seems to have been left behind.

Sydney Smith on the East

Our trouble is that we drink too much tea. I see in this the slow revenge of the Orient, which has diverted the Yellow River down our throats.

J.B. Priestley

Taffy was a Welshman,
Taffy was a thief,
Taffy came to my house
And stole a piece of beef.

I went to Taffy's house,
Taffy wasn't in,
I jumped upon his Sunday hat
And poked it with a pin.

Taffy was a Welshman,
Taffy was a sham,
Taffy came to my house
And stole a leg of lamb.

I went to Taffy's house,
Taffy wasn't there,
Hung his coat and trousers
To roast before a fire.

Taffy was a Welshman
Taffy was a cheat,
Taffy came to my house
And stole a piece of meat.

I went to Taffey's house,
Taffy wasn't home;
Taffy came to my house
And stole a marrow bone.
    English nursery rhyme

A Welshman is a man who prays on his knees on Sunday and preys on his friends the rest of the week.

> Insult, probably of English origin

…an impotent people, sick with inbreeding, Worrying the carcase of an old song.

> R. S. Thomas, Welsh poet and clergyman, An Acre of Land, 'Welsh Landscape'

They are all the same. They're short, they're fat and they're fundamentally corrupt.

> Rod Richards, junior Welsh Office minister, on Welsh Labour councillors, 1995

The land of my fathers. My fathers can have it.

> Dylan Thomas on Wales

There are still parts of Wales where the only concession to gaiety is a striped shroud.

> Gwyn Thomas

The Welsh are so damn Welsh that it looks like affectation.

> Sir Walter Alexander Raleigh to D. B. Wyndham Lewis

It profits a man nothing to give his soul for the whole world … But for Wales!

> Sir Thomas More, in Robert Bolt's A Man for All Seasons

Fucking Welsh.

> Tony Blair, reported by his press secretary Alistair Campbell

Other people have a nationality. The Irish and the Jews have a psychosis.

Brendan Behan

Put an Irishman on the spit and you can always get another Irishman to turn him.

George Bernard Shaw

I return your seasonal greeting card with contempt. May your hypocritical words choke you and may they choke you early in the New Year, rather than later.

Professor Kennedy Lindsay, a Vanguard member of the Northern Assembly, returning a Christmas card from the Minister for Foreign Affairs, Dr Garret FitzGerald, in the Irish Times

Ireland is the old sow that eats her farrow.

James Joyce, A Portrait of the Artist as a Young Man

The problem with Ireland is that it's a country full of genius, but with absolutely no talent.

Hugh Leonard

An Irish queer is a fellow who prefers women to drink.

Sean O'Faolain

The moment the very name of Ireland is mentioned, the English seem to bid adieu to common feeling, common prudence, and common sense, and to act with the barbarity of tyrants, and the fatuity of idiots.

Sydney Smith

But of all nations in the world the English are perhaps the least a nation of pure philosophers.
Walter Bagehot

You must look out in England that you are not cheated by the charioteers.
Marcus Tullius Cicero

...where the Greeks had modesty, we have cant; where they had poetry, we have cant; where they had patriotism, we have cant; where they had anything that exalts, delights, or adorns humanity, we have nothing but cant, cant, cant.
Thomas Love Peacock, Crotchet Castle, *on the English*

The English are the people of consummate cant.
Friedrich Nietzsche, Twilight of the Idols

A ready means of being cherished by the English is to adopt the simple expedient of living a long time. I have little doubt that if, say, Oscar Wilde had lived into his nineties, instead of dying in his forties, he would have been considered a benign, distinguished figure suitable to preside at a school prize-giving or to instruct and exhort scoutmasters at their jamborees. He might even have been knighted.
Malcolm Muggeridge

The English people on the whole are surely the nicest people in the world, and everyone makes everything so easy for everybody else, that there is almost nothing to resist at all.
D.H. Lawrence, Dull London

The English have an extraordinary ability for flying into a great calm.
  Alexander Woollcott

The English don't mind people pissing on them, provided it's from a great height.
  George Walden

Thirty millions, mostly fools.
  Thomas Carlyle, when asked what the population of England was. Attrib.

I speak Spanish to God, Italian to women, French to men, and German to my horse.
  Charles V, Holy Roman Emperor. Attrib.

An ass in Germany is a professor in Rome.
  German song

Life is too short to learn German.
  Richard Porson

Life is never so bad that Germany is better.
  Jeremy Clarkson

German humour is no laughing matter.
  Mark Twain

Ah, so next time we shall not be able to hear them coming.
  Pierre Mendes-France, former French Prime Minister, on news that German soldiers' jackboots were now fitted with rubber soles, 1960

German is a language which was developed solely to afford the speaker the opportunity to spit at strangers under the guise of polite conversation.

National Lampoon

The devil take these people and their language! They take a dozen monosyllabic words in their jaws, chew them, crunch them and spit them out again, and call that speaking. Fortunately they are but nature fairly silent, and although they gaze at us open-mouthed, they spare us long conversations.

Heinrich Heine on the English

From every Englishman emanates a kind of gas, the deadly choke-damp of boredom.

Heinrich Heine

Unmitigated noodles.

Kaiser Wilhelm II of Germany on the English

One thing I will say for the Germans, they are always perfectly willing to give somebody else's land to somebody else.

Will Rogers

How much disgruntled heaviness, lameness, dampness, dressing gown – how much beer there is in the German intelligence.

Friedrich Nietzsche, Twilight of the Idols

The perfidious, haughty, savage, disdainful, stupid, slothful, inhospitable, inhuman, English.

Julius Caesar Scaliger on England

The English are, in my opinion, perfidious and cunning, plotting the destruction of the lives of foreigners, so that even if they humbly bend the knee, they cannot be trusted.
Leo de Rozmital, 1456

You must hate a Frenchman as you hate the devil.
Horatio Nelson

The English often kill themselves. It is a malady caused by the humid climate.
Napoleon Bonaparte

That sweet enemy.
Sir Philip Sidney on France

A country the size of a piece of snot.
Chen Tan-Sun, Taiwanese Foreign Minister, on Singapore

The immense popularity of American movies abroad demonstrates that Europe is the unfinished negative of which America is the proof.
Mary McCarthy, American novelist

In the USA 'First' and 'Second' class can't be painted on railroad cars, for all passengers, being Americans, are equal and it would be 'un-American.' But paint Pullman on a car and everyone is satisfied.
Owen Wister on the American class system

An Englishman's way of speaking absolutely classifies him. The moment he talks he makes some other Englishman despise him.
Alan Jay Lerner, My Fair Lady

The English take their pleasures sadly, after the fashion of their country.
Maximilien de Béthune, Duc de Sully

We are terribly afraid that some Americans spit on the floor, even when that floor is covered by good carpets. Now all claims to civilization are suspended till this secretion is otherwise disposed of. No English gentleman has spit upon the floor since the Heptarchy.
Sydney Smith

England is ... a country infested with people who love to tell us what to do, but who very rarely seem to know what's going on.
Colin MacInnes, novelist

Oh, if the Queen were a man, she would like to go and give those horrid Russians whose word one cannot trust such a beating.
Queen Victoria, letter to Disraeli

On the Continent people have good food: in England people have good table manners.
George Mikes

The Japanese have perfected good manners and made them indistinguishable from rudeness.
Paul Theroux

The French have made of ingratitude – as of most things in life – an art.
Charles Krauthammer, Washington Post

A family with the wrong members in control – that, perhaps, is as near as one can come to describing England in a phrase.
George Orwell, The Lion and the Unicorn, 'The Ruling Class'

In Italy for thirty years under the Borgias they had warfare, terror, murder, bloodshed – they produced Michelangelo, Leonardo da Vinci and the Renaissance. In Switzerland they had brotherly love, five hundred years of democracy and peace, and what did they produce…? The cuckoo clock.
Orson Welles, The Third Man

Since both its national products, snow and chocolate, melt, the cuckoo clock was invented solely in order to give tourists something solid to remember it by.
Alan Coren on Switzerland

I look upon Switzerland as an inferior sort of Scotland.
Sydney Smith

Oats. A grain, which in England is generally given to horses, but in Scotland supports the people.
Samuel Johnson, Dictionary of the English Language

It requires a surgical operation to get a joke well into a Scotch understanding.
Sydney Smith

It is never difficult to distinguish between a Scotsman with a grievance and a ray of sunshine.
P. G. Wodehouse

Norway, too, has noble wild prospects; and Lapland is remarkable for prodigious noble wild prospects. But, Sir, let me tell you, the noblest prospect which a Scotchman ever sees, is the high road that leads him to England.

Samuel Johnson, A Journey to the Western Islands of Scotland

The best thing that comes out of Yorkshire is the road to Lancashire.

Dame Thora Hird

Never ask a man if he comes from Yorkshire. If he does, he will tell you without asking. If he does not, why humiliate him?

Sydney Smith

I have been trying all my life to like Scotchmen, and am obligated to desist from the experiment in despair.

Charles Lamb

His sayings are generally like women's letters; all the pith is in the postscript.

William Hazlitt on Charles Lamb

The Scotchman is one who keeps the Sabbath and every other thing he can lay his hands on.

Lyndon Johnson

You've forgotten the grandest moral attribute of a Scotsman, Maggie, that he'll do nothing which might damage his career.

J.M. Barrie, What Every Woman Knows

DR Johnson: Sir, it is a very vile country.

MR S: Well, sir, God made it.

DR Johnson: Certainly he did, but we must remember that He made it for Scotchmen.

Samuel Johnson, A Journey to the Western Islands of Scotland

The national sport of England is obstacle racing. People fill their rooms with useless and cumbersome furniture, and spend the rest of their lives in trying to dodge it.

Herbert Beerbohm Tree

I am willing to love all mankind, except an American.

Samuel Johnson

Kick all America in the guts: they need it ... Spit on every neurotic ... All that arty and literacy crew, I know them, they are smoking, steaming shits.

D. H. Lawrence on America

The English think of an opinion as something which a decent person, if he has the misfortune to have one, does all he can to hide.

Margaret Halsey, American writer

American society is pyramid-shaped: the further down you go, the wider people grow. Half of America spends its time eating; the other half spends its time trying not to eat.

Craig Brown, the Daily Telegraph

Really nice...it made the spirits sink.

D.H. Lawrence on Australia and Australians, in Kangaroo

So you're going to Australia!…What are you going to sing?
All I can say is – sing'em muck! It's all they can understand!
Dame Nellie Melba, Australian soprano, speaking to Clara Butt

The average American is just like a child.
Richard Nixon

It raises the average IQ of both countries.
*Robert Muldoon, Prime Minister of New Zealand, commenting on an
exodus of New Zealanders emigrating to Australia*

Acquaintances seemed to steer slap through his consciousness
and were gone with the wind.
D.H. Lawrence comparing the Australian mind with the Flying Dutchman

Pass a law to give every single whingeing bloody Pommie his
fare home to England. Back to the smoke and the sun shining
ten days a year and shit in the streets. Yer can have it.
Thomas Keneally, The Chant of Jimmie Blacksmith

I find it hard to say, because when I was there it seemed to be
shut.
Clement Freud on being asked his opinion of New Zealand

You must remember that the Australian voter has a short
memory span … less than 14 days in most cases.
John Howard, Australian Prime Minister

Walking is uniquely un-American.
Bill Bryson

What America calls 'globalisation' the rest of the world call
'Americanisation'.
Henry Louis Gates Jnr

God damn America for treating our citizens as less than human. God damn America for as long as she acts like she is God and she is supreme.

Jeremiah Wright, the senior pastor at Barack Obama's church

Frustrate a Frenchman, he will drink himself to death; an Irishman, he will die of angry hypertension; a Dane, he will shoot himself; an American, he will get drunk, shoot you, then establish a million dollar aid programme for your relatives. Then he will die of an ulcer.

Stanley Rudin

Of course, America had often been discovered before Columbus, but it had always been hushed up.

Oscar Wilde

American intellectuals became afraid to collect their thoughts lest they be accused of unlawful assembly.

Historian Charles Beard on McCarthyite hysteria in America

The English approach to ideas is not to kill them but to let them die of neglect.

Jeremy Paxman

There is no expedient to which a man will not resort to avoid the real labour of thinking.

Sir Joshua Reynolds

The human mind treats a new idea the same way the body treats a strange protein: it rejects it.

Anatomist P.B. Medawar

Many people would sooner die than think. In fact, they do.
Bertrand Russell

Poor Mexico, so far from God and so near to the United States!
Porfirio Diaz

England is perhaps the only great country whose intellectuals are ashamed of their own nationality.
George Orwell

Canada is useful only to provide me with furs.
Madame de Pompadour after the fall of Quebec

The gloomy region, where the year is divided into one day and one night, lies entirely outside the stream of history.
W.W. Reade on Canada, 1872

Canada is a country built against any common, geographical, historic or cultural sense.
Pierre Trudeau, Canadian Prime Minister

I don't even know what street Canada is on.
Al Capone

The people of Crete unfortunately make more history than they can consume locally.
Andrei Dimitrievich Sakharov

Bolivians are merely metamorphosed llamas who have learned to talk but not think.
Chilean Admiral Jose Toribio Merino

God made serpents and rabbits and Armenians.
Turkish insult

Do not trust a Hungarian unless he has a third eye in his forehead.
Czech insult

Half an Italian is one too many in a house.
German and French insult

I saw the new Italian navy. Its boats have glass bottoms so they can see the old Italian navy.
Peter Secchia, President Bush's nominee for US Ambassador to Italy, during Senate confirmation hearings, 1989

In Milan traffic lights are instructions. In Rome they are suggestions. In Naples they are Christmas decorations.
Italian Defence Minister, Antonio Martino

Americans will put up with anything provided it doesn't block traffic.
Dan Rather

Apart from cheese and tulips, the main product of Holland is advocaat, a drink made from lawyers.
Alan Coren, The Sanity Inspector

There are few virtues which the Poles do not possess and there are few errors they have ever avoided.
Winston Churchill

Beer is the Danish national drink and the Danish national weakness is another beer.
Clementine Paddleford

Did hogs feast or did Lithuanians have a feast here?
Polish saying

The Greeks — dirty and impoverished descendants of a bunch of la-de-da fruit salads who invented democracy and then forgot how to use it while walking around dressed up like girls.
P.J. O'Rourke, in the National Lampoon

Just compare with the vast monuments of this vital aqueduct network those useless pyramids or the good-for-nothing tourist attractions of the Greeks.
Frontinus, superintendent of Roman aqueducts

Realizing that they will never be a world power, the Cypriots have decided to settle for being a world nuisance.
George Mikes

It will be golden elephants next.
Clare Short, Development Minister, on demands by the British colony of Montserrat for compensation after the island was devastated by a volcano, 1997

Bongo-Bongo land.
Alan Clark, then an Employment Minister, on the provenance of an African delegation, 1985

The indigested vomit of the sea
Fell to the Dutch by just propriety.
    Andrew Marvell, The Character of Holland

A nation is a society united by a delusion about its ancestry
and by a common hatred of its neighbours.
    William Ralph Inge, A Perpetual Pessimist

If I had to choose between betraying my country and
betraying my friend, I hope I should have the guts to betray
my country.
    E.M. Forster, Two Cheers for Democracy, 'What I Believe'

Patriotism is the last refuge of the scoundrel.
    Samuel Johnson

When Dr Johnson described patriotism as the last refuge of
the scoundrel, he ignored the enormous possibilities of the
world Reform.
    US Senator Roscoe Conkling

Reform? Reform? Aren't things bad enough already?
    The Duke of Wellington

Progress might have been all right once, but it has gone on
too long.
    Ogden Nash

You gotta live somewhere.
    Jimmy Brogan, a suggested motto for Cleveland, USA

They say that men become attached even to Widnes.
    A.J.P. Taylor, in the Observer

Come, friendly bombs, and fall on Slough
It isn't fit for humans now.

… Come, friendly bombs, and fall on Slough
To get it ready for the plough.
The cabbages are coming now;
The earth exhales.
   John Betjeman, Continual Dew, 'Slough'

Suburbia is where the developer bulldozes out the trees, then names the streets after them.
   Bill Vaughan

Erith isn't twinned with anywhere, but it does have a suicide pact with Dagenham.
   Linda Smith

In 1956 the population of Los Angeles was 2,243,901. By 1970 it had risen to 2,811,801, 1,650,917 of whom are currently up for a series.
   Fran Lebowitz on Los Angeles

The difference between yoghurt and Los Angeles is that yoghurt has a living culture.
   Sean Penn

She's blended right in – not necessarily a compliment around here.
   A member of the public after seeing Gwyneth Paltrow in London's Kilburn High Road

He chose to live in Manchester, a wholly incomprehensible choice for a free man to make.
Mr Justice Melford Stevenson, of a man in a divorce case

I see you come from Slough. You can go back there. It is a terrible place.
Mr Justice Melford Stevenson, to a prisoner acquitted of rape

Can pigs grow wings and fly, unwonton birds?
Can the salt sea grow black with grazing herds?
Can the lean thistle blossom into figs?
Or Oxford aught produce save fools and prigs?
Geoffrey Howard on Oxford

Home of lost causes, and forsaken beliefs, and unpopular names, and impossible loyalties!
Matthew Arnold on Oxford

So this is Winnipeg. I can tell it's not Paris.
Bob Edwards on Winnipeg

From 20,000 feet in the air, on the way to Paris.
Australian Prime Minister Paul Keating, asked the best way to see Darwin, Northern Territory

What the hell would I want to go to a place like Mombassa for? I just see myself in a pot of boiling water with all these natives dancing around me.
Mel Lastman, Mayor of Toronto

Why should Ontario pay for Quebec's fucking?
George Drew, Ontario Premier, during a parliamentary debate on family allowances

I have the feeling this is all going to end very badly.
General Charles de Gaulle, to an aide, on first seeing California

One has no great hopes from Birmingham. I always say there is something direful in the sound.
Jane Austen, Emma

When a man is tired of Birmingham he is entirely right.
Hannah Betts

Getting drunk is the quickest way out of it.
Anonymous High Court Judge on Manchester

Manchester is, in the main, dull and workmanlike, the majority of its people live between the workshop, the racing columns of the newspapers, the organized banality of the music hall and the mean street ... in the outer bourgeois and banking Manchester there is another phase. The people in those peripheral garden areas are not so much purse-proud as purse-conscious. They sign their cheques with the strength of men who never stooped to a cash transaction. Of lofty city feeling, there is little in any class.
D.L.Kelleher, The Glamour of Manchester, 1920

Not such a nice place.
Queen Elizabeth II on Manchester, during a visit to St Petersburg, 1994

The grotesque chaos of a Labour council – a Labour Council – hiring taxis to scuttle around a city handing out redundancy notices to its workers.
Neil Kinnock, attacking Militant-Labour-run Liverpool, 1985

They will steal the very teeth of your mouth as you walk the streets. I know it from experience.
> *Judge William Arabin on the people of Uxbridge*

An excessive predilection for welfarism has created a peculiar, and deeply unattractive, psyche among many Liverpudlians. They see themselves whenever possible as victims, and resent their victim status; yet at the same time they wallow in it. Part of this flawed psychological state is that they cannot accept that they might have made any contribution to their misfortunes, but seek rather to blame someone else for it, thereby deepening their sense of shared tribal grievance against the rest of society.
> *Editorial in the* Spectator. *The editor, Boris Johnson, took responsibility. It was alleged that the journalist Simon Heffer was involved in drafting the column*

Here we are, in one of the most depressed towns in Southern England, a place that is arguably too full of drugs, obesity, underachievement and Labour MPs.
> *Boris Johnson on Portsmouth*

The New Deal saved West Virginia from a fate worse than . . . I don't know what. Worse than being West Virginia I guess.
> *Gore Vidal*

An inverted pyramid of piffle.
> *Boris Johnson on allegations against himself*

Underneath this superficial tinsel, there's real tinsel
> *Anonymous on Las Vegas*

New York .... That unnatural city where everyone is an exile, none more so than the American.

Charlotte Perkins Gilman

London, that great cesspool into which all the loungers of the Empire are irresistibly drained.

Sir Arthur Conan Doyle, A Study in Scarlet

Rome's just a city like anywhere else. A vastly overrated city, I'd say. It trades on belief just as Stratford trades on Shakespeare.

Anthony Burgess, Inside Mr Enderby

The Niagara Falls is simply a vast, unnecessary amount of water going the wrong way and then falling over unnecessary rocks.

Oscar Wilde

The river Rhine, it is well known,
Doth wash your city of Cologne;
But tell me, Nymphs, what power divine
Shall henceforth wash the river Rhine?

Samuel Taylor Coleridge, Cologne

The young Cambridge group, the group that stood for 'freedom' and flannel trousers and flannel shirts open at the neck, and a well-bred sort of emotional anarchy, and a whispering, murmuring sort of voice, and an ultra-sensitive sort of manner.

D.H. Lawrence, Lady Chatterley's Lover

You will hear more good things on the outside of a stagecoach from London to Oxford than if you were to pass a twelve-month with the undergraduates, or heads of colleges, of that famous university.

William Hazlitt, The ignorance of the Learned

Oxford is on the whole more attractive than Cambridge to the ordinary visitor; and the traveller is therefore recommended to visit Cambridge first, or to omit it altogether if he cannot visit both.

Baedeker's Great Britain

Too often travel, instead of broadening the mind, merely lengthens the conversation.

Elizabeth Drew

Bugger Bognor.

George V, alleged last words when told by his doctor that he would soon be well enough to visit Bognor Regis; also claimed as the king's response to the proposal to rename the town Bognor Regis in honour of its recuperative effect on His Majesty

Brighton looks like a town which is helping police with their enquiries.

Keith Waterhouse, in the Evening Standard

Very flat, Norfolk.

Noel Coward, Private Lives

Roast beef in human form.

Horace Walpole on the inhabitants of Norfolk

Shake a bridle over a Yorkshireman's grave and he will rise
and steal a horse.
Lancashire saying

California is a place in which a boom mentality and a sense of
Chekhovian loss meet in uneasy suspension.
Joan Didion

If I owned Texas and Hell, I would rent out Texas and live in Hell.
General Philip Sheridan

In Marseilles they make half the toilet soap we consume in
America, but the Marseillaise only have a vague theoretical
idea of its use, which they have obtained from books of travel.
Mark Twain

Great God! this is an awful place.
Captain Robert Falcon Scott on the South Pole —arguably reverentially

Bastards sitting in their offices
And bastards trying to boss you around
Bastards up there in Canberra
You expect those bastards to be bastards
But what gets me
Is having bastards all around you
Bastards on your own side who turn out to be bastards.
I guarantee if they started a society
To rid the world of bastards
In six months the bastards
Would take over.
Len Fox, Gumleaves and People

Dost thou not know, My son, with what little wisdom the world is governed?

Count Oxenstierna (c.16220) to the young King Eustavus Adolphus

We have screwed up. Not a little but a lot. No country in Europe has screwed up as much as we have. It can be explained. We have obviously lied throughout the past 18 to 24 months. It was perfectly clear that what we were saying was not true ... I almost perished because I had to pretend for 18 months that we were governing. Instead we lied morning, noon and night.

Ferenc Gyurcsany, Hungarian Prime Minister, recorded in a private meeting to his party in 2006. The broadcast caused riots

This is a great day for France.

Richard Nixon, in Paris for the funeral of President Pompidou

If I had known Henry was going to be President I would have sent him to school.

A 19th-century President of Bolivia's mother

There exists no politician in India daring enough to attempt to explain to the masses that cows can be eaten.

Indira Gandhi

No party in Ireland is prepared to accept anything except the impossible.

W. C. Gladstone

It is by the goodness of God that in our country we have those three unspeakably precious things: freedom of speech, freedom of conscience, and the prudence never to practise either of them.
Mark Twain

A liberal is just a conservative who hasn't been mugged.
Hilton Hamman, South African self-defence expert

A liberal is a man too broad-minded to take his own side in a quarrel.
Robert Frost

A liberal is someone whose interests are not threatened at the moment.
Ann Leslie

Have I said something foolish?
Phocion, to his friend, Diogenes Laertius, after the crowd applauded a point in his speech, 150 BC

The people would be just as noisy if they were going to see me hanged.
Oliver Cromwell, referring to a noisy crowd of admirers

Democracy means government by discussion but it is only effective if you can stop people talking.
Clement Attlee

Politics is the gentle are of getting votes from the poor and campaign contributions from the rich by promising to protect each from the other.
Edward Bennet Williams, US political campaign organiser

Politics is nothing more than a means of rising in the world.
Samuel Johnson

He brings to the fierce struggle of politics the tepid enthusiasm of a lazy summer afternoon at a cricket match.
Aneurin Bevan on Clement Attlee

Too bad all the people who know how to run the country are busy driving cabs and cutting hair.
George Burns

One fifth of the people are against everything all the time.
Robert Kennedy

It's a sure sign of political backwardness when any movement is led by students.
A. J. P. Taylor

Every great cause begins as a movement, becomes a business, and eventually deteriorates into a racket.
Eric Hoffer

Get on; get honest; get honour.
Anonymous reflection on the order of attainment for those seeking to rise in the world

What the state has, is theft. What the state says is lies.
Friederich Nietzsche

There's a reason why everybody lies. It works. It's what allows society to function. It's what separates us from beasts. When you care about someone, you lie to them.
Dr Gregory House, from the US drama House

The soft bigotry of low expectations.
  George W. Bush on the welfare state

Our human stock is threatened ... These mothers ... single parents from classes 4 and 5, are now producing a third of all births. If we do nothing the nation moves towards degeneration.
  Sir Keith Joseph, Conservative politician.

For every difficult intractable problem there's a solution that's neat, plausible and wrong.
  H.L. Mencken

Only constant repetition will finally succeed in imprinting an idea on the memory of the crowd.
  Adolf Hitler, Mein Kampf

Would that the Roman people had one neck!
  Emperor Caligula

I was elected by a bunch of fat, stupid, ugly old ladies that watch soap operas, play bingo, read tabloids and don't know the metric system.
  Tom Alcieri on his election as a Republican member of the New Hampshire state legislature

Democracy has been served – the people have spoken, (*sotto voce*) the bastards.
  Wendell Willkie on hearing of his defeat by President Roosevelt

There is nothing more tyrannical than a strong popular feeling among a democratic people.
  Anthony Trollope

Drop dead, you little cretin.
> Nicolas Sarkozy after a man rejected his handshake in a crowd and shouted
> 'Don't touch me, you will make me dirty'

An idea isn't responsible for the people who believe in it.
> Don Marquis

The public buys its opinions as it buys its meat, or takes in its milk, on the principle that it is cheaper to do this than to keep a cow.
> Samuel Butler

A committee is a group of people who individually can do nothing but as a group decide nothing can be done.
> Fred Allen

That garrulous monk.
> Benito Mussolini on Adolf Hitler

The broad mass of a nation ... will more easily fall victim to a big lie than to a small one.
> Adolf Hitler, Mein Kampf

A group is always more easily deceived than an individual.
> Pio Baroja

Well, you might try getting crucified and rising again on the third day.
> Talleyrand on what might impress the French peasantry

Out of the crooked timber of humanity no straight thing can ever be made.
> Immanuel Kant

The people long eagerly for just two things – bread and circuses.

Juvenal, Satires

Without exaggerating, the miners' leaders were the stupidest men in England, had we not had frequent occasion to meet the mine owners.

Lord Birkenhead

Whenever you hear a politician say 'something must be done' grab your wallet and your first-born; they are both in danger.

John Charmley

The urge to pass new laws must be seen as an illness, not much different from the urge to bite old women. Anyone suspected of suffering from it should either be treated with the appropriate pills or, if it is too late for that, elected to parliament and paid a huge salary, with endless holidays, to do nothing whatever.

Auberon Waugh

There ain't nothing in the middle of the road but yellow lines and dead armadillos.

Texan politician on 'middle of the road' politics

The hottest places in hell are reserved for those who in times of great moral crisis who maintain their neutrality.

Dante

If you want to keep something a secret, proclaim it in the Chamber of the House of Commons.

Enoch Powell

I prefer the cacophony of the playground to the tortured prose of Whitehall but both answer to a need: that of a child to say something and a bureaucrat to say nothing.
Simon Jenkins

Saying sorry is becoming fashionable ... because it's something government can do without raising taxes.
Joe Rogaly

The bulk of mankind is as well qualified for flying as for thinking.
Jonathan Swift

I'll give you my opinion of the human race ... Their heart's in the right place, but their head is a thoroughly inefficient organ.
W. Somerset Maugham

The majority of minds are no more to be controlled by strong reason than plumb-pudding is to be grasped by sharp pincers.
George Eliot

Those who know their minds do not necessarily know their hearts.
Francois de la Rochefoucauld

The public is an old woman. Let her maunder and mumble.
Thomas Carlyle

The great Unwashed.
Lord Henry Brougham. Attrib.

The whole aim of practical politics is to keep the populace alarmed (and hence clamorous to be led to safety) by menacing it with an endless series of hobgoblins, all of them imaginary.
H.L. Mencken

Freedom's just another word for nothing left to lose.
Kris Kristofferson, American actor and singer

Life is just one damned thing after another.
Elbert Hubbard, American writer

What is there to make so much of in the Thames? I am quite tired of it. Flow, flow, flow, always the same.
William Douglas, 4th Duke of Queensberry

My little friend Grildig, you have made a most admirable panegyric upon your country; you have clearly proved that ignorance, idleness, and vice, are the proper ingredients for a qualifying legislator; that laws are best explained, intercepted, and applied, by those whose interest and abilities lie in perverting, confounding, and eluding them...I cannot but conclude the bulk of your natives to be the most pernicious race of little odious vermin that nature ever suffered to crawl upon the surface of the earth.
Jonathan Swift, Gulliver's Travels. King of Brobdingnag on the English

Steele might become a reasonably good writer if he would pay a little attention to grammar, learn something about the propriety and disposition of words and incidentally, get some information on the subject he intends to handle.
Jonathan Swift on Richard Steele

A monster, gibbering shrieks and gnashing imprecations against mankind – tearing down all shreds of modesty, past all sense of manliness and shame: filthy in word, filthy in thought, furious, raging, obscene.

William Thackeray on Jonathan Swift

Thackeray settled like a meat-fly on whatever one had got for dinner; and made one sick of it.

John Ruskin on William Thackeray

The Cynic Parasite.

Benjamin Disraeli on William Thackeray

SIR,

I have received your letter with indignation and with scorn return you this answer.... I scorn your proffer; I disdain your favour; I abhor your treason; and am so far from delivering up this island to your advantage, that I shall keep it to the utmost of my power, and, I hope, to your destruction. Take this for your final answer, and forbear any further solicitations; for if you trouble me with any more messages of this nature, I will burn your paper, and hang up your messenger. This is the immutable resolution, and shall be the undoubted practice, of him who accounts it his chiefest glory to be his Majesty's most loyal and obedient subject.

DERBY

The Earl of Derby, a Royalist holding the Isle of Man, to General Henry Ireton, Cromwell's son-in-law

That the said Charles Stuart being admitted King of England, and therein trusted with a limited power to govern by and according to the laws of the land and not otherwise ... Yet, nevertheless, out of a wicked design to

erect and uphold in himself an unlimited and tyrannical
power, to rule according to his will and to overthrow the
rights and liberties of the people ... hath trayterously and
maliciously levied war against the present Parliament and
the people therein represented ... By which cruel and
unnatural wars by him the said Charles Stuart levied,
continued and renewed as aforesaid, much innocent blood
of the free people of this nation hathe been spilt, many
families have been undone, the publick treasure wasted and
exhausted, trade destructed and miserably decayed, vast
expense and damage to the nation incurred and many parts
of the land spoyled, some of them even to desolation ...
And the said John Cook ... Doth for the said treasons and
crimes, on behalf of the said people of England, impeach
the said Charles Stuart as tyrant, traytor, murtherer and a
publick and implacable enemy to the commonwealth of
England ...

> From the 'charge of High Treason and other High Crimes exhibited to the
> High Court of justice by John Cook Esq. Solicitor General appointed by the
> said Court, for and on behalf of the People of England against Charles
> Stuart King of England.

A man so various, that he seem'd to be
Not one, but all mankind's Epitome.
Stiff in Opinions, always in the wrong;
Was Everything by starts, and Nothing long:
But, in the course of one revolving Moon,
Was Chymist, Fidler, Statesman, and Buffoon;
Then all for Women, Painting, Rhiming, Drinking,
Besides ten thousand Freaks that died in thinking.
Blest madman, who could every hour employ,
With something New to wish, or to enjoy!

Railing and praising were his usual Theams;
And both (to show his judgment) in Extreams:
So over Violent, or over Civil,
That every Man, with him, was God or devil.
In squandering Wealth was his peculiar Art:
Nothing went unrewarded but Desert.

John Dryden on Zimri (the Duke of Buckingham), Absalom and Achitophel

The difference between genuine poetry and the poetry of
Dryden, Pope, and all their school, is briefly this: their poetry
is conceived and composed in their wits, genuine poetry is
conceived and composed in the soul.

Matthew Arnold

What shall we do with this bauble? There, take it away.

Oliver Cromwell, dismissing Parliament, 1653

....consider into the commission of what crimes, impieties,
wickednesses, and unheard of villanies, we have been led,
cheated, cozened, and betrayed, by that grand impostor, that
loathsome hypocrite, that detestable traitor, that prodigy of
nature, that opprobrium of mankind, that landscape of
iniquity, that sink of sin, and that compendium of baseness,
who now calls himself our Protector. What have we done.
Nay, what have we not done, which either hellish policy was
able to contrive, or brutish power to execute? We have
trampled underfoot all authorities; we have laid violent hands
upon our own Sovereign; we have ravished our Parliaments;
we have deflowered the virgin liberty of our nation; we have
put a yoke, an heavy yoke of iron, upon the necks of our own
countrymen; we have thrown down the walls and bulwarks of
the people's safety; we have broken often repeated oaths,
vows, engagements, covenants, protestations; we have

betrayed our trusts; we have violated our faiths; we have
lifted up our hands to heaven deceitfully; and that these our
sins might want no aggravation to make them exceedingly
sinful, we have added hypocrisy to them all; and ... like the
audacious strumpet, wiped our mouths, and boasted that we
have done no evil ...

*Anabaptist address to Charles II, attacking Cromwell shortly before his
death*

You have better proofs of your descent, my Lord, than the
register of marriage, or any troublesome inheritance of
reputation. There are some hereditary strokes of character by
which a family may be as clearly distinguished as by the
blackest features of the human face. Charles the First lived
and died a hypocrite. Charles the Second was a hypocrite of
another sort, and should have died upon the same scaffold. At
the distance of a century, we see their different characters
happily revived, and blended in your Grace. Sullen and severe
without religion, profligate without gaiety, you live like
Charles the Second, without being an amiable companion,
and, for aught I know, may die as his father did, without the
reputation of a martyr.

*'JUNIUS', letter to the Duke of Grafton, the descendant of an illegitimate
son of Charles II*

I'th'isle of Britain, long since famous grow
For breeding the best cunts in Christendom,
There reigns, and oh! Long may he reign and thrive,
The easiest King and best bred man alive.
Him no ambition moves to get renown
Like the French fool, that wanders up and down
Starving his people, hazarding his crown.

Peace is him aim, gentleness is such,
And love his loves, for he loves fucking much.
Nor are his high desires above his strength:
His sceptre and his prick are of length:
And she may sway the one who plays with th'other,
And make him little wiser than his brother.
Poor prince! thy prick, like the buffoons at Court,
Will govern thee because it makes thee sport.
'Tis sure the sauciest prick that e'er did swive,
The proudest, peremptoriest prick alive…

> *John Wilmot, Earl of Rochester,* A Satyr on Charles II. The hector of France to the cully of Britain

Here lies our mutton-loving King
Whose word no man relies on
Who never said a foolish thing
And never did a wise one.

> *John Wilmot on Charles II*

This is very true: for my words are my own, and my actions are my ministers'.

> *Charles II*

Becket parts company from Henry II and Louis VII, after a stormy meeting.

> *From* The Becket Leaves

I think, father, that many men who are called great patriots in the House of Commons are really great humbugs. For my part, when I get into Parliament, I will pledge myself to no party, but write upon my forehead in legible characters 'To Be Let'.

> *Tom Sheridan to his father, Richard Brinsley Sheridan*

And under it, Tom, write 'Unfurnished'.

> *Richard Sheridan's reply*

Sir, the atrocious crime of being a young man, which the honourable gentleman has, with such spirit and decency, charged upon me, I shall neither attempt to palliate nor deny; but content myself with wishing that I may be one of those whose follies may cease with their youth, and not of those who continue ignorant in spite of age and experience. Whether youth can be attributed to any man as a reproach, I will not, Sir, assume the province of determining: but surely, age may justly become contemptible, if the opportunities which it brings have passed away without improvement, and vice appear to prevail when the passions have subsided. The wretch who, after having seen the consequences of a thousand errors, continues still to blunder, and in whom age has only added obstinacy to stupidity, is surely the object either of abhorrence or contempt; and deserves not that his grey head should secure him from insults. Much more, Sir, is he to be abhorred, who, as he has advanced in age, has receded from virtue, and become more wicked with less temptation: who prostitutes himself for money which he cannot enjoy, and spends the remains of his life in the ruin of his country.

> *William Pitt, speech, after entering Parliament, to Horace Walpole, who had mocked his youth*

With death doomed to grapple
Beneath this cold slab, he
Who lied in the Chapel
Now lies in the Abbey.
Lord Byron on William Pitt

Not a gentleman; dresses too well.
Bertrand Russell on Anthony Eden

Posterity will do justice to that unprincipled maniac.
Gladstone – extraordinary mixture of envy, vindictiveness,
hypocrisy and superstition, and with one commanding characteristic – whether Prime Minister or Leader of the
Opposition, whether preaching, praying, speechifying or
scribbling – never a gentleman.
Benjamin Disraeli on W. E. Gladstone

Disraeli lacked two qualities, failing which true eloquence is
impossible. He was never quite in earnest, and he was not
troubled by dominating conviction.
Henry Lucy, journalist

Honest in the most odious sense of the word.
Benjamin Disraeli on W. E. Gladstone

Among prigs there is a freemasonry which never fails. All the
prigs spoke of him as the coming man.
Benjamin Disraeli on W. E. Gladstone

I don't object to the Old Man always having the ace of
trumps up his sleeve, but merely to his belief that God
Almighty put it there.
Henry Labouchere on W. E. Gladstone

An old man in a hurry.
>   *Lord Randolph Churchill on W. E. Gladstone*

Gladstone ... founded the great tradition ... in public to speak the language of the highest and strictest principle, and in private to pursue and possess every sort of woman.
>   *Peter Wright on W.E. Gladstone*

Mr Peter Wright,
Your Garbage about Mr Gladstone in 'Portraits and Criticisms' has come to our knowledge. You are a liar. Because you slander a dead man, you are a coward. Because you think the public will accept invention from such as you, you are a fool.
GLADSTONE
I associate myself with this letter.
H.N. GLADSTONE
>   *W. E. Gladstone's sons*

My name is George Nathaniel Curzon.
I am a most superior person.
My face in pink, my hair is sleek.
I dine at Blenheim once a week.
>   *Anonymous on Lord Curzon,* The Masque of Balliol

He is, without exception, the most notorious liar in all our country. He lies out of every pore in his skin. Whether he is sleeping or walking, on foot or on horseback, talking with his neighbours or writing for a newspaper, a multititudinous swarm of lies, visible, palpable, and tangible, are buzzing and settling about him like flies around a horse in August.
>   *Sir Francis Bond Head on William Lyon Mackenzie*

He spent his whole life in plastering together the true and the false and therefrom extracting the plausible.
Stanley Baldwin on David Lloyd George

Not even a public figure. A man of no experience. And of the utmost insignificance.
Lord Curzon on Stanley Baldwin

A lot of hard-faced men who look as if they had done very well out of the war.
Stanley Baldwin, referring to the post-First-World-War Commons

To save your world you asked this man to die:
Would this man, could he see you now, ask why?
W. H. Auden, Epitaph for an Unknown Soldier

He has a brilliant mind, until he makes it up.
Margot Asquith on Sir Stafford Cripps, Autobiography

I cannot say. I am not a doctor.
Edward Heath, declining to speculate on why Mrs Thatcher disliked him

Sit down, man. You're a bloody tragedy.
James Maxton, Scottish Labour leader, heckling Ramsay MacDonald during the latter's last Commons speech. Attrib.

Mr Macmillan is the best Prime Minister we have.
R.A. Butler on Harold Macmillan. Although often quoted in the form above, Butler simply answered 'yes' to the question: 'Would you say that this is the best Prime Minister we have?'

Above any other position of eminence, that of Prime Minister is filled by fluke.
Enoch Powell

Defeat comes from God, victory comes from the
Government.
Aneurin Bevan on Winston Churchill

I must say that (Profumo) never struck me as a man at all like
a cloistered monk; and that Miss Keeler is a professional
prostitute. There seems to me to be a basic improbability
about the proposition that their relationship was purely
platonic. What are whores about? *(turning to Macmillan)* What
is to happen now? We cannot just have business as usual. I
myself feel that the time will come very soon when my Right
Honourable Friend ought to make way for a much younger
colleague. I feel that ought to happen. I certainly will not
quote at him the savage words of Cromwell, but perhaps
some word of Browning might be appropriate:
   '...let him never come back to us!
   There would be doubt, hesitation and pain.
   Forced praise on our part – the glimmer of twighlight,
   Never glad confident morning again.'
Nigel Birch MP on Harold Macmillan: Commons speech.

His style ... is not very literary, and he lacks force.
The Daily News, on Winston Churchill's Maiden Speech

I have only one purpose, the destruction of Hitler, and my life
is much simplified thereby. If Hitler invaded Hell, I would
make at least a favourable reference to the Devil in the House
of Commons.
Winston Churchill

I have never seen a human being who more perfectly
represented the modern conception of a robot.
Winston Churchill on Vyacheslav Molotov

He never spares himself in conversation. He gives himself so generously that hardly anybody else is permitted to give anything in his presence.
Aneurin Bevan on Churchill

Neil Kinnock's speeches go on for so long because he has nothing to say, so he has no way of knowing when he's finished saying it.
John Major

This is a government born in treachery, surviving by subterfuge, double-dealing and fraud, Janus-faced and brazen, slippery and underhand, a dismaying blend of incompetence and low cunning, doomed to end in shame and recrimination.
Paul Johnson, writing on John Major's government in the Spectator, *1993*

It is easier to cancel a nuclear submarine than a civil servant's parking space.
Simon Jenkins

I stuffed their mouths with gold!
Aneurin Bevan, explaining how he persuaded doctors to accept the National Health Service. Attrib.

They never miss an opportunity to miss an opportunity
Conor Cruise O'Brien on the Ulster Unionists

Beaverbrook is so pleased to be in the Government that he is like the town tart who has finally married the Mayor!
Beverley Baxter on Lord Beaverbrook

They say that common sense comes from the North.
Professor Laski hit Newark from the South. It was a Saturday
night meeting in the Market Square. Several hundred
spectators represented the typical elements of the constituency – agriculture, mining, brewing, malting, and engineering.
They were all there. Professor Laski appeared on a sort of
French Revolution cart filled with a microphone instead of a
guillotine. Dressed in a tight-fitting, hip-slinky overcoat of the
sort that dance-band leaders wear, he addressed the crowd
with an air of quite remarkable superiority. For the better
part of an hour he sprayed us with an oleaginous stream of
rhetorical oratory, full of sly half-truths and old womanish
digs at Mr Churchill; the British Empire, as apparently
typified by the Conservative Party; Mr Brendan Bracken, who
clearly was an ant in the Laski pants; and the British idea of
freedom with which the little professor did not apparently
agree. No doubt it was not in his blood. Mr Laski was
infinitely condescending. He even told the assembled citizens
of Newark, most of whom, presumably, were supposed to be
his supporters, that they would know a great deal more about
their country if they read history books, but then, of course,
they never did read history books. One got the impression
that Mr Laski regarded Newark as a sort of rural dead end, a
feudal sump, a place of beer and bacon but no brains. In fact,
it was quite obvious that Newark was expected to regard
itself as highly flattered by this opportunity to bask in the
pinkly iridescent rays of the Laski sun...The Air Vice Marshall
certainly looked the part on the platform. But there, alas, was
Professor Laski, swaying slightly before the microphone, his
hands in his pockets, his eyes glinting behind his large
spectacles in a sort of dreamy mysticism, evidently lost in a
Laski version of Utopia, and ecstasy of involved phrases and

cheap cracks at Mr Churchill, with, now and then, that sort of erudite aside into ancient political history in which the book worm politicians of 'intellectual' Labour delight. Mr Laski is a small man, what you might call narrow-chested . He is not an imposing figure. He does not look as though he had ever shouldered a pack or done a day's manual labour. But the Laski mind overshadowed the Laski physique, and even occasionally diverted one's eye for the Laski dance-band overcoat.

James Wentworth Day on Harold Laski, in Harvest Adventure

His sentences burble from his lips . . . a susurration of clichés barely turning a leaf . . . Each phrase is laced with laudanum . . . political musak, a background hum. We search in vain for the knob to turn them off . . . Put Mr Ashdown in a Labour cabinet and he would sink gently to the bottom, leaving only silver bubbles on the surface.

Simon Jenkins on Paddy Ashdown, in The Times

It is all a bit like reading The Perfect Storm reset in a bathtub.

Craig Brown on Paddy Ashdown's diaries

A mind not so much open as permanently vulnerable to a succession of opposing certainties.

Hugo Young on David Howell, in One of Us

She would be outshone by the candles on a birthday cake.

'Black Dog' on Dawn Primarolo MP, in the Mail on Sunday

A man who could start a fight in an empty room.

Anonymous on Gerald Kaufman MP

Jesus Christ, in any case, is a Name Which Makes News...
From Lord Beaverbrook's point of view, his was essentially a
success story. From humble origins (though, as the son of
God, he might be considered to have exalted connections) he
achieved a position of outstanding power and influence. The
Crucifixion was a set-back, certainly, but the Resurrection
more than compensated for it. Thenceforth, the movement he
founded progressed almost as fast as the circulation of the
Daily Express...

His astonishing career, from carpenter's son to an
accepted position on God's right hand, exemplified Lord
Beaverbrook's favourite proposition that dazzling opportunities await whoever has the shrewdness, energy and pertinacity
to see and seize them. Not even the sky was the limit. It was
as a successful propagandist that Jesus Christ won Lord
Beaverbrook's particular admiration. Without the advantages
of a chain of newspapers, lacking financial resources and
powerful earthly connections, he still managed to put across
his ideas so effectively that nearly two thousand years later
they are still ringing in mankind's ears. It is not surprising
that so outstanding a feat should have impressed another
operator in the field of propaganda who, with so many
additional advantages, saw every cause he espoused founder,
every individual he attacked thrive, and most of those he
praised fall in public esteem . . . The main propagandist
weapons he used were 'personality, example and oratory'. It
is significant that so old a hand at the game as Lord
Beaverbrook should have omitted any reference to the truth
of what was being propagated as a factor in its successful
propagation. Here, he was following his own practice.

Malcolm Muggeridge, reviewing The Divine Propagandist, a life of
Christ *by Lord Beaverbrook*

He was swaggering in a predatory way towards the susceptible of this conference like a gigolo eyeing the passenger deck.

Edward Pearce on Michael Portillo, in the Guardian

Is there no beginning to your talents?

Clive Anderson to Jeffrey Archer

Calling Jeffrey Archer's fictional characters cardboard is an insult to the British packaging industry.

Peter Preston

Whenever I want a good read I get one of Jeffrey's novels, and stand on it, so I can reach the good books.

Jeffrey Archer's fellow politician, Steven Norris

Lord Archer of Weston-Super-Mare, the only seaside peer that Danny La Rue hasn't performed on.

Neil Shand

The prigs who attack Jeffrey Archer should bear in mind that we all, to some extent, reinvent ourselves. Jeffrey has just gone to a bit more trouble.

Barry Humphries

A numbing fusillade of platitudes… his brain permanently on line to a fad lexicon…Mr Blair uses abstract nouns as a wine writer uses adjectives, filling space with a frothy concoction devoid of meaning.

Simon Jenkins on Tony Blair, in The Times

If Roy Jenkins appeared to be trying to cup the breasts of peasant girls, Tony Blair looks as if he were trying to stop him.
Simon Hoggart, 1994

With Tony you have to take the smooth with the smooth.
Anonymous senior Labour politician on his leader

Mr Blair is a man of hidden shallows.
Hugo Gurdon, in the Daily Telegraph

He made particularly good toast.
Michael Gasgoigne on Tony Blair – Blair was his 'fag' at Fettes school

My advice is quit while you're behind.
Tony Blair to William Hague

Tory MPs are willing to be led, in the way that Henry VIII was willing to be married.
Bruce Anderson

He's only worked up about the fuel crisis because he's got four bandwagons to run.
Rory Bremner on William Hague

The deals on wheels Prime Minister.
Michael Howard as Conservative leader on Tony Blair

He has something of the night about him.
Tory MP Ann Widdecombe on her former boss and Home Secretary Michael Howard, 1997

All the attributes of a populist except popularity.
Bruce Anderson on Michael Howard

This grammar school boy will take no lessons from that public school boy.
Michael Howard to Tony Blair

You can't expect a boy to be vicious till he's been to a good school.
Saki

You were the future once.
David Cameron to Tony Blair

As Blair and his impertinent young political pups wage war on old Labour . . . as they seek to kill off their fathers, these political adolescents boost themselves with a dangerous amnesic and, thus drugged, the courageous volunteers, damned with piss-proud erections, dare to obliterate the reality that the most 'radical and regenerative Labour government' that brought us the welfare state, was led by old men.
Leo Abse, former Labour MP

For Hon. Members opposite the deterrent is a phallic symbol. It convinces them that they are men.
George Edward Cecil, Baron Wigg, 1964, on the nucleal deterrent

Characterizing fellow MPs' fondness for nuclear weapons as a phallic fixation was too complicated a thought for the speaker to rule 'out of order' on the spot; decisions have to be made on the spur of the moment, and Speakers rarely revisit their rulings. A reading of *Hansard* since the *Official Report* commenced in 1861 yields a bewildering variety of judgements. What is or is not acceptable as Parliamentary scorn seems to depend on the Speaker's digestion on the day in question. Take, for instance, rulings on how far a Member may go in calling another Member a liar. The following have been disallowed:

1862 a Member's statement was 'entirely false and without foundation' (Speaker: The hon Member should express himself in proper language.')

1863   'scandalous and unfounded'
1868   'doing dodges'
1870   'false'
1881   'hardly credible'
1883   'resorting to trickiness'
1884   'shuffling'
1886   'dishonest and hypocritical'
1887   'foul calumny' and 'gigantic falsehood'
1888   'flippant mendacity'
1909   'cold and calculated lie'
1914   'mendacious'
        'infamous lie'
        'wilful falsehood'
1932   'perverter of the truth'
1945   'dishonest evasion'
1946   'abdominal lies'
1952   'a wicked misstatement of the truth'

1953   'dishonest'
1961   'untrue'
1963   'duplicity'
1966   'deliberate fabrication'
1967   'twister'
1976   'fiddling the figures'
1978   'arch confidence trickster'
        'spoke with a forked tongue'
1987   'economical with the truth'
1988   'numerological inexactitude'
        'organized mendacity'
1992   'telling porkies' (Speaker: I think we will not have
        that word. It escaped my notice last week. I had to
        look it up in the dictionary, but now I know what it
          means the hon Member should please withdraw it.')
1993   'dishonest'

But these slipped through:

1864   'a calumnious [sic] statement'
1946   'devoid of any truth'
1959   'cooking the figures'
1988   'shameless lack of candour'
1994   'tissue of lies'

And this lived a half-life, appearing in the first edition of
Hansard then disappearing from a Defence minister's lips, and
the bound volume, after the Speaker conveniently declared it
could not be verified on audio recordings:
2008   'absolute bollocks'

It is similarly out of order to accuse another Member of being drunk. MPs have tried with little success to get round this; all the following having been ruled out of order:

1935   'Have you been drinking?'
1945   'Take him out, he's drunk!'
1951   'alcoholic jeers'
       'not sober...'
1974   'the appearance of being slightly inebriated'
1976   'a semi-drunken Tory brawl'
1983   'in this condition' (Claire Short, MP, of the minister
       Alan Clark. The editor of this book was there. He
       was drunk. But the Deputy Speaker reprimanded Short.)
1987   'in a drunken stupor'

However, in 1974 James Wellbeloved did slip past the Chair this half-retraction: I am not suggesting that they are drunk, I am merely suggesting that they are giving a very good imitation of it.'

Comparing another Member with an animal is also unwise. In 1976 the Speaker (Selwyn Lloyd) was clear: 'I always object to the use of animal terminology when applied to Members of this House.' He was banning a description by an MP of the Members opposite as 'laughing hyena'. Withdrawing the words, the MP substituted 'laughing Ken Dodds opposite', which the Chair found satisfactory. How Lloyd would have viewed Michael Foot's description of Norman Tebbit as a 'semi house-trained polecat' we shall never know. *Hansard*'s first recorded animalistic references consisted only of noises. This, and terms in the list which follows, have been ruled out of order:

1872	'amid the general confusion were heard imitations of the crowing of cocks, where at the Speaker declared the scenes unparliamentarily, and gross violations of order'
1884	'bigoted, malevolent young puppy'
1885	'jackal'
1886	'Tory skunks'
1923	'chameleon politician'
1930	'insolent young cub'
1931	'lie down, dog!'
	'noble and learned camels'(of the Lords)
1936	'swine'
1946	'silly ass'
1948	'dirty dog'
1949	'stool pigeons'
1952	'you rat'
1953	'cheeky young pup'
1955	'rat'
1977	'snake'
1978	'bitchy' (of Mrs Thatcher)
1985	'baboons'
	'his shadow spokesman's monkey'
1986	'political weasel and guttersnipe'
1987	'the morals of tom cats'
1989	'political skunk'

And these were allowed by the Chair:

1989	'the attention span of a gerbil'
	'the wolf of Dagenham'
1992	'the hamster from Bolsover' (of Dennis Skinner)
	'cruel swine' (of Kenneth Baker)

But perhaps the most surprising permission was the Speaker's declining to stop an MP describing Margaret Thatcher as 'behaving with all the sensitivity of a sex-starved boa constrictor'.

I have been helped in the selection of these examples by the research of parliamentary writer Phil Mason, whose book *Nothing Good Will Ever Come of It* quotes more than a century of MPs' recorded predictions, most of them hilariously off-target, and who has edited (with me) *Mission Accomplished* (JR Books, 2007). Drawing on Mason's files, there follows a selection of various other Speakers' rulings on arguably unparliamentarly language:

DISALLOWED

1861   'very insolent and scornful' (of the Chancellor)

1867   'returned by the refuse of a large constituency' (of an MP)

1872   'three peaceful shepherds had already turned their pipes behind him'. (Speaker: not becoming expression')

1875   'Villains' (Samuel Plimsoll describing shipowners)

1877   'Speaker: 'It is not proper to impute what of straight-forwardness or courage to any Member or to imply that a Member was not actuated by the feelings of a gentleman'

1878   'damnable character'

1880   Speaker: It is not in accordance with Parliamentary usage to say that members of this House are on the side of Atheism, irreligion and immorality.'

1881   'poltroon'

1884   'seditious blasphemer'
        'ruffianism'

1885   'insolence'
        'indecent purpose'

1887	'damned lot of cads'
	'bad, mean, pettifogging' (of the House of Lords)
1888	'Judas'
1897	'tommy rot'
1900	'language of the pot-house'
1901	'fool'
	'orgy of unbridled ruffianism'
1902	'pharisees and hypocrites,
1906	'the offscourings of Bristol' (of constituents)
1908	'vicious and vulgar'
	'coward and a cad'
1910	'half pantaloon and half highwayman'
1911	'traitor'
1914	'swindlers' (of government)
	'vulgar cad'
1924	'leader of a murder gang' (of a minister)
1926	'the minister of death' (of Minister of Health)
	'a mind on all fours with a London County Council sewer'
1928	'Pecksniffian cant'
1931	'blethering'
	'impertinent dog'
	'dirty rot'
	'sponger'
1939	'bunch of robbers'
1944	'unspeakable blackguard'
1946	'source of infection'
1949	'freelance demagogue'
1950	'yahoos opposite'
1951	'rabble', 'stooge'
1955	'nosey parker'
1956	'murderer'

	'traitorous defeatist'
1958	'I'll see you outside'
	'stinker'
1959	'dunderhead'
	'smart Alec'
1960	'oafish'
1961	'lousy'
	'slippery'
	'get back to the gutter'
	'white livered'
1965	'Quisling'
	'sheer, concentrated humbug'
1968	'A British Herr Himmler'
	'scoundrel'
1969	'mean bastards'
1972	'the Right honourable cheat'
1975	'bunch of damned hypocrites'
	'buffoon'
	'grubby and squalid'
1976	'idiots'
	'racialists'
	'hooligan'
1978	'arch confidence trickster'
	'ignorant bigot'
	'the biggest basket of them all' (of Prices minister)
1980	'mass murderer'
1983	'two-faced'
1984	'supercilious git'
	'mealy-mouthed hypocrisy'
	'a load of bullshit'
	'pompous sod' (Dennis Skinner of David Owen. Skinner offered to withdraw 'pompous')

1985	'creeps'
1986	'bollocks'
	'cretin'
	'twerp'
	'boring old twat'
	'wimp'
1987	'bugger all'
	'giggling idiot'
	'go to hell'
	'arrogant bastards'
	'fat bounder' (of Nigel Lawson)
	'bumptious balloon' (of Nigel Lawson)
	'Pakistani umpire'
1988	'bugger'
1988	'political shyster'
	'tweak his goolies'
	'poached bullshit'
	'sneak'
	'berk'
	'wicked'
	'cheat'
	'objectionable lout'
1989	'freak'
	'barmy'
1990	'ignorant twat'
	'poppycock, bunkum and balderdash'
	'scabs'
	'freeloading scroungers'
	'paid hack'
	'arrogant little shit'
	'spiv'
	'parasite'

'Mr Oil Slick'
'front bench yobo'
'jerk'
'kinnocchio'

1991 'trifler and opportunist'
1992 'little squirt'
'like a 50p piece: two-faced and seven-sided'
'hack, obedient, lickspittle Tory member'
'clever little sod'
'stool pigeons'
1994 'shifty' (when used to describe a member but allowed for a policy)
'unctuous slob'
'ethically challenged'
'prat'
'stupid cow'
1995 'dimwit'
'nitwit'
1998 'gormless alien'
'the honourable anorak'
'piddling' The alternative offered, 'two-bit' was also ruled out of order
1999 'riff raff' (compare with 'waifs and strays',
1996, which was challenged and deemed in order)
2000 (to do) 'sod all'
2001 'con man'
2002 'coward'

'crap' was allowed in July 1991, but ruled out of order just 5 months later.

ALLOWED

1931	'nonsensical twaddle' (Speaker: Use of nonsensical 'a matter of taste'. No judgement on twaddle)
	'bunk'
	'humbug'
1936	'tripe'
1947	'clear your ears out'
1949	'official stooge'
	'Quisling'
1953	'unclean'
1957	'near treachery'
	'bribery'
1958	'blather'
1959	'a card sharper and confidence trickster'
1966	'tame hacks'
1968	'go back to Moscow'
1970	'carpet bagger'
1971	'shower' (the Government)
1978	'political thug'
1985	'snivelling little git'
1986	'a Government of petty crooks'
	'old Etonian twerp'
	'Gauleiter'
	'pathetic Member'
	'wally'
	'weak-minded'
1987	'a boot up the backside'
	'arrogant little basket'
1988	'wet-necked twits'
	'two-faced as hell'
1989	'be quiet, silly old fool'
	'absolute bull'

'fathead'
'utter crap'
'street hooligan'
'yankee lickspittle'
'freaks' (as a description of opposing members. In
the same year, the singular was ruled out of order as
this was deemed to reflect upon an individual member)

Since 1990:

'twit'
'don't be so bloody stupid'
'bloodthirsty louts'
'too bloody mean'
'you mean and silly woman'
'shut up, you old windbag'
'[the minister] does not give a fart'
'witless, blind and stupid...'
'Polly Pot in No 10' (of Mrs Thatcher)

1990 'pig's bladder on a stick' *(see below, under Tony Banks MP)*
1991 'bloodthirsty louts' (again, allowed as it did not refer
to a particular individual)
1992 'mad fool, loony half-mad cretin'
'millionaire's mammy boy' (ruled 'not wholly
unparliamentary')
1995 'twaddle'
1996 'chancer'
'waifs and strays'
'school sneaks'
1997 'claptrap'
1998 'Sweet FA' (Mr Speaker confessed to be 'not certain
whether this was unparliamentary, but most
undesirable')
[speaking] 'with forked tongue'

1999   'Stepford Wives' (as a description of opposing members)
        'Quislings' (the ruling in 1965 outlawing the same
insult was on the singular which made all the difference)
2000   'chopping off their goolies'
2004   'knackered'
2005   'bonkers'
2006   'total cock-up'
        'toe-rags' (used to describe fraudsters not other
        members)
2007   'shit' (when used as a noun)

And finally:

> 'that amiable dumb bell' (of Sir Geoffrey Howe).
>
> *The mild-mannered Sir Geoffrey Howe, Margaret Thatcher's first Chancellor of the Exchequer and later Foreign Secretary, finally turned against her in November 1990. His resignation speech is quoted at some length beneath, not for the savagery of its invective – the restrained prose makes for a less than scorching read – but for its effect, which was the more explosive in coming from a much-put-upon and undemonstrative politician and close and very senior colleague. Many would trace Thatcher's downfall back to this Commons moment, which to witness was stunning …*

I find to my astonishment that a quarter of a century has passed since I last spoke from the backbenches . . . The Prime Minister and I have shared something like 700 meetings of Cabinet or shadow Cabinet during the past 18 years, and some 400 hours alongside each other, at more than 30 international summit meetings. For both of us, I suspect, it is a pretty daunting record. *[Sir Geoffrey reflects on his time as Margaret Thatcher's first Chancellor of the Exchequer]* . . . Not one of our economic achievements would have been possible without the courage and leadership of my Right hon. Friend

– and, if I may say so, they possibly derived some little benefit from the presence of a Chancellor who was not exactly a wet himself. ... *[Sir Geoffrey explains that he accepted the need, as Foreign Secretary, to stand up for British interests in Europe; but the Prime Minister is failing to understand Britain's relationship with European allies]* . . . And it is here, I fear, that my right hon. Friend the Prime Minister increasingly risks leading herself and others astray in matters of substance as well as of style. [It is] essential . . . not to retreat into a ghetto of sentimentality about our past . . . We must at all costs avoid presenting ourselves yet again with an over-simplified choice, a false antithesis, a bogus dilemma, between one alternative, starkly labelled "co-operation between independent sovereign states" and a second, equally crudely labelled alternative, "centralised, federal super-state", as if there were no middle way in between. *[Sir Geoffrey accuses the Prime Minister of using the language of victory and surrender]* . . . The European enterprise is not and should not be seen like that – as some kind of zero sum game . . . [a] . . . nightmare image sometimes conjured up by my right hon. Friend, who seems sometimes to look out upon a continent that is positively teeming with ill-intentioned people, scheming, in her words, to "extinguish democracy", to "dissolve our national identities" and to lead us "through the back-door into a federal Europe". What kind of vision is that for our business people, who trade there each day, for our financiers, who seek to make London the money capital of Europe or for all the young people of today? *[Sir Geoffrey criticises Margaret Thatcher for appearing to rule out a compromise plan for a "common" European currency to complement national currencies – the "hard ecu"– and for casually dismissing its prospects]* ... How on earth are the Chancellor and the Governor of the Bank of England, commending the hard ecu as they strive to, to be taken as serious participants in the debate against that kind of background noise? ... It is rather like sending your opening batsmen to the crease only for them to find, the moment the first balls are bowled, that their bats have been broken before the game by the team captain. *[Sir Geoffrey quotes from a correspondent critical of the Prime Minister's impetuous public utterances]* My correspondent concluded : "This is a desperately serious situation for our country." And sadly, I have to agree. The tragedy is — and it is for me personally, for my party, for our whole people and for my Right hon. Friend herself, a very real tragedy — that the Prime Minister's perceived attitude towards Europe is running increasingly serious risks for the future of our nation ... In my letter of resignation, which I tendered with the utmost sadness and dismay, I said: "Cabinet Government is all about trying to persuade one another from within". That was my commitment to Government by persuasion ... but ... the task has become futile: trying to stretch the meaning of words beyond what was credible, and trying to pretend that there was a common policy when every step forward risked being subverted by some casual comment or impulsive answer. The conflict of loyalty ... to my Right hon. Friend the Prime Minister ... and ... to what I perceive to be the true interests of the nation, has become all too great. I no longer believe it possible to resolve that conflict from within this Government. That is why I have resigned. In doing so, I have done what I believe to be right for my party and my country. The time has come for others to consider their own response to the tragic conflict of loyalties with which I have myself wrestled for perhaps too long.

Sir Geoffrey Howe, *resigning.*

Like being savaged by a dead sheep.
*Denis Healey, referring to the attack by Sir Geoffrey Howe on his Budget
proposals, in the* Listener

You cannot make a man by standing a sheep on its hind legs.
But by standing a flock of sheep in that position you can make
a crowd of men.
Max Beerbohm, Zuleika Dobson

What men call social virtues, good fellowship, is commonly
but the virtue of pigs in a litter, which lie in close together to
keep each other warm.
Henry David Thoreau

I would rather consult my valet than the Conservative
conference.
Arthur Balfour

They are gnats on an elephant's backside.
John Prescott on workers at New Labour's Millbank HQ, 1997

He loses his temper on Monday and doesn't find it again till
Friday.
Anonymous civil servant about John Prescott

There is something utterly nauseating about a system of
society which pays a harlot 25 times as much as it pays its
Prime Minister, 250 times as much as it pays its Members of
Parliament, and 500 times as much as it pays some of its
ministers of religion.
Harold Wilson on the case of Christine Keeler

From Lord Hailsham we have had a virtuoso performance
in the art of kicking a friend in the guts. When self-
indulgence has reduced a man to the shape of Lord
Hailsham, sexual continence involves no more than a sense
of the ridiculous.

> *Reginald Paget MP on Lord Hailsham, following the Profumo scandal*

'What have you done?' cried Christine,
'You've wrecked the whole party machine!
'To lie in the nude 'may be terribly rude,
'But to lie in the house is obscene!'

> *Anonymous on John Profumo, about the Profumo scandal*

. . . a pig, an ass, a dunghill, the spawn of an adder, a basilisk,
a lying buffoon, a mad fool with a frothy mouth . . . a
lubberly ass . . . a frantic madman . . .

> *Martin Luther on Henry VIII*

My Dear Sir,
In times like the present, it is impossible to allow private
feelings to take the place of a public sense of duty. I think
your conduct as dangerous in Parliament as it is in your own
county. Were you my own brother, therefore, I could not give
you my support.

> *Thomas Liddell to J.G. Lambton, who was contesting the Durham con-
> stituency, letter*

My Dear Sir Thomas,
In answer to your letter, I beg to say that I feel gratitude for
your frankness, compassion for your fears, little dread of your
opposition, and no want of your support.

> *J.G. Lambton to Thomas Liddell, in reply*

Gentlemen, I received yours and am surprised by your insolence in troubling me about the Excise. You know, what I very well know, that I bought you. And I know, what perhaps you think I don't know, you are now selling yourselves to somebody Else; and I know, what you do not know, that I am buying another borough. May God's curse light upon you all: may your houses be as open and common to all Excise Officers as your wives and daughters were to me, when I stood for your scoundrel corporation.

Yours, etc., Anthony Henley

Letter from Anthony Henley, MP for Southampton (1727-34), to his constituents, following their protests over the Excise Bill

The Right Honourable gentleman is indebted to his memory for his jests, and to his imagination for his facts.

Richard Brinsley Sheridan, replying to a speech in the House of Commons by Henry Dundas. Attrib.

Mr Speaker, I said the honourable member was a liar it is true and I am sorry for it. The honourable member may place the punctuation where he pleases.

Richard Brinsley Sheridan on being asked to apologise for calling a fellow MP a liar. Attrib.

Lord Talbot's horse, like the great planet in Milton, danced about in various rounds his wandering course. At different times, he was progressive, retrograde, or standing still. The progressive motion I should rather incline to think the merit of the horse, the retrograde motion, the merit of the Lord.

John Wilkes on the conduct of the Earl of Talbot's horse at the coronation of George III, in the North Briton, *1762*

. . . two vultures sick for battle,
Two scorpions under one wet stone,
Two bloodless wolves whose dry throats rattle,
Two crows perched on the murrained cattle,
Two vipers tangled into one.

> *Percy Bysshe Shelley,* similes for two political characters of 1819 – *the Home Secretary Sidmouth, and Foreign Secretary and Leader of the Commons, Castlereagh*

Why is a pump like Viscount Castlereagh? –
Because it is a slender thing of wood,
That up and down its awkward arm doth sway,
And coolly spout and spout and spout away,
In one weak, washy, everlasting flood.

> *Thomas Moore on Viscount Castlereagh*

Therefore I charge Mr Hastings with having destroyed, for private purposes, the whole system of government by the six provincial Councils, which he had no right to destroy.

I charge him with taking bribes of Gunga Govind Sing.

I charge him with not having done that bribe-service which fidelity, even in iniquity, requires at the hands of the worst of men.

I charge him with having robbed those persons of whom he took the bribes.

I charge him with having fraudulently alienated the fortunes of widows.

I charge him with having, without right, title or purchase, taken the lands of orphans and given them to wicked persons under him.

I charge him with having removed the natural guardians of a minor Raja, and given his zamindary to that wicked person, Deby Sing.

I charge him – his wickedness being known to himself
and all the world – with having committed to Deby Sing the
management of three great provinces; and with having
thereby wasted the country, destroyed the landed interest,
cruelly harassed the peasants, burnt their houses, seized their
crops, tortured and degraded their persons, and destroyed
the honour of the whole female race of that country.

> *Edmund Burke, peroration on Warren Hastings, 1788*

Burke was a damned wrong-headed fellow, through his whole
life jealous and obstinate.

> *Charles James Fox on Edmund Burke. Attrib.*

I met Murder on the way – He had a mask like Castlereagh ...

> *Percy Bysshe Shelley, The Mask of Anarchy*

Posterity will ne'er survey
A nobler grave than this;
Here lie the bones of Castlereagh:
Stop here traveller, and piss.

> *Lord Byron on Viscount Castlereagh, who killed himself*

Pitt is to Addington
As London is to Paddington.

> *George Canning. Paddington was then a village outside London*

The Right Honourable Gentleman's smile is like the silver
fittings on a coffin.

> *Benjamin Disraeli on Sir Robert Peel*

You owe the Whigs a great gratitude, my Lord, and therefore
I think you will betray them. For your Lordship is like a
favourite footman on easy terms with his mistress. Your
dexterity seems a happy compound of the smartness of an
attorney's clerk and the intrigue of a Greek of the lower
empire.

Benjamin Disraeli on Lord Palmerston

If a traveller were informed that such a man was the Leader
of the House of Commons, he might begin to comprehend
how the Egyptians worshipped an insect.

Benjamin Disraeli on Lord John Russell

. . . a systematic liar and a beggarly cheat; a swindler and a
poltroon . . . He has committed every crime that does not
require courage.

Benjamin Disraeli on the Irish agitator Daniel O'Connell

He is a liar. (Cheers) He is a liar in action and in words. His life
is a living lie. He is a disgrace to his species. What state of
society must be that could tolerate such a creature – having the
audacity to come forward with one set of principles at one
time, and obtain political assistance by reason of those
principles, and at another to profess diametrically the reverse?
His life, I say again, is a living lie. He is the most degraded of
his species and kind; and England is degraded in tolerating or
having upon the face of her society a miscreant of his
abominable, foul and atrocious nature. (Cheers)…It will not be
supposed…when I speak to D'Israeli as the descendant of a
Jew, that I mean to tarnish him on that account. They were
once the chosen people of God. There were miscreants
amongst them however, also, and it must certainly have been

from one of these that D'Israeli descended. (Roars of laughter)
He possesses just the qualities of the impenitent thief who died
upon the cross, whose name, I verily believe, must have been
D'Israeli. (Roars of laughter) For aught I know, the present
D'Israeli is descended from him, and, with the impression that
he is, I now forgive the heir-at-law of the blasphemous thief
who died upon the Cross. (Loud cheers and roars of laughter)

> *Daniel O'Connell on Benjamin Disraeli, at a meeting of trades unions in Dublin*

London, May 6 [1835]
Mr O'Connell:
Although you have long placed yourself out of the pale of civilization, still I am one who will not be insulted, even by a Yahoo,
without chastising it ... Listen, then, to me. If it had been
possible for you to act like a gentleman, you would have
hesitated before you made your foul and insolent comments ... I
admire your scurrilous allusions to my origin. It is quite clear
that the 'hereditary bondman' has already forgotten the clank of
his fetter ... With regard to your taunts as to my want of success
in my election contests, permit me to remind you that I had
nothing to appeal to but the good sense of the people ... My
pecuniary resources, too, were limited; I am not one of those
public beggars that we see swarming with their obtrusive boxes
in the chapels of your creed, nor am I in possession of a princely
revenue wrung from a starving race of fanatical slaves ...

We shall meet at Philippi; and ... I will seize the first
opportunity of inflicting upon you a castigation which will
make you at the same time remember and repent the insults
you have lavished upon
BENJAMIN DISRAELI

> *Benjamin Disraeli to Daniel O'Connell*

As I sat opposite the Treasury Bench, the Ministers reminded me of one of those marine landscapes not very unusual on the coast of South America. You behold a range of exhausted volcanoes, not a flame flickers on a single pallid crest, but the situation is still dangerous. There are occasional earthquakes, and ever and anon the dark rumbling of the sea.

Benjamin Disraeli on the Liberal Government

He made his conscience not his guide but his accomplice.

Benjamin Disraeli on W.E. Gladstone

He has not a single redeeming defect.

Benjamin Disraeli on W.E. Gladstone

There is not a criminal in an European gaol, there is not a cannibal in the South Sea Islands, whose indignation would not rise and boil at the recital of that which has been done, which has too late been examined, but which remains unavenged; which has left behind all the foul and all the fierce passions that produced it, and which may again spring up, in another murderous harvest, from the soil soaked and reeking in blood, and in the air tainted with every imaginable deed of crime and shame. That such things should be done once, is a damming disgrace to the portion of our race which did them; that a door should be left open for their ever-so-barely possible repetition would spread that shame over the whole ...

W.E. Gladstone on the Turks, Bulgarian Horrors and the Question of the East

If Gladstone fell into the Thames, that would be a misfortune, and if anybody pulled him out that, I suppose, would be a calamity.

Benjamin Disraeli on W.E. Gladstone, after being asked to distinguish misfortune and calamity

He was without any rival whatever, the first comic genius
who ever installed himself in Downing Street.
Michael Foot on Benjamin Disraeli

A sophistical rhetorician, inebriated with the exuberance of
his own verbosity, and gifted with an egotistical imagination,
that can at all times command an interminable and inconsis-
tent series of arguments, malign an opponent and glorify
himself.
Benjamin Disraeli on W.E. Gladstone, parodying his style

Mr Gladstone speaks to me as if I were a public meeting.
Queen Victoria on W.E. Gladstone

... an old, wild, and incomprehensible man ...
*Queen Victoria on W. E. Gladstone's fourth and last appointment as Prime
Minister*

Cannes, March 15, 1893
Far away from my native Land, my bitter indignation as a
Welshwoman prompts me to reproach you, you bad, wicked,
false, treacherous Old Man! ...You have no conscience, but I
pray that God may even yet give you one that will sorely
smart and trouble you before you die. You pretend to be
religious, you old hypocrite! That you may more successfully
pander to the evil passions of the lowest and most ignorant of
the Welsh people ...You think you will shine in history, but it
will be a notoriety similar to that of Nero. I see someone pays
you the unintentional compliment of comparing you to
Pontius Pilate, and I am sorry, for Pilate, though a political
time-server, was, with all his faults, a very respectable man in
comparison with you ...You are certainly cleverer. So also is
your lord and master the Devil. And I cannot regard it as

sinful to hate and despise you, any more than it is sinful to abhor Him. So with full measure of contempt and detestation, accept these compliments from

'A DAUGHTER OF OLD WALES'

> *Anonymous letter to W. E. Gladstone, following his proposals to change the Welsh church*

The ordinary women of Wales are generally short and squat, ill-favoured and nasty.

> *David Mallet to Alexander Pope*

If you weren't such a great man you'd be a terrible bore.

> *Mrs W. E. Gladstone to her husband*

Mr Gladstone read Homer for fun, which I thought served him right.

> *Winston Churchill on W. E. Gladstone*

I am dead: dead, but in the Elysian fields.

> *Benjamin Disraeli on his move to the House of Lords. Attrib.*

The House of Lords is like heaven — you want to get there some day, but not while there is any life in you.

> *Lord Denning, Master of the Rolls*

This is a rotten argument, but it should be good enough for their lordships on a hot summer afternoon.

> *Civil Servant's note on a ministerial brief read out by mistake in the House of Lords, quoted in* The Way the Wind Blows *by Lord Home of the Hirsel*

They that hated the Bishops hated them worse than the devil, and they that loved them loved them not so well as their dinner.

> Lucius Cary, 2nd Viscount Faulkland on a Lords vote to deprive bishops of
> voting rights in 1661

It is very easy, my Lord, to swing about in the House of Lords, and to be brave five years after the time, and to point out to their Lordships the clear difference between moral and physical fear, and to be nodded to by the Duke of Wellington, but I am not to be paid by such coin.

> Sydney Smith, letter to The Times, attacking the Bishop of London, Charles
> James Blomfield, for his support of the Ecclesiastical Commission of 1836

It's easy to be brave from a distance.

> Aesop

I made his honour my most humble acknowledgements for the good opinion he was pleased to conceive of me; but assured him, at the same time, that my birth was of the lower sort, having been born of plain honest parents, who were just able to give me a tolerable education; that nobility among us was altogether a different thing from the idea he had of it; that our young noblemen are bred from their childhood in idleness and luxury; that as soon as years will permit, they consume their vigour, and contract odious diseases, among lewd females; and when their fortunes are almost ruined, they marry some woman of mean birth, disagreeable person, and unsound constitution, merely for the sake of money, whom they hate and despise; that the productions of such marriages are generally scrofulous, rickety, or deformed children; by which means the family seldom continues above three generations, unless the wife takes care to provide a healthy father, among her neighbours or domestics, in order to improve and continue the breed; that a weak, diseased body, a meagre countenance, and sallow complexion, are the true marks of noble blood; and a healthy, robust appearance is so disgraceful in a man of quality, that the world concludes his real father to have been a groom or coachman. The imperfections of his mind run parallel with those of his body, being a composition of spleen, dullness, ignorance, caprice, sensuality, and pride.

Without the consent of this illustrious body no law can be enacted, repealed, or altered; and these nobles have likewise the decision of all our possessions, without appeal.

Jonathan Swift, Gulliver's Travels, 'Gulliver on the English nobility'

A fully equipped Duke costs as much to keep as two Dreadnoughts, and Dukes are just as great a terror, and they last longer.
David Lloyd George

The House of Lords is like a glass of champagne that has stood for five days.
Clement Attlee. Attrib.

Every man has a House of Lords in his own head. Fears, prejudices, misconceptions – those are the peers, and they are hereditary.
David Lloyd George

Historical throwbacks and hillbilly inbreds.
Tony McNulty MP on hereditary peers

An ermine-lined dustbin, an up-market geriatric home with a faint smell of urine.
Austin Mitchell on the House of Lords

Let me be thankful, God, that I am not
A Labour Leader when his life-work ends,
Who contemplates the coronet he got
By being false to principles and friends;
Who fought for forty years a desperate fight
With words that seared and stung and slew like swords,
And at the end, with victory in sight,
Ate them – a mushroom viscount in the Lords.
    William Kean Seymour, Viscount Demos

He occasionally stumbled over the truth, but hastily picked
himself up and hurried on as if nothing had happened.
    Winston Churchill on Stanley Baldwin

Like a cushion, he always bore the impress of the last man
who sat on him.
    David Lloyd George on Lord Derby; also attrib. to Lord Haig

The two most powerful men in Russia are Tsar Nicholas II
and the last person who spoke to him.
    Anonymous

This goat-footed bard, this half-human visitor to our age from
the hag-ridden magic and uncharted woods of Celtic
antiquity.
    John Maynard Keynes on David Lloyd George, Essays and Sketches in
    Biography, *1933*

The tenth possessor of a foolish face.
    David Lloyd George on any aristocrat

When they circumcised Herbert Samuel they threw away the wrong bit.
David Lloyd George. Attrib.

He could not see a belt without hitting below it.
Margot Asquith on David Lloyd George

The Right Honourable gentleman has sat so long on the fence that the iron has entered his soul.
David Lloyd George on Sir John Simon. Attrib

The Right Honourable and Learned Gentleman has twice crossed the floor of this House, each time leaving behind a trail of slime.
David Lloyd George on Sir John Simon

Death is the most convenient time to tax rich people.
David Lloyd George

My one ardent desire is that after the war he should be publicly castrated in front of Nurse Cavell's statue.
Lytton Strachey on David Lloyd George

The manners of a cad and the tongue of a bargee.
Herbert Asquith on Joseph Chamberlain

It is fitting that we should have buried the Unknown Prime Minister by the side of the Unknown Soldier.
Herbert Asquith at Andrew Bonar Law's funeral. Attrib.

If I am a great man, then a good many of the great men of history are frauds.
Andrew Bonar Law. Attrib.

I must follow them; I am their leader.
  Andrew Bonar Law

I met Curzon in Downing Street, from whom I got the sort
of greeting a corpse would give to an undertaker.
  Stanley Baldwin. Attrib.

One could not even dignify him with the name of a stuffed
shirt. He was simply a hole in the air.
  George Orwell on Stanley Baldwin

I think Baldwin has gone mad. He simply takes one jump in
the dark; looks around and then takes another.
  Lord Birkenhead on Stanley Baldwin

I would rather be an opportunist and float, than go to the
bottom with my principles round my neck.
  Stanley Baldwin

Decided only to be undecided, resolved to be irresolute,
adamant for drift, solid for fluidity, all-powerful to be
impotent.
  Winston Churchill on Stanley Baldwin

He saw foreign policy through the wrong end of a municipal
drainpipe.
  *Winston Churchill on Neville Chamberlain; also attrib. to David Lloyd
  George*

A retail mind in a wholesale business.
  David Lloyd George on Neville Chamberlain

You have sat too long here for any good you have been doing.
Depart, I say, and let us have done with you. In the name of
God, go!
Leopold Amery to Neville Chamberlain, using Cromwell's words

He is no better than a Mayor of Birmingham, and in a lean
year at that. Furthermore he is too old. He thinks he
understands the modern world. What should an old hunk like
him know of the modern world?
Lord Hugh Cecil on Neville Chamberlain

He has the lucidity which is the by-product of a fundamentally sterile mind ... Listening to a speech by Chamberlain is
like paying a visit to Woolworth's; everything in its place and
nothing above sixpence.
Aneurin Bevan on Neville Chamberlain

The people of Birmingham have a specially heavy burden for
they have given the world the curse of the present British
Prime Minister.
Sir Stafford Cripps on Neville Chamberlain

There but for the grace of God goes God.
Winston Churchill on Sir Stafford Cripps

Wherever Sir Stafford Cripps has tried to increase wealth and
happiness, grass never grows again.
Colm Brogan, Our New Masters

Well, he seemed such a nice old gentleman, I thought I would
give him my autograph as a souvenir.
Adolf Hitler on Neville Chamberlain

He was a meticulous housemaid, great at tidying up.

A.J.P. Taylor on Neville Chamberlain

He is one of those orators of whom it was well said, 'Before they get up they do not know what they are going to say; when they are speaking, they do not know what they are saying; and when they sit down, they do not know what they have said.'

Winston Churchill on Charles Beresford

I remember, when I was a child, being taken to the celebrated Barnum's Circus, which contained an exhibition of freaks and monstrosities; but the exhibit on the programme which I most desired to see was the one described 'The Boneless Wonder'. My parents judged that the spectacle would be too revolting and demoralizing for my youthful eyes, and I have waited fifty years to see The Boneless Wonder sitting on the Treasury Bench.

Winston Churchill on Ramsay MacDonald

Winston had devoted the best years of his life to preparing his impromptu speeches.

F. E. Smith on Winston Churchill

Begotten of froth out of foam.

Herbert Asquith on Winston Churchill

Tell the Lord Privy Seal I am sealed to my privy, and can only deal with one shit at a time.

Winston Churchill when interrupted on the toilet in his wartime bunker and told the Lord Privy Seal wished to see him. Attrib.

WANTED! Dead or alive! Winston Churchill. 25 years old. 5 feet 8 inches tall. Indifferent build. Walks with a bend forward. Pale complexion. Red-brownish hair. Small toothbrush moustache. Talks through his nose and cannot pronounce the letter 'S' properly.
> *Jan Smuts on Winston Churchill*

I thought he was a young man of promise; but it appears he was a young man of promises.
> *Arthur James Balfour, writing in his diary of Winston Churchill's entry into politics*

A promising young man should go into politics so that he can go on promising for the rest of his life.
> *Robert Byrne*

His impact on history would be no more than the whiff of scent on a lady's purse.
> *David Lloyd George on Arthur Balfour*

A glass of port in his hand and a fat cigar in his mouth, with a huge and bloody red steak which he puts in his mouth in big chunks, and chews and chatters and smokes until the blood trickles down his chin – and to think this monster comes of a good family.
> *Joseph Goebbels on Winston Churchill*

A sheep in sheep's clothing.
> *Winston Churchill on Clement Attlee*

He is a man suffering from petrified adolescence.
> *Aneurin Bevan on Winston Churchill*

A tardy little marionette.
>*Randolph Churchill on Clement Attlee*

Dear Randolph, utterly unspoilt by failure.
>*Noel Coward on Randolph Churchill*

A triumph of modern science – to find only part of Randolph that wasn't malignant and remove it.
>*Evelyn Waugh on Randolph Churchill after an operation*

An empty taxi arrived at 10 Downing Street, and when the door was opened Attlee got out.
>*Winston Churchill (attrib.) on Clement Attlee. But Kenneth Harris (Attlee, 1982) says Churchill denied the quote: 'Mr Attlee is an honourable and gallant gentleman, and a faithful colleague who has served his country well at the time of her greatest need. I should be obliged if you would make it clear whenever an occasion arises that I would never make such a remark about him and I strongly disapprove of anyone who does'*

I welcome this opportunity of pricking the bloated bladder of lies with the poniard of truth.
>*Aneurin Bevan on Winston Churchill*

He will be as great a curse to this country in peace as he was a squalid nuisance in time of war.
>*Winston Churchill on Aneurin Bevan*

Christopher, I don't think Mr Mikardo is such a nice man as he looks.
>*Winston Churchill to his parliamentary private secretary, Christopher Soames, about Ian Mikardo, who was a famously ugly MP. Sir Edward Heath told us that this remark was made after a debate in the House of Commons in which Mr Mikardo 'pressed the Prime Minister about anti-Semitic practices at the Mid-Ocean Club, Bermuda, somewhat to the irritation of the Prime Minister'*

Always in the wrong, always surrounded by crooks, a most unsuccessful father – simply a 'Radio personality' who outlived his prime.
  Evelyn Waugh on Winston Churchill

Mr Waugh, I always feel, is an antique in search of a period, a snob in search of a class, perhaps even a mystic in search of a beatific vision.
  Malcolm Muggeridge on Evelyn Waugh

A difficulty for every solution.
  Herbert Samuel on the civil service

No amount of cajolery, and no attempts at ethical and social seduction, can eradicate from my heart a deep burning hatred for the Tory Party ... So far as I am concerned they are lower than vermin.
  Aneurin Bevan

A party of great vested interests ... corruption at home, aggression to cover up abroad ... sentiment by the bucket-load, patriotism by the imperial pint.
  Winston Churchill (while still a Liberal) on the Conservative Party

An overripe banana, yellow outside, squishy in.
  Sir Reginald Paget on Anthony Eden

Might as well have a corncob up his arse.
  Alan Clark MP on Douglas Hurd MP

A podgy puffball.
  Alan Clark MP on Kenneth Clarke MP

He is not only a bore, but he bores for England.
Malcolm Muggeridge on Sir Anthony Eden

Muggeridge, a garden gnome expelled from Eden, has come to rest as a gargoyle brooding over a derelict cathedral.
Kenneth Tynan on Malcolm Muggeridge

I'd like it translated, if you want to say anything.
Harold Macmillan during an address to the UN General Assembly after Nikita Khrushchev, seated opposite, disagreed so vehemently that he took off his shoe and banged the heel on the table

It was almost impossible to believe he was anything but a down-at-heel actor resting between engagements at the decrepit theatres of minor provincial towns.
Bernard Levin on Harold Macmillan, The Pendulum Years

Greater love hath no man than this, that he lay down his friends for his life.
Jeremy Thorpe after Harold Macmillan's 1962 Cabinet reshuffle

One can never escape the suspicion, with Mr Macmillan, that all his life was a preparation for elder statesmanship.
Frank Johnson on Harold Macmillan, in The Times

He is going around the country stirring up apathy.
William Whitelaw on Harold Wilson

If ever he went to school without any boots it was because he was too big for them.
Ivor Bulmer-Thomas on Harold Wilson's claims to an impoverished childhood

Only the future is certain, the past is always changing.
Paul Flynn MP (Lab) on New Labour propaganda

Harold Wilson said Labour was a crusade or it was nothing. I try not to think about his assertion. The logical implications are too painful.
Roy Hattersley, 1997

He was always the sort of Socialist who would do anything for the workers except eat like them.
Bruce Anderson on Roy Hattersley, in the Spectator

When I woke up to the [1997] election result my first thought was New Labour – New Zealand.
Richard Littlejohn, Daily Mail

Nouvelle cuisine was French for 'fucking hell, is that all you get?' This is Nouvelle Labour.
Rory Bremner

New Labour is like when a gorgeous woman accepts your dinner invitation and then tells you at the end of the evening she's a lesbian.
Alan McGee

Being elected a Labour MP is the only job you can get that actually makes you redundant.
AA Gill

God cannot alter the past; only historians do that.
Simon Jenkins

Historians are like deaf people who go on answering questions that no one has asked them.

> *Leo Tolstoy*

As far as the 14th Earl is concerned, I suppose Mr Wilson, when you come to think of it, is the 14th Mr Wilson.

> *Sir Alec Douglas-Home, responding to Harold Wilson's sneers after*
> *renouncing his peerage as the 14th Earl of Home to become Prime Minister*

Harold Wilson was one of the men who ruined post-war Britain. He was a small posturing visionless politician, personally pleasant to his friends and even his enemies, amusing, irreverent and apparently kind. But his public work was a long strung-out disaster, overlaid by the impression at the time that it was at least dextrously accomplished.

> *Hugo Young, in the* Guardian, *1995*

SIR ALEC DOUGLAS-HOME: Tell me, Mr Chairman, what do you think would have happened if Mr Khrushchev had been assassinated and not President Kennedy?
CHAIRMAN MAO: I do not believe Mr Onassis would have married Mrs Khrushchev.

> *Exchange at an official dinner*

The Minister of Technology flung himself into the Sixties technology with the enthusiasm (not to say the language) of a newly-enrolled Boy Scout demonstrating knot-tying to his indulgent parents.

> *Bernard Levin on Tony Benn,* The Pendulum Years

If I rescued a child from drowning, the press would no doubt headline the story 'Benn grabs child.'

> *Tony Benn*

The Bertie Wooster of Marxism.

Anonymous, about Tony Benn

Words cannot express my regret at the news that Anthony Wedgwood Benn has decided to retire from parliament. My regret is that he left it so late.

Gerald Kaufman MP

A little boy sucking his misogynist thumb and blubbing and carping in the corner of the front bench below the gangway is a mascot which parliament can do without.

Nicholas Fairbairn MP on Edward Heath

A perfectly good second-class chemist, a Beta chemist ... she wasn't an interesting person, except as a Conservative ... I would never, if I had amusing, interesting people staying, have thought of asking Margaret Thatcher.

Dame Janet Vaughan (former tutor at Somerville College, Oxford) on Margaret Thatcher

Headstrong, obstinate and dangerously self-opinionated.

ICI personnel report on the 22-year-old Margaret Roberts (later Thatcher)

The enemy within.

Margaret Thatcher on trades unions

Mrs Thatcher is a woman of common views but uncommon abilities.

Julian Critchley on Margaret Thatcher

The one thing I learnt as Margaret Thatcher's chief whip was that there is no limit to the capacity of human beings to absorb flattery.

John (Lord) Wakeham

. . . the powers of a first-rate man and the creed of a second-rate man.

Walter Bagehot on Sir Robert Peel

She is happier getting in and out of museums or theatre seats. She seems to derive more pleasure from admiring new missiles than great works of art. What else can we expect from an ex-Spam hoarder from Grantham presiding over the social and economic decline of the country?

Tony Banks on Margaret Thatcher

If she has a weakness it is for shopkeepers, which probably accounts for the fact that she cannot pass a branch of Marks and Spencers without inviting the manager to join her private office.

Julian Critchley on Margaret Thatcher

The Prime Minister tells us that she has given the French president a piece of her mind – not a gift I would receive with alacrity.

Denis Healey on Margaret Thatcher

Cette femme Thatcher! Elle a les yeux de Caligule, mais elle a la bouche de Marilyn Monroe.
(That woman Thatcher! She has the eyes of Caligula, but the mouth of Marilyn Monroe.)

Francois Mitterand on Margaret Thatcher – widely attrib. But her biographer, Charles Moore, says the original limeric was "the voice of Marylyn Monroe and the eyes of Stalin"

I wouldn't say she is open-minded on the Middle East, so much as empty-headed. She probably thinks Sinai is the plural of Sinus.

Jonathan Aitken MP on Margaret Thatcher

I wish that cow would resign.

Richard Needham MP, Northern Ireland minister, overheard on a telephone, on his Prime Minister, Margaret Thatcher. Informed of this, she responded that if this was the worst her ministers were saying, she was lucky

They'll have the same as me.

Margaret Thatcher (in puppet form in the TV satire 'Spitting Images') while dining with her ministers. The waiter had taken her order for a steak and inquired "and the vegetables?"

An extraordinary affair. I gave them their orders and they wanted to stay and discuss them.

The Duke of Wellington, describing his first Cabinet as Prime Minister

Like the deadly Upas tree, beneath whose branches nothing grows.

Denis Healey on Margaret Thatcher's deadening effect upon her Cabinet

She's a handbag economist who believes that you pay as you go.

New Yorker *on Margaret Thatcher*

She approaches the problems of our country with all the one-dimensional subtlety of a comic strip.

Denis Healey on Margaret Thatcher

La Pasionaria of middle-class privilege.

Denis Healey on Margaret Thatcher

Pétain in petticoats.

Denis Healey on Margaret Thatcher

Rhoda the Rhino.
Denis Healey on Margaret Thatcher

The great she-elephant.
Julian Critchley on Margaret Thatcher

Jezebel.
Revd Ian Paisley on Margaret Thatcher

The Immaculate Misconception.
Norman St John-Stevas on Margaret Thatcher

Attila the Hen.
Clement Freud on Margaret Thatcher

David Owen in drag.
Rhodesia Herald on Margaret Thatcher

The trouble is that when she speaks without thinking she says what she thinks.
Norman St John-Stevas on Margaret Thatcher

One of the things that politics has taught me is that men are not a reasoned or reasonable sex.
Margaret Thatcher

'Her Majesty does not notice what other people are wearing.'
A Palace official's alleged response when (after being embarrassed by arriving for her weekly meeting with the Queen wearing an identical outfit) Mrs Thatcher had asked her office to suggest the Palace give her prior notice of Her Majesty's proposed dress.

I wasn't lucky. I deserved it.
Margaret Thatcher, aged nine, after receiving a school prize

On the last Sunday of the 1983 General Election campaign I represented the Labour Party at a 'Question Time' organized by TVS in Gillingham, Kent, and filmed before an audience. Whilst I was responding to a question about Margaret Thatcher, a member of the audience interrupted with a shout of 'At least she's got guts'. I responded immediately by saying 'It's a pity that others had to lose theirs at Goose Green to prove it.'

Neil Kinnock, letter to the editor of this book. Mr Kinnock points out that there were demands that he withdraw his statement. He didn't, he says, 'not least because several people in, or associated with, the Forces took the trouble to let me know that they thought I should stand by what I said'

The self-appointed king of the gutter.

Michael Heseltine on Neil Kinnock after the above attack on Margaret Thatcher

If I was in the gutter and I ain't, he'd still be looking up at me from the sewer.

Neil Kinnock on Michael Heseltine

He reminds me of a Scottish Buddha, the very essence of immobility with a faint smile of perfect self-contentment upon his face.

John Major on John Smith

I did lower the ceiling somewhat.

Cecil Parkinson, scandal-hit Conservative politician, after explaining how you should leave politics when you've reached your ceiling

John Major himself now veers towards the ridiculous, whether flourishing his meaningless Citizen's Charter, tinkering with the Honours List, litigating alongside his cook, half-attacking Margaret Thatcher in the *Independent* – then backing down in fear and confusion – bickering with his archbishops or giving two cheers (one, really) for his embattled Queen. Not a man to go tiger-shooting with, even if the brutes were drugged or indeed stuffed. If I saw the Captain with a gun I would head for cover … John Major, in my estimation, is not the man to frog-march his party towards what he conceives to be his destiny … Major is what he is: a man from nowhere, going nowhere, heading for a well-merited obscurity as fast as his mediocre talents can carry him …

Paul Johnson, in the Spectator, *March 1993*

Cecil Parkinson, you're director of a fertilizer company. How deep is the mess you're in?

Jeremy Paxman's first question to former Conservative party chairman on the BBC's 1997 General Election results programme

John Major, Norman Lamont: I wouldn't spit in their mouths if their teeth were on fire.

Rodney Bickerstaffe of UNISON, 1992, who said this was based on a Scottish insult he learned in his youth: 'I wouldn't piss down his throat if his chest was on fire'

Only some ghastly, dehumanised moron would want to get rid of the Routemaster bus.

Ken Livingstone, Mayor of London. (He did)

You don't have to put up with dreadful human beings sitting alongside you.

> Steven Norris MP, Minister of Transport, explaining the superiority of the motor car over public transport

They lack fragrance on the whole. They're definitely not desert island material ... they all look as though they are from the 5th Kiev Stalinist machine-gun parade.

> Nicholas Fairbairn MP on women MPs

If you vote for Kinnock you're voting against Christ.

> Dame Barbara Cartland explaining why British voters should not vote Labour

A Conservatist government is an organized hypocrisy.

> Benjamin Disraeli

How can one best summon up the exquisite, earnest tedium of the speech of Sir Geoffrey Howe in yesterday's South African debate? It was rather like watching a much-loved family tortoise creeping over the lawn in search of a distant tomato.

> David McKie on Sir Geoffrey Howe

If you were hanging from a ledge by your fingers, he'd stamp on them.

> Edward Pearce on James Callaghan

The outstanding surviving example of English baroque.

> Michael White on Norman St John-Stevas

The Honourable Member for two tube stations.
Nicholal Fairbairn on Frank Dobson (MP for Holborn and St Pancras)

A bull in search of a china shop.
Unnamed union boss on Charles Clarke

Whenever Claire Short wrestles with her conscience, she wins.
Ben Macintyre

The man who takes the weight out of lightweight.
Bruce Anderson on Charles Kennedy

Like a fist fight in a hydrangea bush.
Craig Brown on buxom Dame Jill Knight wearing a floral print

His delivery at the dispatch-box has all the bite of a rubber duck.
Marcia (Lady) Falkender on John Moore

Peter Mandelson has the insolent manner of one born to the top rung but three.
Gore Vidal

Having a conversation with Mr Mandelson was rather like walking down stairs and missing the last step. You were uninjured but remained disconcerted.
Alan Watkins

Like Woody Allen without the jokes.
Simon Hoggart on Sir Keith Joseph

John Stuart Mill rewritten by Ernest Hemingway.
Chris Patten on David Owen

A tango dancer who's opened his legs to President Clinton.
Chinese government description of Chris Patten (last governor of Hong Kong)

You've stolen my fucking budget.
Gordon Brown to Tony Blair. Attrib.

There is nothing that you could say to me now that I could ever believe.
Gordon Brown to Tony Blair. Attrib.

If we can't take this lot apart in the next few years we shouldn't be in the business of politics at all.
Tony Blair handing over the premiership to Gordon Brown

He can't defeat Cameron.
Michael (Lord) Levy, Blair's chief fundraiser, quoting Tony Blair on his successor, Brown. Blair denied saying this

An analogue politician in a digital age.
David Cameron on Gordon Brown

A liar.
Blair's view of Brown according to Lord Levy

A tiny dot on this world.
Robert Mugabe on Gordon Brown

The House has noticed the Prime Minister's remarkable transformation in the past few weeks from Stalin to Mr Bean, creating chaos out of order, rather than order out of chaos.
Vincent Cable, MP to Gordon Brown

A Shakespearean tragedy.
Jonathan Powell, Tony Blair's chief of staff, describing Gordon Brown, to Boris Johnson, later Mayor of London. Johnson was on a bicycle, stopped at traffic lights. Powell denies the remark

Tempers of an indescribable nature ... so unhappy in himself ... [a] tragedy on a personal level as well as on a party, government and country level ... the Prime Minister looks so unhappy within his own body.
Frank Field MP on Gordon Brown

It doesn't matter how deep your intelligence or convictions, or how ingrained your sense of vocation and election, if you look sick when someone laughs at you, you aren't up to the job.
Howard Jacobson on Gordon Brown

Well that's a lie.
Cherie Blair (overheard) on hearing Gordon Brown say he had considered it a privilege to work with Tony Blair. She denied the remark

A fucking disaster.
Alleged remark by John Hutton, Business Secretary, anticipating Gordon Brown's premiership

At Downing Street upon the stair
I met a man who wasn't Blair.
He wasn't Blair again today.
Oh how I wish he'd go away!

> *Limerick attributed to a cabinet minister (anonymous) describing Gordon Brown's occupancy of 10 Downing Street*

Psychologically flawed.

> *A 'source close to' Prime Minister Tony Blair, on his Chancellor of the Exchequer, Gordon Brown, 1998. Alastair Campbell, Blair's Press Secretary denies the attribution*

Faintly autistic.

> *Reference (unspecific) by journalist Mary Ann Sieghart, to which George Osborne, Conservative Shadow-Chancellor replied "We're not getting on to Gordon Brown yet."*

He can brighten a room just by leaving it.

> *Peter Lilly on Gordon Brown*

Frustrating, annoying, bewildering and prickly … could go off like a bloody volcano.

> *John Prescott quoting colleagues opinion of Gordon Brown*

John is John.

> *Tony Blair on John Prescott*

[Tony Blair] doesn't like the full-frontal approach. It puts him off his tea.

> *John Prescott on Tony Blair*

One of the Number Ten mekons.

John Prescott of David Miliband, the Foreign Secretary - a comparison with the big-brained, shrivelled-bodied, green alien dictator in the 1950s Eagle *comic*

A semi-detached member of the cabinet.

Description of Tory politician John Biffen by Margaret Thatcher's Press Secretary, Bernard Ingham

The sewer and not the sewerage.

John Biffen on Bernard Ingham

Silly old fucker.

Alastair Campbell on Bernard Ingham

Boulton pretty sour as ever ... Robinson a jerk.

Alastair Campbell (diary entry) on Adam Boulton, Political Editor of Sky News *and Nick Robinson, BBC Political Editor*

A big twat.

Alastair Campbell on Martin Sixsmith, a Whitehall director of communications

A desiccated calculating machine.

Aneurin Bevan, usually regarded as a jibe at Hugh Gaitskell

He schemed, revised history ... the king of all larrikins, a coarse auto-didact with a tongue that could clip a hedge.

Conrad Black, owner of the Daily Telegraph, *on former Australian Prime Minister, Paul Keating*

A feral calculator.
Paul Keating on John Hewson, 1993 Australian general election

Like being flogged with a warm lettuce.
Australian Prime Minister Paul Keating, referring to an attack by the Opposition leader, John Hewson

He's wound up like a thousand day clock.
The then Australian Prime Minister, Paul Keating, about his Liberal Party opponent John Howard

What we have is a dead carcass, swinging in the breeze, but nobody will cut it down to replace him.
Paul Keating on John Howard

. . . the brain-damaged Leader of the Opposition.
Paul Keating on John Howard

From this day onwards, Howard will wear his leadership like a crown of thorns and in parliament I will do everything to crucify him.
Paul Keating on John Howard

I am not like the Leader of the Opposition. I did not crawl out of the Cabinet room like a mangy maggot.
Paul Keating on John Howard

I was implying that the Honourable Member was like a lizard on a rock – alive but looking dead.
Paul Keating on John Howard

I suppose that the Honourable Gentleman's hair, like his intellect, will recede into the darkness.
Paul Keating on shadow treasurer Andrew Peacock

It is the first time the Honourable Gentleman has got out from under the sunlamp.
Paul Keating on Andrew Peacock

Just because you swallowed a fucking dictionary when you were about fifteen doesn't give you the right to pour a bucket of shit over the rest of us.
Paul Keating to a member of his Cabinet

What for? Then I'd be like you.
Paul Keating, to Australian Prime Minister Gough Whitlam. Whitlam had just said to him 'that was a good speech. You should go back, comrade, and get yourself an honours degree.'

More Australian Parliamentary Expressions

ALLOWED
'The honourable Member for Crofts harbour with controversial views'
(Northern Territory)

'I am talking to the butcher, not the maggot on the block'
(Tasmania)

'Carry on like a pommy soccer larrikin'
(Tasmania)

'The Hungarian drink waiter'
(Tasmania)

'Go back to your sewer you sewer rat'
(Tasmania)

'Bulldust'
(Northern territory)

'You silly old moo'
(Victoria)

DISALLOWED
'Any of the hoons on the backbench'
(Northern Territory)

'Afghans who giggle and interject'
(Victoria, Lower House)

'Brains of a cabbage'
(Northern Territory)

'Carping whinging crap'
(Northern Territory)

'Covering up for bloody porky'
(Northern Territory)

'Educated wank'
(Northern Territory)

'It is bloody 10 o'clock and I want to go home too'
(Northern Territory)

'It is unusual for him to be alive'
(New South Wales)

'Tinfoil Tootsie'
  (Queensland)

'Total pig ignorance of this government'
  (Northern Territory)

'You are a messenger for the *Toorak Times*'
  (Victorian Assembly)

'So dishonest he could not lie straight in bed'
  (Northern Territory)

'Just because you like a rat looking over the Weet-bix'
  (Northern Territory)

'…has the power to take his Tonka Toys and drive them at his
own whim through Darwin'
  (Northern Territory)

'You are a slime, Fred'
  (Northern Territory)

'You are pathetic, Fred'
  (Northern Territory)

All he could hear was a whining noise. I could have told him
that it was his wife'
  (Victoria)

'…you miss your bloody plane tomorrow'
  (Northern Territory)

'You are mad. You smoke too much ganja'
  (Northern Territory)

'...off having liquid teas and maybe they should lie down for a little while'
  (Northern Territory)

Canadian Parliamentary Expressions

ALLOWED
'Misleading Albertans'
  (Alberta)

'I am indeed glad to welcome the Hon. Gentleman back from his long siesta'
  (Alberta)

DISALLOWED
'Goose farmer'
  (Alberta)

'He chickened out, the bum'
  (Alberta)

'Shafting Albertans'
  (Alberta)

'Wonder Woman and the Romper Room brats'
  (Canadian House of Commons)

'Vote grégaire de ses moutons' (herd-vote of his sheep)
  (Quebec)

'Well let me tell you, you curly little chum'
   (Saskatchewan)

Other Nation's Parliamentary Expressions

DISALLOWED
'What else can we expect from a party associated with the assassination of Mahatma Gandhi?'
   (Gujarat)

'There will be hurling of shoes'
   (Rajasthan)

'Drown yourself in a handful of water'
   (Rajasthan)

'Chief Minister himself is an agent of fertilizers'
   (India, Lok Sabha)

'Government has put oil in its ears' (ie, isn't listening)
   (Rajasthan)

'Shitty Government'
   (Western Samoa)

'Our sea coast is like the property of a Brahmin widow, which there is no one to look after'
   (Gujarat)

'Even the judges have started running brothels'
   (India, Lok Sabha)

They are nothing else but a load of kippers – two-faced, with no guts.

Eric Heffer on the Conservative Government

A Liar and A Cheat.

Guardian headline, on the news that former Tory Minister Neil Hamilton had withdrawn his libel case against the paper, 1996

It would be wrong to suggest Neil Hamilton is his own worst enemy when there are so many people better qualified for the post.

Craig Brown, in the Daily Telegraph

He Lied and Lied and Lied.

Guardian headline, on the news that former Tory Minister Jonathan Aitken had withdrawn his libel case against the paper, 1997

We had lost the art of communication – but not, alas, the gift of speech.

Gordon Brown, then Shadow Chancellor, on the Labour Party's 1983 election campaign, 1997

Jail him! – Aitken: serial liar, cheat, coward. His marriage is over and he faces a £2 million legal bill. It is not punishment enough. He must be sent to jail…he is unfit to mop the floor in a soup kitchen. He is not just a failure as a politician. He is a failure as a human being.

The Mirror *on Jonathan Aitken*

A semi-house-trained polecat.

Michael Foot on Norman Tebbit

Far better to keep your mouth shut and let everyone think you're stupid than to open it and leave no doubt.
> *Norman Tebbit to Dennis Skinner*

The weak are a long time in politics.
> *Neil Shand on John Gummer*

Up Yours Delors!
> *Sun headline, attacking the President of the European Commission, Jaques Delors*

Drittsekk
> *Thorbjorn Berntsen on John Gummer. British newspapers translated the word as 'shitbag', but the Royal Norwegian Embassy suggests a better translation is 'twerp'*

Putney said 'up your hacienda, Jimmy.'
> *David Mellor to James Goldsmith, shortly after losing his seat in Putney in the 1997 General Election*

He is undoubtedly living proof that a pig's bladder on a stick can be elected as a member of parliament.
> *Tony Banks on fellow MP Terry Dicks*

When I first came into this House I formed the opinion that the Honourable gentleman was a jerk. I have not changed that opinion.
> *Neil Kinnock, asked in the Commons Chamber by the late Robert Adley if, during his political career, there was anything on which he had not changed his opinion*

When I hear the name Richard Body I hear the sound of white coats flapping.
> *John Major on one of his own MPs, 1994. Attrib.*

A political leader worthy of assassination.
Irving Layton on Pierre Trudeau

I was my best successor but I decided not to succeed myself.
Pierre Trudeau on his decision not to seek another term as Canadian Prime Minister

A man who looks as if he has two flies fucking in his mouth.
Boris Yeltsin on his adviser Sergei Filatov

An improbable creature, like a human giraffe, sniffing down his nostril at mortals beneath his gaze.
Richard Wilson on Charles de Gaulle

He has missed a wonderful opportunity to keep his mouth shut.
Jacques Chirac on Ariel Sharon

A horrible voice, bad breath and a vulgar manner – the characteristics of a popular politician.
Aristophanes

The junk food of political journalism ... all reshuffle stories are crap.
Alistair Campbell, the Prime Minister's Press spokesman, to journalists, 1998

It is inexcusable for scientists to torture animals; let them make their experiments on journalists and politicians.
Henrik Ibsen

I invariably miss most of the lines in the last act of an Ibsen play; I always have my fingers in my ears waiting for the loud retort that means the heroine has just Passed On.

Dorothy Parker on Henrik Ibsen

I know what a statesman is. He's a dead politician. We need more statesmen.

Robert C. Edwards. Attrib.

A politician is a statesman who approaches every question with an open mouth.

Adlai Stevenson

Only in politics would Ken Livingstone appear to be an interesting man. Anywhere else he would be recognised as a bore.

Sebastian Faulks

When a politician changes his position it's sometimes hard to tell whether he has seen the light or felt the heat.

Robert Fuoss

Politicians are people who, when they see light at the end of the tunnel, order more tunnel.

John Quinton Banker

Nothing in politics is ever more certain than 60/40.

Adam Boulton, Political Editor of Sky News

In our time, political speech and writing are largely the defence of the indefensible.

George Orwell, Politics and the English Language

Few things are as immutable as the addiction of political groups to the ideas by which they have once won office.

John Kenneth Galbraith, The Affluent Society

In a dying civilisation, political prestige is the reward not of the shrewdest diagnostician but of the man with the best bedside manner.

Eric Ambler

He only had one idea and that was wrong.

Benjamin Disraeli, on a now-forgotten MP

Since a politician never believes what he says, he is surprised when others believe him.

Charles de Gaulle. Attrib.

A common definition of gaffe is when a politician tells the truth.

Alexander Chancellor

In politics there is no honour.

Benjamin Disraeli

The word 'politics' is derived from the word 'poly', meaning 'many', and the word 'ticks', meaning 'blood sucking parasites'.

Larry Hardiman

The reason there are so few female politicians is that it is too much trouble to put make-up on two faces.

Maureen Murphy

It is now known ... that men enter local politics solely as a result of being unhappily married.

Cyril Northcote Parkinson, Parkinson's Law

Politics, as a practice, whatever its profession, had always been the systematic organization of hatred.
Henry Adams, The Education of Henry Adams

Politicians can forgive almost anything in the way of abuse; they can forgive subversion, revolution, being contradicted, exposed as liars, even ridiculed, but they can never forgive being ignored.
Auberon Waugh, in the Observer

The only really safe pleasure for a parliamentarian is a bag of boiled sweets.
Julian Critchley

Whoever could make two ears of corn or two blades of grass to grow upon a spot of ground where only one grew before would deserve better of mankind and do more essential service to his country than the whole race of politicians put together.
Jonathan Swift

I have found some of the best reasons I ever had for remaining at the bottom simply by looking at the men at the top.
Frank More Colby

... and as to you, sir, treacherous in private friendship ... and a hypocrite in public life, the world will be puzzled to decide whether you are an apostate or an imposter, whether you have abandoned good principles, or whether you ever had any?
Tom Paine to George Washington

That dark designing sordid ambitious vain proud arrogant and vindictive knave.
General Charles Lee on George Washington

The moral character of Jefferson was repulsive. Continually puffing about liberty, equality and the degrading curse of slavery he brought his own children to the hammer and made money out of his debaucheries.

Alexander Hamilton, American politician, on Thomas Jefferson, third President of the USA

His attachment to those of his friends whom he could make useful to himself was thoroughgoing and exemplary.

John Quincy Adams on Thomas Jefferson

He looked at me as if I was a side dish he hadn't ordered.

Ring Lardner Jr., on President William Howard Taft

DEPEW: I hope if it's a girl Mr Taft will name it for his charming wife.

TAFT: If it is a girl, I shall, of course, name it for my lovely helpmate of many years. And if it is a boy, I shall claim the father's prerogative and name it Junior. But if, as I suspect, it is only a bag of wind, I shall name it Chauncey Depew.

William Howard Taft, before his election as President, and Chauncey Depew

He was a man of splendid abilities but utterly corrupt. Like rotten mackerel by moonlight, he shines and stinks.

John Randolph on fellow-US-politician Edward Livingstone

Sir, divine providence takes care of his own universe. Moral monsters cannot propagate. Impotent of everything but malevolence of purpose, they cannot otherwise multiply miseries than by blaspheming all that is pure and prosperous and happy. Could demon propagate demon, the universe might become a pandemonium; but I rejoice that the Father of Lies can never become the Father of Liars. One adversary of God and man is enough for one universe.

Tristram Burges on US congressman John Randolph, who was reputed to be impotent

You pride yourself upon an animal faculty, in respect of which the slave is your equal and the jackass infinitely your superior.

John Randolph to Tristram Burges, in reply to the above

It's a kangaroo ticket – stronger in the hindquarters than in the front.

A Texan Democrat on the merits of the nominations as presidential and vice-presidential candidates of Franklin Roosevelt and John Garner, in 1932

A real Centaur: part man, part horse's ass.

Dean Acheson on President Johnson

President Robbins was so well adjusted to his environment that sometimes you could not tell which was the environment and which was President Robbins.

Randall Jarrell

Why, if a man were to call my dog McKinley, and the brute failed to resent to the death the damning insult, I'd drown it.

William Cowper Brann on William McKinley

Reader, suppose you were an idiot; and suppose you were a member of Congress; but I repeat myself.

Mark Twain

Don't just do something – stand there.

President Ronald Reagan to a group of officials (attrib.)

'Do you pray for the senators, Dr Hale?' 'No, I look at the senators and I pray for the country.'
Edward Everett Hale

The trouble with Senator Long is that he is suffering from halitosis of the intellect.
Harold L. Ickes on Huey Long

Six inches deep - and six miles wide at the mouth.
Popular jibe comparing William Jennings Byron, American populist party's presidential candidate (known as The Boy Orator of the Platte), with the River Platte

[He] stirred whiskey with a thick forefinger, his socks drooped, his suits were green-hued, his ties were indifferent, and his breath was chronically bad. Hunched forward as he talked, he droned on in a flat voice, pronouncing Anthony Eden 'Ant-ny'.
Walter Isaacson and Evan Thomas on John Foster Dulles

The policeman and the trashman call me Alice. You cannot.
Alice Roosevelt Longworth, when Senator Joseph McCarthy called her Alice

The meanest kind of bawling and blowing office-holders, office-seekers, pimps, malignant, conspirators, murderers, fancy-men, custom-house clerks, contractors, kept-editors, spaniels well-train'd to carry and fetch, jobbers, infidels, disunionists, terrorists, mail-riflers, slave-catchers, pushers of slavery, creatures of the President, creatures of would-be Presidents, spies, bribers, compromisers, lobbyers, spongers, ruin'd sports, expell'd gamblers, policy-backers, monte-dealers, duellists, carriers of conceal'd weapons, deaf men, pimpled men, scarr'd inside with vile disease, gaudy outside with gold chains made from other people's money and

harlots' money twisted together; crawling, serpentine men,
the lousy combinings and born freedom-sellers of the earth.
> *Walt Whitman on a Democratic National Convention of the 1850s*

A large shaggy dog just unchained scouring the beaches of the
world and baying at the moon.
> *Robert Louis Stevenson on Walt Whitman*

A man of taste, arrived from Mars, would take one look at
the convention floor and leave forever, convinced he had seen
one of the drearier squats of Hell ... a cigar-smoking, stale-
aired, slack-jawed, butt-littered, foul, bleak, hardworking,
bureaucratic death gas of language and faces ... lawyers,
judges, ward heelers, mafiosos, Southern goons and grandees,
grand old ladies, trade unionists and finks; of pompous words
and long pauses which lie like a leaden pain over fever.
> *Norman Mailer on the Democratic National Convention of 1960*

My dear McClellan: If you don't want to use the army I
should like to borrow it for a while.
Yours respectfully, A. Lincoln
> *Abraham Lincoln to General McClellan, accused of inactivity in the*
> *American Civil War*

Filthy Story-Teller, Despot, Liar, Thief, Braggart, Buffoon,
Usurper, Monster, Ignoramus Abe, Old Scoundrel, Perjurer,
Robber, Swindler, Tyrant, Field-Butcher, Land-Pirate.
> *Harper's Weekly on Abraham Lincoln*

God damn your god damn old hellfiered [sic] god damned
soul to hell god damn you and god damn your god damned
family's god damned hellfiered god damned soul to hell and
good damnation gad damn them and god damn your god
damned friends to hell.

> Peter Muggins, American citizen, in a letter to President Abraham Lincoln

He is not known except as a slang-whanging stump-speaker
of which all parties are ashamed.

> The Albany Atlas and Argus, on Lincoln's Gettysburg Address, 1863

A horrid looking wretch he is, sooty and scoundrelly in
aspect, a cross between the nutmeg dealer, the horse
swapper, and the night man, a creature fit evidently for petty
treason, small stratagems and all sorts of spoils.

> Charleston Mercury on Lincoln 1863

Lincoln is the leanest, lankest, most ungainly mass of legs and
arms and hatchet face ever strung on a single frame. He has
most unwarrantably abused the privilege, which all politicians
have, of being ugly.

> Houston Telegraph on Lincoln, 1863

… the small intellect, growing smaller . . .[the Republicans]
take up a fourth-rate lecturer who cannot speak good grammar
and who . . . delivers hackneyed, illiterate compositions.

> New York Herald on Lincoln, 1860 election

Anything more dull and commonplace it wouldn't be easy to
reproduce.

> The Times on President Lincoln's Gettysburg Address, 1863

His argument is as thin as the homeopathic soup that was made by boiling the shadow of a pigeon that had been starved to death.
Abraham Lincoln on Stephen A. Douglas

His speeches leave the impression of an army of pompous phrases moving over the landscape in search of an idea. Sometimes these meandering words would actually capture a straggling thought and bear it triumphantly, a prisoner in their midst, until it died of servitude and overwork.
Senator William McAdoo on Warren Harding, US President

Deformed Sir, The Ugly Club in full meeting have elected you an honorary member of the Hood-Favored Fraternity. Prince Harry was lean, Falstaff was fat. Thersites was hunchbacked, and Slowkenlengus was renowned for the eminent miscalculation which Nature had made in the length of the nose; but it remained for you to unite all species of deformity and stand forth as The Prince of Ugly Fellows.
Anonymous letter to Abraham Lincoln

He writes the worst English that I have ever encountered. It reminds me of a string of wet sponges; it reminds me of tattered washing on the line; it reminds me of stale bean soup, of college yells, of dogs barking idiotically through endless nights. It is so bad that a sort of grandeur creeps into it. It drags itself out of the dark abysm of pish and crawls insanely up the topmost pinnacle of posh. It is rumble and bumble. It is flap and doodle. It is balder and dash.
H.L. Mencken on Warren Harding

The only man, woman or child who wrote a simple declarative sentence with seven grammatical errors is dead
E.E. Cummings on hearing of Warren Harding's death

He had a bungalow mind.
Woodrow Wilson on Warren G. Harding, his successor as President

He's thin, boys. He's thin as piss on a hot rock.
Senator William E. Jenner, on W. Averell Harriman, Governor of New York

McKinley has a chocolate éclair backbone.
Theodore Roosevelt on William McKinley

Wilson and his conscience were on terms of such incessant intimacy that any little disagreement between them could easily be resolved ... the belief that God, Wilson and the People would triumph in the end ... led him to look upon his own inconsistencies as mere transient details in the one great impulse toward right and justice.
Harold Wilson on Woodrow Wilson's state of mind at the Versailles Treaty negotiations

A Byzantine logothete.
Theodore Roosevelt on Woodrow Wilson

A taste for charming and cultivated friends and a tendency to bathe frequently causes in them the deepest suspicion.
Theodore Roosevelt on members of the 'Free Silver' populist movement

His idea of getting hold of the right end of the stick is to snatch it from the hands of someone who is using it effectively, and to hit him over the head with it.
George Bernard Shaw on Theodore Roosevelt

Thomas E. Dewey is just about the nastiest little man I've ever known. He struts sitting down.
Mrs Clarence Dykstra

How can they tell?
> *Dorothy Parker on being told that Calvin Coolidge was dead*

Nero fiddled, but Coolidge only snored.
> *H. L. Mencken on US President Calvin Coolidge*

He looks as if he had been weaned on a pickle.
> *Alice Roosevelt Longworth on Calvin Coolidge*

Democracy is that system of government under which the people, having 35,717,342 native-born adult whites to choose from, including thousands who are handsome and many of whom are wise, pick out a Coolidge to be head of state.
> *H. L. Mencken on Calvin Coolidge*

Hoover, if elected, will do one thing that is almost incomprehensible to the human mind: he will make a great man out of Coolidge.
> *Clarence Darrow during the 1928 American presidential campaign*

My choice early in life was either to be a piano-player in a whorehouse or a politician. And to tell the truth, there's hardly any difference.
> *Harry S. Truman*

Not worth a pitcherful of warm piss.
> *John Nance Garner, FDR's vice-president, on the importance of his position. The quote is often amended to 'warm spit' and often misattributed*

As an intellectual he bestowed upon the games of golf and bridge all the enthusiasm and perseverance that he withheld from books and ideas.
> *Emmet John Hughes on Dwight David Eisenhower*

An intellectual is a man who takes more words than necessary to tell more than he knows.

Dwight Eisenhower

I guess it proves that in America anyone can be President.

Gerald Ford on his appointment

Roosevelt proved a man could be president for life; Truman proved anybody could be president; and Eisenhower proved we don't need a President.

Anonymous

When his library burned down it destroyed both books. Dole hadn't finished colouring in the second.

Jack Kemp on Bob Dole, before he became Dole's running mate in the 1996 Presidential Election

Bob says he offers real leadership – he's right, backwards nor forwards.

Kemp on Dole

He has never met a tax he hasn't hiked.

Kemp on Dole

The candidate of pain, austerity and sacrifice.

Kemp on Dole

It is the greatest honour of my life to have been asked to run by the greatest American hero.

Kemp, accepting Dole's invitation to be his vice-presidential running-mate

You don't want to get in a wrestling match with a pig. You both get dirty, and the pig likes it.

Bob Dole

Always be sincere, whether you mean it or not.
Charles Percy, US Senator

Mothers all want their sons to grow up to be President but they don't want them to become politicians in the process.
John F. Kennedy

The enviably attractive nephew who sings an Irish ballad for the company and then winsomely disappears before the table-clearing and dishwashing begin.
Lyndon B. Johnson on John F. Kennedy

Lyndon acts like there was never going to be a tomorrow.
Lady Bird Johnson on her husband

I'd much rather have that fellow inside my tent pissing out than outside my tent pissing in.
Lyndon B. Johnson, explaining why he retained J. Edgar Hoover at the FBI

Trust him as much as you would trust a rattlesnake with a silencer on its rattle.
Dean Acheson on J. Edgar Hoover, head of the FBI

Do you realize the responsibility I carry? I'm the only person standing between Nixon and the White House.
John F. Kennedy to Arthur Schlesinger during the 1960 presidential campaign

Nixon is the kind of politician who would cut down a redwood tree and then mount the stump to make a speech for conservation.
Adlai Stevenson on Richard Nixon. Attrib.

Richard Nixon is a no-good lying bastard. He can lie out of both sides of his mouth at the same time and if he ever caught himself telling the truth he'd lie just to keep his hand in.
Harry S. Truman

So – did any of you guys do any fornicating over the weekend?
Richard Nixon, to David Frost's media team before an interview

Would you buy a second hand car from this man?
Mort Sahl on Richard Nixon. Attrib.

Nixon, pull out like your father should have.
Graffiti on Richard Nixon

Richard Nixon is a pubic hair in the teeth of America.
Graffiti on Richard Nixon

In political life mud sticks, then stains and eventually becomes part of the fabric.
Mayor Koch

Gerry Ford is so dumb that he can't fart and chew gum at the same time.
Lyndon B. Johnson on Gerald Ford (often misquoted)

Gerry Ford is a nice guy, but he played too much football with his helmet off.
Lyndon B. Johnson on Gerald Ford

He's so dumb he couldn't tip shit out of a boot if the instructions were written on the heel.
Lyndon Johnson on Gerald Ford

He looks like the guy in a science fiction movie who is the first to see the Creature.
> *David Frye on Gerald Ford*

I love all my children, but some of them I don't like.
> *Lillian Carter, mother of Jimmy Carter*

A hippie is someone who looks like Tarzan, walks like Jane and smells like Cheetah.
> *Ronald Reagan*

A triumph of the embalmer's art.
> *Gore Vidal on Ronald Reagan*

Not only a barbarian, but flaky.
> *Ronald Reagan on Colonel Muammar Gaddafi*

He doesn't make snap decisions but he doesn't overthink either.
> *Nancy Reagan on her husband*

If the President's penis is straight, it is the only thing about his administration that is.
> *Mark Steyn on rumours of an intimate nature concerning Bill Clinton*

Bill Clinton does not have the moral fibre to be a mass murderer.
> *Henry Kissinger*

He is the bride at every wedding and the corpse at every funeral he attends.
> *Todd Purdum on Bill Clinton, post-presidency*

I have difficulty in looking humble for extended periods of time.
Henry Kissinger

I am being frank about myself in this book. I tell of my first mistake on page 850.
Henry Kissinger

When you bore people they think it's their fault.
Henry Kissinger on being famous

Satire died the day they gave Henry Kissinger the Nobel Peace Prize. There were no jokes left after that.
Tom Lehrer

A joke that doesn't make you laugh about someone you don't know told by a man who went to Oxford.
AA Gill on satire

I think I speak for everyone when I say what a shame it is that only one of these guys can lose.
David Letterman on the 2000 Presidential election campaign between George W. Bush and Al Gore

I am Al Gore and I used to be the next President of the United States.
Al Gore, to an audience of students

Al Gore is an old person's idea of what a young person should be.
Michael Kinsey

The Bush people ... have virtually got rid of Magna Carta and *habeas corpus*. In a normal republic I would probably have raised an army and overthrown them. It will take a hundred years to put it all back ... those neocons, lawyers, the big corporations – worse than that – the extremists – want to get rid of the great power of oversight of the executive. See what they'll try to do to Obama. They're crooks. They're just gangsters. They are the enemy of the United States. There's no such thing as a war on terrorism. It's idiotic. There are slogans. It's advertising, which is the only art form we've invented and developed. It's lies.

Gore Vidal on the George W. Bush administration

He struggles to exude authority.   He furrows his brow, trying to look more sagacious, but he ends up looking as if he has indigestion.   Appearing confused at his own speech, he seems like a first-grade actor in a production of *James and the Giant Peach*.   Are his blinks Morse code for "Oh, man, don't let that teleprompter break"?

Maureen Dowd on George W. Bush

On some great and glorious day, the plain folks of the land will reach their heart's desire at last, and the White House will be adorned with a moron.

H.L. Mencken

Candidates without ideas hiring consultants without convictions to run campaigns without content.

President Gerald Ford talking about US Presidential race

Too few have the courage of my convictions.

Robert M. Hutchins (Margaret Thatcher made a similar remark about her Cabinet)

Cheer up, only one of them can win.

Bumper sticker in the US Election 1992

She's every American's ex-wife.
P.J. O'Rourke on Hillary Clinton

I think her strategy is more or less insane … I'd always rather liked her. She's a perfectly able lawyer … But this long campaign, this daily search for the grail, has driven her crazy.
Gore Vidal on Hillary Clinton's campaign for the Democratic Presidential nomination

A congenital liar.
William Safire on Hillary Clinton

I've never met anyone in America who has the slightest respect for him. He went to a private school and came bottom of his class. He smashed up his aeroplane and became a prisoner of war, which he is trying to parlay into 'war hero.'
Gore Vidal on John McCain

It's the sort of thing parents might chant encouragingly to a child slow on the potty-training.
Christopher Hitchens on Barack Obama's campaign slogan of 'Yes we can'

I want to cut his nuts off.
Rev. Jesse Jackson on Barack Obama

A goddamned fool he was on television talking about mortgages, and it was quite clear he didn't know what a mortgage is. His head rattles as he walks.
Gore Vidal on John McCain

They never open their mouths without subtracting from the sum of human knowledge.
Thomas Reed, Speaker of the House of Representatives, on members of Congress

The facile leather-tongued oracle of the ordinary bourgeois intelligence.
Karl Marx on Jeremy Bentham

The world would not be in such a snarl,
had Marx been Groucho instead of Karl.
Irving Berlin on Karl Marx

The left always has an orgasm when it sees a crowd.
Simon Jenkins

As with the Christian religion, the worst advertisement for Socialism is its adherents.
George Orwell

We should have had socialism in this country long ago, if it were not for the bloody people who became socialists.
George Bernard Shaw

They are political Calibans on Prospero's island, chanting their subversive songs only to each other.
Jenny McCartney on the Left

The trouble with socialism is that it takes up too many evenings.
Oscar Wilde

Its relationship to democratic institutions is that of the death-watch-beetle — it is not a Party, it is a conspiracy.
Aneurin Bevan on the Communist Party

Russian communism is the illegitimate child of Karl Marx and Catherine the Great.
Clement Attlee

I shall be an autocrat: that's my trade. And the good Lord will forgive me: that's his.
Catherine the Great. Attrib.

Russia is a collapse, not a revolution.
D. H. Lawrence

Every revolution evaporates and leaves behind it only the slime of a new bureaucracy.
Franz Kafka

It would have been better if the experiment had been conducted in some small country, to make it clear it was a Utopian idea.
Boris Yeltsin on Communism

Change? Change? Why do we need change?
Things are quite bad enough as they are.
Lord Salisbury, British Prime Minister

The DAILY HERALD
is unkind. It has been horrid
About my nice new war.
I shall burn the DAILY HERALD.

I think, myself,
That my new war
Is one of the nicest we've had;
It is not war really,
It is only a training for the next one,
And saves the expense
Of Army Manoeuvres.
Besides, we have not declared war;

We are merely restoring order —
As the Germans did in Belgium,
And as I hope to do later
In Ireland.
I never really liked
The late Tsar;
He was very weak and reactionary...
As I said in a great speech
After the last great war,
I begin to fear That the nation's heroic mood
Is over.
Only three years ago
I was allowed to waste
A million lives in Gallipoli,
But now
They object
To my gambling
With a few thousand men
In Russia!
It does seem a shame.
I shall burn the DAILY HERALD.

> Osbert Sitwell, 'A Certain Statesman' (Churchill), in the
> Daily Herald, 1919

I offer a toast to this gracious lady. Up your bottom.

> Andri Gromyko, Soviet Foreign Minister, to Mrs Dean Rusk at the 1979
> Vienna Summit, after he had refused the assistance of a translator

We will bury you.

> Nikita Khrushchev at a Kremlin reception

A pig-eyed bag of wind.

> Frank L. Howley on Nikita Khrushchev

When you are skinning your customers, you should leave some on to grow so that you can skin them again.
Nikita Khrushchev to British businessmen

Who? Whom?
V I Lenin. In idiom and context the meaning is clearer: that in any controversial proposal the operative question is Who is screwing whom?

The Pope! How many divisions has he got?
Joseph Stalin, when urged by Pierre Lavel to tolerate Catholicism in the USSR to appease the Pope

Pathological exhibits ... human scum ... paranoics, degenerates, morons, bludgers ... pack of dingos ... industrial outlaws and political lepers ... ratbags. If these people went to Russia, Stalin wouldn't even use them for manure.
Arthur Calwell, Australian Minister of Immigration, on Australian Communists

That all men are equal is a proposition to which at ordinary times, no sane individual has ever given his assent.
Aldous Huxley, Proper Studies

Stupid asses.
Karl Marx and Friedrich Engels on the proletariat, private correspondence

This war, like the next war, is a war to end war.
David Lloyd George on the First World War

You can't say civilization don't advance, however, for in every war they kill you a new way.
Will Rogers, Autobiography

War is the national industry of Prussia.
Honoré Gabriel Riquetti, Comte de Mirabeau. Attrib.

When God wants to punish a nation, he makes them invade Afghanistan.
Afghan saying

It's God's responsibility to forgive Bin Laden … it's our responsibility to arrange the meeting.
Slogan on a US marine's bumper sticker

Military intelligence is a contradiction in terms.
Groucho Marx

There they are cutting each other's throats, because one half of them prefer hiring their servants for life, and the other by the hour.
Thomas Carlyle on the American Civil War. Attrib.

Military justice is to justice, as military music is to music.
Groucho Marx

War is God's way of teaching Americans geography.
Ambrose Bierce

Peace: in international affairs, a period of cheating between two periods of fighting.
Ambrose Bierce

If I were fierce, and bald, and short of breath,
I'd live with scarlet Majors at the base,
And speed glum heroes up to the line of death.
You'd see me with my puffy petulant face,
Guzzling and gulping in the best hotel,
Reading the Roll of Honour. 'Poor young chap,'
I'd say – 'I used to know his father well;
Yes, we've lost heavily in this last scrap.'
And when the war is done and youth stone dead,
I'd toddle safely home and die – in bed.

    Siegfried Sassoon, Counter-Attack, 'Base Details'

Patriots always talk of dying for their country, and never of
killing for their country.

    Bertrand Russell

A soldier is a man whose business it is to kill those who never
offended him, and who are the innocent martyrs of other
men's iniquities. Whatever may become of the abstract
question of the justifiableness of war, it seems impossible that
the soldier should not be a depraved and unnatural thing.

    William Godwin

War hath no fury like a non-combatant.

    C. E. Montague, Disenchantment

Lions led by donkeys.

    Max Hoffmann on the British army in the First World War

Restraint? Why are you so concerned with saving their lives?
The whole idea is to kill the bastards. At the end of the war if
there are two Americans and one Russian left alive, we win.

    US General Thomas Power, Head of Strategic Air Command

Standing at the head of his troops, his drawn salary in his hand.
> *Henry Labouchere on the Duke of Clarence*

Ours is composed of the scum of the earth.
> *Duke of Wellington on the British army*

These boys have fought for four years. They deserve their fun.
> *Joseph Stalin on reports of the mass rape of German women by Russian soldiers*

Marijuana smokers, drug addicts, long-hairs, homosexuals and unionists.
> *General Augusto Pinochet, describing the West German army*

This man is depriving a village somewhere of an idiot.
> *Extract from Royal Navy and Marines Fitness Report, 1997*

The only thing more boring than sickness is fitness.
> *Karl Lagerfeld*

I don't know what effect these men will have on the enemy, but, by God, they terrify me.
> *Duke of Wellington on his troops*

He never commanded more than ten men in his life – and he ate three of them.
> *General Weston on Adolphus Greely, on Greely's being made a general. Much of his life had been spent as an Artic explorer*

Jellicoe was the only man on either side who could lose the war in an afternoon.
> *Winston Churchill*

He would kill his own mother just so that he could use her skin to make a drum to beat his own praises.
Margot Asquith on Winston Churchill

If Kitchener was not a great man, he was, at least, a great poster.
Margot Asquith

The General is suffering from mental saddle sores.
Harold L. Ickes on Huey Long

He really deserves some sort of decoration . . . a medal inscribed 'For Vaguery in the Field'.
John Osborne, Look Back in Anger

In defeat unbeatable; in victory unbearable.
Winston Churchill on Viscount Montgomery

Don't talk to me about naval tradition. It's nothing but rum, sodomy, and the lash.
Winston Churchill

The British soldier can stand up to anything except the British War Office.
George Bernard Shaw

One to mislead the public, another to mislead the Cabinet, and the third to mislead itself.
Herbert Asquith, explaining why the War Office kept three sets of figures

Maybe it would have been better if neither of us had been born.
Napoleon Bonaparte, looking at the tomb of Jean-Jacques Rousseau

What have we acquired? What, but a bleak and gloomy solitude, an island thrown aside from human use, stormy in winter and barren in the summer; an island which not even the Southern savages have dignified with habitation; where a garrison must be kept in a state that contemplates with envy the exiles of Siberia; of which the expense will be perpetual and the use only occasional; and which, if fortune smiles upon our labours, may become a nest of smugglers in peace, and in war the refuge of future buccaneers.

Samuel Johnson on the Falkland Islands

The Falklands thing was a fight between two bald men over a comb.

Jorge Luis Borges on the Falklands War

Imperialist running dogs.

Approved Chinese term for Americans in print and on radio

Who cares about a little terrorist in Afghanistan?

Paul Wolfowitz, Deputy Defense Secretary, on concerns about al-Qaeda, April 2001

A crew of pirates are driven by a storm they know not whither; at length a boy discovers land from the topmast; they go on shore to rob and plunder; they see a harmless people, are entertained with kindness; they give the country a new name; they take formal possession of it for their king; they set up a rotten plank or a stone for a memorial; they murder two or three dozen natives; bring away a couple more by force for a sample; return home and get their pardon. Here commences a new dominion acquired with a title by divine right. Ships are sent with the first opportunity; the natives driven out or destroyed; their princes tortured to discover their gold; a free reeking with the blood of its inhabitants; and this execrable crew of butchers, employed in so pious an expedition, is a modern colony, sent to convert and civilize an idolatrous and barbarous people.

> *Jonathan Swift,* Gulliver's Travels 'Gulliver on the English system of colonizing'

Civilized men arrive in the Pacific, armed with alcohol, syphilis, trousers and the Bible.

> *Havelock Ellis*

They send in all their troops to drain the products of industry, to seize all the treasures, wealth and prosperity of the country. Like a vulture with their harpy talons grappled in the vitals of the land, they flap away the lesser kites and they call it protection. It is the protection of the vultures to the lamb.

> *Richard Brinsley Sheridan on the East India Company*

When empires are on the rise, they sacrifice their finest. When they are on the decline, they sacrifice their NCOs.

> *Menachem Begin*

Columbus was not a learned man, but an ignorant. He was not an honourable man, but a professional pirate ... His voyage was undertaken with a view solely to his own advantage, the gratification of an incredible avarice. In the lust of gold he committed deeds of cruelty, treachery and oppression for which no fitting names are found in the vocabulary of any modern tongue. To the harmless and hospitable peoples among whom he came he was a terror and a curse ...

> *Ambrose Bierce on Christopher Columbus*

I admire him, I frankly confess it; and when his time comes I shall buy a piece of the rope for a keepsake.

> *Mark Twain on Cecil Rhodes*

It is nauseating to see Mr Gandhi, a seditious Middle Temple lawyer, now posing as a fakir of a type well known in the East, striding half naked up the steps of the Viceregal Palace, while he is still organizing and conducting a defiant campaign of civil disobedience, to parley with the representative of the King Emperor.

Winston Churchill on Mahatma Gandhi

I think it would be a good idea.

Mahatma Gandhi on being asked his view of Western civilization. Attrib.

Gandhi was very keen on sex. He renounced it when he was 36, so thereafter it was never very far from his thoughts.

Woodrow Wyatt on Mahatma Gandhi

I am sure that Dickie has done marvellously. But it is curious that we should regard as a hero the man who liquidated the Empire which other heroes such as Clive, Warren Hastings, and Napier won for us. Very odd indeed.

Harold Nicolson on Earl Mountbatten

[He] speaks like a Buddha and thinks like a serpent ... His soul is possessed by British colonialism. Nothing can distract him from his perfidy ... The truth has come to light ... Chris Patten will stand condemned down the ages.

Wen Wei Po, the Communist-run newspaper in Hong Kong, on Chris Patten, the Governor

This democracy knows you as the poisoner of the streams of human intercourse, the formenter of war, the preacher of hate, the unscrupulous enemy of human society.

A. G. Gardner on the publisher Lord Northcliffe

They are only ten.
Lord Northcliffe, notice to remind staff on his newspaper of the mental age of readers

A single sentence will suffice for modern man: he fornicated and read the papers.
Albert Camus, The Fall

We live under a government of men and morning newspapers.
Wendell Phillips

A journalist is a person who works harder than any other lazy person in the world.
Anonymous

Facing the press is more difficult than bathing a leper.
Mother Teresa

Bye! I won't miss you.
Cherie Blair, leaving Downing Street for the last time, to the attendant press corps

I have spent half my life trying to get away from journalism, but I am still mired in it – a low trade and a habit worse than heroin, a strange seedy world full of misfits and drunkards and failures.
Dr Hunter S. Thompson

Somewhere along the line, many Americans relegated the media to a notch on the morality scale only slightly above that of child molesters.
Gregory Kane in the Baltimore Sun

A journalist is a reporter out of a job.
Mark Twain

A foreign correspondent is someone who flies around from hotel to hotel and thinks that the most interesting thing about any story is the fact that he has arrived to cover it.
Tom Stoppard, Night and Day

A drink-soaked former Trotskyist popinjay.
George Galloway MP on Christopher Hitchens

Made natural history by metamorphosing from a butterfly to a slug.
George Galloway MP on Christopher Hitchens

Ready to fight to the last drop of other people's blood.
George Galloway on Christopher Hitchens

You did write like an angel and now you're working for the devil. Damn you and damn all your words.
George Galloway on Christopher Hitchens

A mouthpiece for those miserable, malevolent incompetents who could not even pick up the bodies of their own citizens in New Orleans.
George Galloway on Christopher Hitchens and the US Republican administration

Ba'athist, short-arse, sub-Leninist, Eastend carpet-bagger.
Christopher Hitchens on George Galloway

Every journalist who is not too stupid or too full of himself to notice what is going on knows that what he does is morally indefensible. He is a kind of confidence man, preying on people's vanity, ignorance, or loneliness, gaining their trust and betraying them without remorse.
Janet Malcolm

The way I had it is all gone now. The bars are gone, the drinkers, gone. There remain the smartest, healthiest newspeople in the history of the business. And they are so boring that they kill the business right in front of you.
Jimmy Breslin

To a newspaperman, a human being is an item with skin wrapped around it.
Fred Allen

You cannot hope to bribe or twist,
Thank God! the British journalist.
But, seeing what the man will do
Unbribed, there's no occasion to.
Humbert Wolfe

Once a newspaper touches a story, the facts are lost for ever, even to the protagonists.
Norman Mailer

I hesitate to say what the functions of the modern journalist may be, but I imagine that they do not exclude the intelligent anticipation of facts before they occur.
Lord Curzon

I read the newspaper avidly. It is my one form of continuous fiction.
Aneurin Bevan

Trying to determine what is going on in the world by reading newspapers is like trying to tell the time by watching the second hand of a clock.
Ben Hecht

A newspaper is a device unable to distinguish between a bicycle accident and the collapse of civilization.
George Bernard Shaw

The government of bullies, tempered by editors.
Ralph Waldo Emerson on democracy

Some editors are failed writers, but so are most writers.
T. S. Eliot

Emerson's writing had a cold, cheerless glitter like the new furniture in a warehouse, which will come of use by and by.
American author Alexander Smith, in Dreamthorp, *on Ralph Waldo Emerson, American essayist and poet*

What the proprietorship of these papers is aiming at is power, and power without responsibility – the prerogative of the harlot throughout the ages.
Stanley Baldwin on press barons Lord Rothermere and Beaverbrook

Good God, that's done it. He's lost us the tarts' vote.
The 10th Duke of Devonshire on Stanley Baldwin's attack on newspaper proprietors. Attrib.

The press is the enemy.
Richard Nixon

Politicians who complain about the press are like ships' captains who complain about the sea.
Enoch Powell

All the faults of the age come from Christianity and Journalism.
Frank Harris

Christianity, of course, but why journalism?
Arthur James Balfour in reply

Frank Harris has been invited to all the great houses in England once.
Oscar Wilde

You lying BBC; you're photographing things that aren't happening.
Belfast woman to a BBC cameraman

To press journalists, television is like a mendacious, boastful cousin who keeps turning up at family parties with a prettier girl and a more powerful motor that you rather hope will end up in a ditch.
Allison Pearson, in the Evening Standard

Sir: During the short time since the Sun started publishing in Edmonton, I have witnessed your decay from amiable drunk through voyeur and track rat to misogynous, vitriolic pariah ... I cannot but from now on dismiss your scribblings as the libellous drivel of an unbalanced mind.
Robert Hamilton, letter to the Edmonton Sun

I can but wonder what will become of the editor of the Los Angeles Times when the breath leaves his feculent body and death stops the rattling of his abortive brain. He cannot be buried at sea lest he poison the fishes. He cannot be suspended in mid-air, like Mahomet's coffin, lest the circling worlds, in their endeavour to avoid contamination, crash together, wreck the universe and bring about the reign of chaos and Old Night. The damm scoundrel is a white elephant on the hands of the Deity, and I have some curiosity to know what He will do with him.

> *William Cowper Brann*

All newspaper editorial writers ever do is come down from the hills after the battle is over and bayonet the wounded.

> *Anonymous*

An editor is one who separates the wheat from the chaff and prints the chaff.

> *Adlai Stevenson*

Getting information from the internet is like getting a glass of water from Niagara.

> *Arthur C. Clarke*

It's a wonder none of them crash-landed on the magazine.

> Private Eye, *responding to the Editor of* Punch's *comment that 'jokes winged back and forth between the men and women'*

The Times is speechless and takes three columns to express its speechlessness.

> *Winston Churchill on Irish Home Rule*

On the whole I would not say that our Press is obscene. I would say that it trembles on the brink of obscenity.
Lord Longford

Unreconstructed wankers.
Tony Blair's description of the Scottish media, 1997

Journalism consists in buying white paper at two cents a pound and selling it for ten cents a pound.
Cyril Connolly

There is much to be said in favour of modern journalism. By giving us the opinions of the uneducated, it keeps us in touch with the ignorance of the community.
Oscar Wilde

No one ever went broke underestimating the taste of the American public.
H. L. Mencken

Every item in the *Daily Mail* should make our readers hate someone or something, or fear something or someone, a little bit more.
Instruction to a young journalist joining The Daily Mail's Wicked Whispers *diary column*

There is not a more mean, stupid, dastardly, pitiful, selfish, envious, ungrateful animal than the public. It is the greatest of cowards, for it is afraid of itself.
William Hazlitt, On Living to Oneself

Teenage scribblers.
Nigel Lawson, when Chancellor, on City journalists

People with nothing to say and who know how to say it.
  Karl Kraus on journalists

If a person is not talented enough to be a novelist, not smart enough to be a lawyer, and his hands are too shaky to perform operations, he becomes a journalist.
  Norman Mailer

It's great to be with Bill Buckley, because you don't have to think. He takes a position and you automatically take the opposite one and you know you're right.
  John Kenneth Galbraith on William F. Buckley, Jr., right-wing editor of the National Review

Price of *Herald* three cents daily. Five cents Sunday. Bennett.
  Telegram from James Gordon Bennett, American newspaper owner and editor, to William Randolph Hearst, when Hearst, who was trying to buy his paper, asked for a price

A reptile marking his path wherever he goes and breathing a mildew at everything fresh and fragrant; a midnight ghoul preying on rottenness and repulsive filth. A creature hated by his nearest intimates and bearing his consciousness thereof upon his distorted features and upon his despicable soul.
  Walt Whitman on James Gordon Bennett, Editor of the New York Herald

If Max gets to Heaven he won't last long. He will be chucked out for trying to pull off a merger between Heaven and Hell … after having secured a controlling interest in key subsidiary companies in both places, of course.
  H. G. Wells on Lord Beaverbrook

A legend in his own lunchtime.
> Christopher Wordsworth on the journalist Clifford Makins

The Titchmarsh interviewing technique consists of grovelling
… the theme music should really be L'Apres-midi d'un faun.
> Victor Lewis-Smith, newspaper critic, 1994

His improbabilities started with his looks. His long body
seemed to be only basted together, his hair was quills upon
the fretful porcupine, his teeth were Stonehenge, his clothes
looked as if they had been brought up by somebody else.
> Dorothy Parker on Harold Ross, editor of the New Yorker

I have just seen your submission to the Press Complaints
Commission. For sheer, pathetic, childish, toys-out-of-the-
pram crap, it's hard to beat. Tantrums and tiaras, darlings?
Stick them where the sun don't shine.
> Piers Morgan in a letter to Sir Elton John's lawyer

I think we fell out when you said 'I think' and I said 'I don't
give a fuck what you think'.
> Kelvin Mackenzie, former editor of the Sun, to a marketing man at the
> latter's leaving party

Well tell him to take a flying fuck at a rolling doughnut.
> Kelvin Mackenzie to a colleague worried lest Mackenzie upset another
> editor

Switch off now. There's no sex in this programme, unless you
count the Sun newspaper's dirty words, but there will be a
great deal of violence. I'm going to get down there in the
gutter where so many of our journalists crawl, and for maybe
the third time in my life conduct an argument in the sort of

personal terms that have become the norm across such large and fetid tracks of our cynical, venal, genuinely prostituted and foreign-owned Press.

Touch and go though it has been, and through an often messy and occasionally shameful personal life, I've managed to gather around myself some shreds of self-respect, so what I'm about to do is perhaps less obviously foolhardy than it otherwise might seem. And what I am about to do is to make a provenly vindictive and extremely powerful enemy, a sort of serial killer (metaphorically speaking) who has more phials of poison at his command than there are chemists' shops in this troubled land.

This programme is not going out live, so at least I know that I shall reach the end of it in more or less one piece. Not quite a joke – more a nervous simper – because the enemy in question is that drivel-merchant, global huckster and so-to-speak media psychopath Rupert Murdoch, a Hannibal The Cannibal who is in many important ways a deal more powerful in Britain than our own schoolboy Parliament, its minority-elected Government, and even its bumbling Mr Pooter of a Prime Minister. A Government – and God help us – that the Murdoch Press did so much, so dishonestly, to put into power, mostly by means so aslant, so titled, so bent and untrue that they by definition open the trap-door under the world 'democracy'. If we cared twopence about our own culture, we ought to make sure that the next time Murdoch sets foot in this, his fiefdom, he should be arrested and put on public trial ...

In less than an hour's time on this channel, there will be another episode of Lipstick On Your Collar. Let darkness fall upon the land, and England's mountains green be splattered with used condoms, for the series is written by that lecherous

beast known to the toilet-paper papers as Dirty Den, or by
Murdoch's salacious *News of the World* as 'Television's Mr
Filth', or, in an endearing reference to what must be my
other less priapic illness by that sub-literate, homophobic,
sniggering rictus of a lout Gary Bushell of Murdoch's 'The
Sun', Old Flakey. 'Very Lipstick on my dipstick', slurps
Bushell, with the kind of saloon-bar leer that presumably adds
some kind of balance to what one might charitably call his
Talent, all of which you could just about press into the little
space you get when you lift a plastic lavatory brush from its
holder.

> *Dennis Potter on tabloid journalism, on Channel 4, 1993*

A mere ulcer; a sore from head to foot; a poor devil so
completely flayed that there is not a square inch of healthy
flesh on his carcass; an overgrown pimple, sore to the touch.

> Quarterly Review *on William Hazlitt*

Sir, – You have an ugly trick of saying what is not true of any
one you do not like; and it will be the object of this letter to
cure you of it. You say what you please of others: it is time
you were told what you are. In doing this, give me leave to
borrow the familiarity of your style – for the fidelity of the
picture I shall be answerable. You are a little person, but a
considerable cat's-paw; and so far worthy of notice. Your
clandestine connexion with persons high in office constantly
influences your opinions, and alone gives importance to
them. You are the Government Critic, a character nicely
differing from that of a government spy – the invisible link,
that connects literature with the police. It is your business to
keep a strict eye over all writers who differ in opinion with
His Majesty's Ministers, and to measure their talents and

attainments by the standard of their servility and meanness. For this office you are well qualified. Besides being the Editor of the *Quarterly Review*, you are also paymaster of the band of Gentlemen Pensioners; and when an author comes before you in the one capacity, with whom you are not acquainted in the other, you know how to deal with him. You have your cue beforehand. The distinction between truth and falsehood you make no account of: you mind only the distinction between Whig and Tory. Accustomed to the indulgence of your mercenary virulence and party-spite, you have lost all relish as well as capacity for the unperverted exercises of the understanding, and make up for the obvious want of ability by a bare-faced want of principle. The same set of threadbare common-places, the same second-hand assortment of abusive nick-names, the same assumption of little magisterial airs of superiority, are regularly repeated; and the ready convenient lie comes in aid of the dearth of other resources, and passes off, with impunity, in the garb of religion and loyalty ...

... There is something in your nature and habits that fits you for the situation into which your good fortune has thrown you. In the first place, you are in no danger of exciting the jealousy of your patrons by a mortifying display of extraordinary talents, while your sordid devotion to their will and to your own interest at once ensures their gratitude and contempt. To crawl and lick the dust is all they expect of you, and all you can do. Otherwise they might fear your power, for they could have no dependence on your fidelity: but they take you with safety and fondness to their bosoms; for they know if you cease to be a tool, you cease to be anything. If you had an exuberance of wit, the unguarded use of it might sometimes glance at your employers; if you were sincere yourself, you might respect the motives of others; if you had sufficient understanding, you might attempt an argument, and fail in it. But luckily for yourself and your admirers, you are but the dull echo, 'the tenth transmitter' of some hackneyed jest: the want of all manly and candid feeling in yourself only excites your suspicion and antipathy to it in others, as something at which your nature recoils: your slowness to understand makes you quick to misrepresent; and you infallibly make nonsense of what you cannot possibly conceive. What seem your wilful blunders are often the felicity of natural parts, and your want of penetration has all the appearance of an affected petulance!... Such, Sir, is the picture of which you have sat for the outline.

> *William Hazlitt, 'A letter to William Gifford,' editor of the* Quarterly Review

Has there ever been a more confusing face? With an expression half-bovine and half sheep-like he stares out of the screen in such a way as to leave us all uncertain whether he wants to cut our throats or lick our boots.

> *Peregrine Worsthorne on* Sunday Times *editor Andrew Neil, in the* Sunday Telegraph

That is a bit rich coming from a man who looks like a sexually confused, ageing hairdresser: the Teasy Weasy of Fleet Street...

> *Richard Littlejohn, in the* Sun, *on Peregrine Worsthorne after the latter's attack on Andrew Neil*

It would be nice to have an opinion about everything; but if you did, then you would be Andrew Neil, and the problem with Andrew Neil is that he has an opinion about everything.

> *Rory Bremner*

This dodipoule, this didopper ... why, thou arrant butter whoe, thou coteueane & scrattop of scoldes, will thou never leave affecting a dead Carcasse ... a wispe, a wispe, rippe, rippe, you kitchen-stuff wrangler!

Thomas Nashe, a 16th-century pamphleteer and novelist, on Gabriel Harvey, a contemporary writer. The pair conducted a feud so furious that in 1599 the Archbishop of Canterbury ordered all their works to be burned

A great author, notwithstanding his Dictionary is imperfect, his Rambler pompous, his learning common, his ideas vulgar, his Irene a child of mediocrity, his genius worldly, his politics narrow and his religion bigoted.

Robert Potter, a critic, on Samuel Johnson

The reciprocal civility of authors is one of the most risible scenes in the farce of life.

Samuel Johnson, Life of Sir Thomas Browne

Chuang Tzu was born in the 4th Century before Christ. The publication of this book in English, two thousand years after his death, is obviously premature.

Anonymous

It is too early to say.

Zhou Enlai, 20th-century Chinese Party Chairman, asked for his assessment of the 1789 French Revolution

All the universities and all the old writers put together are less talented than my arsehole.

Theophrastus Bombastus von Hohenheim, known as Paracelsus, German alchemist and physician, to his critics

I am sure I have only slightly less high an opinion of
Matthew's literary ability than he does himself.

> *Alan Lomberg, this book's Editor's English teacher in Swaziland, in a school
> report*

The little shit Parris, with his perma-smirk.

> *Alastair Campbell, Tony Blair's former press secretary, on the Editor of this
> book*

The thinking man's Matthew Parris.

> *John Patten, a former geography teacher, on Simon Hoggart,* Guardian
> *parliamentary sketchwriter*

Critics! appall'd I venture on the name,
Those cut-throat bandits in the path of fame.

> *Robert Burns*

Thou eunuch of language ... thou pimp of gender ...
murderous accoucheur of infant learning ... thou pickle-
herring in the puppet show of nonsense.

> *Robert Burns on a critic*

If you imagine a Scotch commercial traveller in a Scotch
commercial hotel leaning on the bar and calling the barmaid
'Dearie' then you will know the keynote of Burns' verse.

> *A. E. Housman on Robert Burns*

Descended from a long line of maiden aunts.

> *A fellow don (anon) on A. E. Housman*

A louse in the locks of literature.

> *Tennyson on Churton Collins, a critic*

I think of Mr Stevenson as a consumptive youth weaving garlands of sad flowers with pale, weak hands.

George Moore on Robert Louis Stevenson

What is Conrad but the wreck of Stevenson floating about in the slipsop of Henry James.

George Moore on Joseph Conrad

... an umbrella left behind at a picnic.

George Moore on W. B. Yeats

That vague formless obscene face.

Oscar Wilde on George Moore

Henry James writes fiction as if it were a painful duty.

Oscar Wilde

He hangs poised for the right word while the wheels of life go round.

Description of Henry James by his cousin

He has a gross and repulsive face but appears *bon enfant* when you talk to him. But he is the dullest Briton of them all.

Henry James on Anthony Trollope

Trollope! Did anyone bear a name that predicted a style more Trollopy?

George Moore on Anthony Trollope

The work of Henry James has always seemed divisible by a simple dynastic arrangement into three reigns. James I, James II, and the Old Pretender.

Philip Guedalla

It's not that he 'bites off more than he can chew' but he chews more than he bites off.

> Clover Adams on Henry James

A church lit but without a congregation to distract you, with every church light and line focused on the high alter. And on the alter, very reverently placed, intensely there, is a dead kitten, an eggshell, a bit of string.

> H. G. Wells on a book by Henry James

He was unperfect, unfinished, inartistic; he was worse than provincial – he was parochial.

> Henry James on Henry David Thoreau

Henry James had turned his back on one of the great events in the world's history, the rise of the United States, in order to report tittle-tattle at tea parties in English country houses.

> W. Somerset Maugham on Henry James

I doubt that the infant monster has any more to give.

> Henry James on Rudyard Kipling

Poor Henry James! He's spending eternity walking round and round a stately park and the fence is just too high for him to peep over and he's just too far away to hear what the countess is saying.

> W. Somerset Maugham

Henry James has a mind so fine that no idea could violate it.

> T. S. Eliot. Attrib.

How unpleasant it is to meet Mr Eliot!
With his features of clerical cut,
And his brow so grim
And his mouth so prim
And his conversation, so nicely
Restricted to What Precisely
And If and Perhaps and But.
T. S. Eliot on himself

To me Pound remains the exquisite showman minus the show.
Ben Hecht on Ezra Pound

Mr Eliot is at times an excellent poet and has arrived at the supreme Eminence among English critics largely through disguising himself as a corpse.
Ezra Pound on T. S. Eliot

A hack writer who would not have been considered fourth rate in Europe, who tried out a few of the old proven 'sure-fire' literary skeletons with sufficient local colour to intrigue the superficial and the lazy.
William Faulkner on Mark Twain

Jane Austen's books, too, are absent from this library. Just that one omission alone would make a fairly good library out of a library that hadn't a book in it.
Mark Twain

I have discovered that our great favourite, Miss Austen, is my countryman ... with whom Mama, before her marriage, was acquainted. Mama says that she was then the prettiest, silliest, most affected, husband-hunting butterfly she ever remembers.
Mary Russell Mitford on Jane Austen, letter to a friend

I think I may boast myself to be, with all possible vanity, the most unlearned and uninformed female who ever dared be an authoress.
Jane Austen on herself

I found out in the first two pages that it was a woman's writing – she supposed that in making a door, you last of all put in the panels!
Thomas Carlyle on Adam Bede *by George Eliot*

I wish her characters would talk a little less like the heroes and heroines of police reports.
George Eliot on Jane Eyre *by Charlotte Bronte*

All the faults of Jane Eyre are magnified a thousandfold, and the only consolation which we have in reflecting upon it is that it will never be generally read.
James Lorimer on Wuthering Heights *by Emily Bronte, in the* North British Review

Literature cannot be the business of a woman's life, because of the sacredness of her duties at home.
Robert Southey on Charlotte Brontë

Oh really. What is she reading?
Dame Edith Evans to a friend who said Nancy Mitford was borrowing her villa in France to finish a book

A woman who writes a book commits two sins; she increases the number of books, and decreases the number of women.
Alphonse Karr

One of the surest signs of his genius is that women dislike his books.

George Orwell on Joseph Conrad

He would not blow his nose without moralizing on conditions in the handkerchief industry.

Cyril Connolly on George Orwell

Conrad spent a day finding the *mot juste* then killed it.

Ford Maddox Ford on Joseph Conrad

I cannot abide Conrad's souvenir shop style and bottled ships and necklaces of romanticist clichés.

Vladimir Nabokov on Joseph Conrad

Freud Maddox Fraud.

Osbert Sitwell on Ford Maddox Ford

An animated adenoid.

Norman Douglas, novelist, on Ford Maddox Ford

One could always baffle Conrad by saying 'humour'. It was one of our damned English tricks he had never learned to tackle.

H. G. Wells on Joseph Conrad

He is the old maid among novelists.

Rebecca West on H. G. Wells

His writing, as he might have said himself, is like lace; the material is of very little consequence, the embroidery is all that counts; and it shares with the lace the happy faculty of coming out sometimes in yards and yards.

Lytton Strachey on Horace Walpole

He has the most remarkable and seductive genius – and I should say about the smallest in the world.
> *Lytton Strachey on Max Beerbohm*

Of course we all know that Morris was a wonderful all-round man, but the act of walking round him has always tired me.
> *Max Beerbohm on William Morris*

The gods bestowed on Max the gift of perpetual old age.
> *Oscar Wilde on Max Beerbohm*

Tell me, when you are alone with Max, does he take off his face and reveal his mask?
> *Oscar Wilde on Max Beerbohm*

One must have a heart of stone to read the death of little Nell without laughing.
> *Oscar Wilde on Charles Dickens's* Old Curiosity Shop

Of Dicken's style it is impossible to speak praise. It is jerky, ungrammatical and created by himself in defiance of the rules. No young novelist should ever dare to imitate the style of Dickens.
> *Anthony Trollope on Charles Dickens*

He has never played any significant part in any movement more significant than that of a fly ... on a wheel.
> Saturday Review *on Charles Dickens*

He's a mediocre man – and knows it, or suspects it, which is worse; he will come to no good, and in the meantime he's treated rudely by waiters and is not really admired even by middle-aged dowagers.
> *Lytton Strachey on E.M. Forster*

A novelist who writes nothing for 10 years finds his reputation rising. Because I keep on producing books they say there must be something wrong with this fellow.

> *J.B. Priestley*

My knowledge of Mr Forster's work is limited to one novel which I dislike, and anyway it was not he who fathered that trite little whimsy about characters getting out of hand, it is as old as the quills, although of course, one sympathizes with his people if they try to wriggle out of that trip to India or wherever he takes them. My characters are all galley-slaves.

> *Vladimir Nabokov on E.M. Forster, The* Paris Review *Interviews*

He is limp and damp and milder than the breath of a cow.

> *Virginia Woolf on E.M. Forster*

We are nauseated by the sight of trivial personalities decomposing in the eternity of print.

> *Virginia Woolf*

I am fairly unrepentant about her poetry. I really think that three quarters of it is gibberish. However, I must crush down these thoughts, otherwise the dove of peace will shit on me.

> *Noel Coward on Dame Edith Sitwell*

I thought nothing of her writing. I considered her a beautiful little knitter.

> *Dame Edith Sitwell on Virginia Woolf*

Mr Lawrence looked like a plaster gnome on a stone
toadstool in some suburban garden . . . he looked as if he had
just returned from spending an uncomfortable night in a very
dark cave.

Dame Edith Sitwell on D.H. Lawrence

The dirtiest most indecent, most obscene thing ever written.
Yes it is, Frieda . . . it is filthy. My god, what a clumsy '*olla
putrida*' James Joyce is! Nothing but old fags and cabbage-
stumps of quotations from the Bible and the rest, stewed in
the juice of deliberate, journalistic dirty-mindedness.

D.H. Lawrence on Ulysses *by James Joyce*

The work of a queasy undergraduate scratching his pimples.

Virginia Woolf on Ulysses *by James Joyce*

She has been a peculiar kind of snob without really belonging
to a social group with whom to be snobbish.

Edmund Wilson on Virginia Woolf

Always striking the two notes: rank and genius.

Virginia Woolf on Osbert Sitwell

I don't care for Osbert's prose; the rhododendrons grow to
such a height in it.

Virginia Woolf on Osbert Sitwell

We have met too late. You are too old for me to have any
effect on you.

James Joyce on meeting W.B. Yeats

The quick brown fox jumps over the lazy dog. How fucking
difficult is that? It's the sentence that bestrides the fucking

book I reviewed for you. It is the sentence I wrote first in my fucking review. It is 35 fucking letters long, which is why I wrote that it was. And so some useless cunt sub-editor decides to change it to 'jumps over *a* lazy dog'. Can you fucking count? Can you see that that makes it a 33 letter sentence? So it looks as if I can't count, and the cunting author of the book, poor Mr Dunn, cannot count. The whole bastard book turns on the sentence being as I wrote it, and that is exactly 35 letters long. Why do you meddle? What do you think you achieve with that kind of dumb-witted smart arsery? Why do you change things you do not understand without consulting? Why do you believe you know best when you know fuck all, jack shit? That is as bad as editing can be. Fuck. I hope you're proud. It will be small relief for the author that nobody reads your poxy magazine. Never ever ask me to write something for you. And don't pay me. I'd rather take 400 quid for assassinating a crack whore's only child in a revenge killing for a busted drug deal – my integrity would be less compromised. Jesus fucking wept. I don't know what else to say.

> British columnist Giles Coren in a memo to the editor of his paper's review-and-listings section when he noticed that a word had been changed in his review of a novel by Mark Dunn.

Dear Mr Pinker, I have read the effusion of Mr Duckworth's reader with not inconsiderable disgust. These vermin crawl over and be-slime our literature with their pulings, and nothing but the day of judgement can, I suppose, exterminate 'em. Thank god one need not, under ordinary circumstances, touch them. Hark to his puling squeak: too 'unconventional'. What in hell do we want but some change from the unbearable monotony of the weekly six shilling Pears soap annual novel; ... the dungminded dungbearded, penny a line, please-the-mediocre-at-all-cost doctrine. You English will get no prose till you enterminate [sic] this breed...

Canting, supercilious, blockhead ... I always supposed from report that Duckworth was an educated man, but I can not reconcile this opinion with his retention of the author of the missive you send me. If you have to spend your life in contact with such minds, God help you ... Why can't you send the publisher's reader to the Serbian front, and get some good out of the war ... Serious writers will certainly give up the use of english altogether unless you can improve the process of publication. In conclusion, you have given me a very unpleasant quarter of an hour, my disgust flows over, though I suppose there is no use in spreading it over this paper. If there is any phrase or form of contempt that you care to convey from me to the reeking Malebolge of the Duckworthian slum, pray, consider yourself at liberty to draw on my account (unlimited credit) and transmit it. Please, if you have occasion to write again, either in regard to this book or any other, please do not enclose the publisher's readers [sic] opinions. Sincerely yours, EZRA POUND P.S . . . . as for altering Joyce to suit Duckworth's readers – I would like trying to fit the Venus de Milo into a piss-pot . . .

> Ezra Pound, acting for James Joyce, to the literary agent James B. Pinker. The reader for the publisher, Duckworth, had complained that Joyce's Portrait of the Artist as a Young Man was 'too discursive, formless, unrestrained', and that 'ugly things, ugly words, are too prominent; indeed at times they seem to be shoved in one's face on purpose unnecessarily'

Why don't you write books people can read?

> Mrs Nora Joyce to her husband, James

An essentially private man who wished his total indifference to public notice to be universally recognised.

> Tom Stoppard on James Joyce

He had a genius for backing into the limelight.
> Lowell Thomas, biographer of T.E. Lawrence

I fancy, for myself, that they are rather out of touch with reality; by reality I mean shops like Selfridges, and motor buses, and the *Daily Express*.
> T.E. Lawrence on expatriate authors living in Paris, such as James Joyce, in a letter to W. Hurley

Arabian Lawrence, who, whatever his claims as a man, was surely a sonorous fake as a writer.
> Kingsley Amis on T.E. Lawrence

...only a frantic pair of moustaches.
> T.E. Lawrence on Ferdinand Foch

A bore and a bounder and a prig. He was intoxicated with his own youth, and loathed any milieu which he couldn't dominate. Certainly he had none of a gentleman's instincts, strutting about Peace Conferences in Arab dress.
> Sir Henry Channon on T.E. Lawrence

It seems that Dr Leavis gave a lecture at Nottingham University on 'Literature in My Time' and declared that apart from D.H.Lawrence there had been no literature in his time. He knocked hell out of everybody, and no doubt had all the Lucky Jims rolling down the aisles. Like Groucho Marx on another academic occasion, whatever it was he was against it. Virginia Woolf was a 'slender talent'; Lytton Strachey 'irresponsible and unscrupulous'; W.H.Auden 'the career type', fixed at 'the undergraduate stage'; Spender 'no talent whatsoever'; Day-Lewis 'Book Society author'; the whole age 'dismal', and outlook 'very poor'. By the time Dr Leavis caught his train back to Cambridge, there was hardly anything left to read in Nottingham. I have not the pleasure of the doctor's acquaintance – he was up at Cambridge just after me – but I have a vague but impressive vision of him, pale and glittering-eyed, shining with integrity, marching out of Downing to close whole departments of libraries, to snatch books out of people's hands, to proclaim the bitter truth that nobody writes anything worth reading. There is Lawrence; there is Leavis on Lawrence; perhaps a disciple, Jones, is writing something – let us say, Jones on Leavis on Lawrence, after that, nothing.

J.B. Priestley on F.R. Leavis

It is sad to see Milton's great lines bobbing up and down in the sandy desert of Dr Leavis's mind with the grace of a fleet of weary camels.

Edith Sitwell on F.R. Leavis, Aspects of Modern Poetry

Then Edith Sitwell appeared, her nose longer than an anteater's, and read some of her absurd stuff.

Lytton Strachey, An evening at Arnold Bennett's House

I do not want Miss Mannin's feelings to be hurt by the fact that I have never heard of her. At the moment I am debarred from the pleasures of putting her in her place by the fact she has not got one.

Edith Sitwell on Ethel Mannin

So you've been reviewing Edith Sitwell's last piece of virgin dung, have you? Isn't she a poisonous thing of a woman, lying concealing, flipping, plagiarizing, misquoting, and being as clever a crooked literacy publicist as ever.

Dylan Thomas on Edith Sitwell

He was a detestable man. Men pressed money on him, and women their bodies. Dylan took both with equal contempt. His great pleasure was to humiliate people.
  A. J. P. Taylor on Dylan Thomas

Somebody's boring me. I think it's me.
  Dylan Thomas after he had been talking continuously for some time

You have but two topics, yourself and me, and I'm sick of both.
  Samuel Johnson on James Boswell

E. M. Forster never gets any further than warming the teapot. He's rare fine hand at that. Feel this teapot. Is it not beautifully warm? Yes, but there ain't going to be no tea.
  Katherine Mansfield on E. M. Forster

I loathe you. You revolt me stewing in your consumption.
  D. H. Lawrence to Katherine Mansfield

He's impossible. He's pathetic and preposterous. He writes like a sick man.
  Gertrude Stein on D. H. Lawrence

Spit on her when you see her, she's a liar out and out. As for him, I reserve my language ... vermin, the pair of'em.
  D. H. Lawrence on Katherine Mansfield and J. Middleton Murry

This awful Whitman. This post-mortem poet. This poet with the private soul leaking out of him all the time. All his privacy leaking out in a sort of dribble, oozing into the universe.
  D. H. Lawrence on Walt Whitman

Interesting, but a type I could not get on with. Obessed with self. Dead eyes and a red beard, long narrow face. A strange bird.

John Galsworthy on D. H. Lawrence

Like a piece of litmus paper he has always been quick to take the colour of the times.

The Observer on Aldous Huxley

You could tell by his conversation which volume of the *Encyclopaedia Britannica* he'd been reading. One day it would be Alps, Andes and Apennines, and the next it would be the Himalayas and the Hippocratic Oath.

Bertrand Russell on Aldous Huxley

Mr Douglas would rather give a child prussic acid than allow it to read The Well of Loneliness ... I offered to provide Mr Douglas with a child, a bottle of prussic acid, a copy of The Well of Loneliness, and – if he kept his word and chose to administer the acid – a handsome memorial in marble to be erected wherever he might appoint, after his execution. The offer, I regret to say, was not accepted.

Aldous Huxley on James Douglas

The stupid person's idea of a clever person.

Elizabeth Bowen writing in the Spectator, on Aldous Huxley

Your manuscript is both good and original; but the part that is good is not original, and the part that is original is not good.

Samuel Johnson to an author

I hate a fellow whom pride, or cowardice, or laziness drives into a corner, and who does nothing when he is there but sit and growl; let him come out as I do, and bark.

Samuel Johnson

There is no arguing with Johnson; for when his pistol misses fire, he knocks you down with the butt end of it.

Oliver Goldsmith on Samuel Johnson

Curse the blasted, jelly-boned swines, the slimy, the belly-wriggling invertebrates, the miserable sodding rotters, the flaming sods, the snivelling, dribbling, dithering, palsied, pulseless lot that make up England. They've got white of egg in their veins, and their spunk is that watery it's a marvel they can breed. Why, why, why, was I born an Englishman!

D. H. Lawrence after a publisher rejected his manuscript of Sons and Lovers

I like to write when I feel spiteful: it's like having a good sneeze.

D. H. Lawrence, review of Art-Nonsense *by Eric Gill, in the* Phoenix

My publisher and I visited your establishment several weeks ago and found you such a preposterous boor that I was moved to discourse upon the likes of you in the attached interview with the *Washington Star*. The next time I am in Paris I intend to spread cream cheese all over your collection.

Letter to George Whitman, proprietor of Shakespeare & Co in Paris, from an American lady

I am only one, only one, only one. Only one being, one at the same time. Not two, not three, only one. Only one life to live, only sixty minutes in one hour. Only one pair of eyes. Only one brain. Only one being. Being only one, having only one pair of eyes, having only one time, having only one life, I cannot read your MS three or four times. Not even one time. Only one look, only one look is enough. Hardly one copy would sell here. Hardly one. Hardly one.

A.J. Fifield, rejecting a manuscript by Gertrude Stein

Gertrude Stein's prose is a cold, black suet-pudding. We can represent it as a cold suet-roll of fabulously reptilian length. Cut it at any point, it is ... the same heavy, sticky, opaque mass all through, and all along.

Wyndham Lewis

...a flabby lemon and pink giant, who hung his mouth open as though he were an animal at the zoo inviting buns – especially when the ladies were present.

Wyndham Lewis on Ford Maddox Ford

I do not think I have ever seen a nastier-looking man ... Under the black hat, when I had first seen them, the eyes had been those of an unsuccessful rapist.

Ernest Hemingway on Percy Wyndham Lewis

He has never been known to use a word that might send a man to a dictionary.

William Faulkner on Ernest Hemingway

Poor Faulkner. Does he really think emotions come from big words?

Ernest Hemingway on William Faulkner

He is the bully on the Left Bank, always ready to twist the milksop's arm.

Cyril Connolly on Ernest Hemingway

Sing a song of critics pockets full of lye
four and twenty critics
hope that you will die
hope that you will peter out
hope that you will fail
so they can be the first one
be the first to hail
any happy weakening
or sign of quick decay...
If you do not like them lads
one thing you can do
stick them up your asses lads
my Valentine to you.

Ernest Hemingway, Valentine – for a Mr Lee Wilson Dodd and Any of His Friends Who Want It. *Wilson Dodd had given Hemingway's* Men without Women *a poor review in the* Saturday Review of Literature

If my books had been any worse I should not have been invited to Hollywood, and if they had been any better I should not have come.

Raymond Chandler

Another damned, thick, square book! Always scribble, scribble, scribble! Eh! Mr Gibbon?

William, Duke of Gloucester, later George III, to Edward Gibbon

In some passages he drew the thread of his verbosity finer than the staple of his argument.

Richard Porson on Edward Gibbon

Gibbon's style is detestable; but it is not the worst thing about him.

Samuel Taylor Coleridge on Edward Gibbon

Gibbon is an ugly, affected, disgusting fellow, and poisons our literary club for me. I class him among infidel wasps and enormous snakes.

James Boswell on Edward Gibbon

That he was a coxcomb and a bore, weak, vain, pushing, curious, garrulous, was obvious to all who were acquainted with him. That he could not reason, that he had no wit, no humour, no eloquence, is apparent from his writings. Nature had made him a slave and an idolater. His mind resembled those creepers which the botanists call parasites and which can subsist only by clinging round the stems and imbibing the juices of stronger plants.

Servile and impertinent, shallow and pedantic, a bigot and a sot, bloated with family pride, and eternally blustering about the dignity of a born gentleman, yet stooping to be a tablebearer, an eavesdropper, a common butt in the taverns of London ... Everything which another man would have hidden, everything the publication of which would have made another man hang himself, was a matter of exaltation to his weak and diseased mind.

Thomas Babington Macaulay on James Boswell

I wish I was as cocksure of anything as Tom Macaulay is of everything.

Lord Melbourne on Thomas Babington Macaulay

You know, when I am gone you will be sorry you never heard me speak.

Sydney Smith to Thomas Babington Macaulay, a non-stop talker

CONCERNED LADY: Oo poor 'ickle fing, did oo hurt oo's 'ickle finger then?
MACAULAY, AGED 4: Thank you, Madam, but the agony has somewhat abated.
Thomas Babington Macaulay, quoted in Wanda Orton's biography

The great apostle of the Philistines.
Matthew Arnold, referring to Thomas Babington Macaulay

He not only overflowed with learning, but stood in the slop.
Sydney Smith on Thomas Babington Macaulay

And still they gazed, and still the wonder grew,
That one small head could carry all he knew.
Oliver Goldsmith of a village schoolmaster

Rogers is not very well . . . Don't you know he has produced a couplet? When he is delivered of a couplet, with infinite labour and pain, he takes to his bed, has straw laid down, the knocker tied up, expects his friends to call and make enquiries, and the answer at the door invariably is 'Mr Rogers and his little couplet are as well as can be expected.' When he produces an Alexandrine he keeps to his bed a day longer.
Sydney Smith on Samuel Rogers

It is long yet vigorous, like the penis of a jackass.
Sydney Smith on an article in the Edinburgh Review *by Henry Brougham*

Reading Proust is like bathing in someone else's dirty water.
Alexander Woollcott on Marcel Proust. Attrib.

Monsieur Zola is determined to show that if he has not genius he can at least be dull.

    Oscar Wilde

A fat little flabby person with the face of a baker, the clothes of a cobbler, the size of a barrelmaker, the manners of a stocking salesman and the dress of an innkeeper.

    Victor de Balabin on Honoré de Balzac, Diary

Everywhere I go I'm asked if university stifles writers. My opinion is that they don't stifle enough of them.

    Flannery O'Connor

This is not a novel to be tossed aside lightly. It should be thrown with great force.

    Dorothy Parker on Benito Mussolini's Claudia Particella, L'Amante del Cardinale: Grande Romanzo dei Tempi del Cardinal Emanuel Madruzzo

'Daddy, what's an optimist?' said Pat to Mike while they were walking down the street together one day. 'One who thought that M. Asquith wasn't going to write any more,' replied the absent-minded professor, as he wound up the cat and put the clock out. That gifted entertainer, the Countess of Oxford and Asquith, author of *'The Autobiography of Margot Asquith'* (four volumes, ready boxed, suitable for throwing purposes), reverts to tripe in a new book deftly entitled *'Lay Sermons'.* I think it must be pleasanter to be M. Asquith than to be any other living human being ... In this book of essays, which has all the depth and glitter of a worn dime, the Countess walks right up to such subjects as Health, Human Nature, Fame, Character, Marriage, Politics, and Opportunities. A rather large order, you might say, but it leaves the lady with unturned hair. Successively, she knocks down and drags out each topic. And there is something vastly stirring in the way in which, no matter where she takes off from, she brings the discourse back to Margot Asquith. Such singleness of purpose is met but infrequently ... The affair between M. Asquith and M. Asquith will live as one of the prettiest love stories in all history.

Dorothy Parker on Lay Sermons *by Margot Asquith, in the* New Yorker

A combination of Little Nell and Lady Macbeth.

Alexander Woollcott on Dorothy Parker

'That's a very good idea, Piglet,' said Pooh. 'We'll practise it now as we go along. But it's no good going home to practise it, because it's a special Outdoor Song Which Has To Be Sung In The Snow.'

'Are you sure?' asked Piglet anxiously.

'Well, you'll see, Piglet, when you listen. Because this is how it begins. The more it Snows-tiddely-pom-'

'Tiddely what?' said Piglet. (He took, as you might say, the words out of your correspondent's mouth.)

'Pom!' said Pooh. 'I put it in to make it hummy.'

And it is that word 'hummy', my darlings, that marks the first place in 'The House at Pooh Corner' at which Tonstant Weader Fwowed up.

Dorothy Parker on The House at Pooh Corner *by A.A. Milne,* Constant Reader *review in the* New Yorker

Oh for the hour of Herod.

Anthony Hope Hawkins on Peter Pan *by J.M. Barrie*

The triumph of sugar over diabetes.

George Jean Nathan on the works of J.M. Barrie

Nothing but a pack of lies.

Damon Runyon on Alice in Wonderland *by Lewis Carroll*

From the moment I picked up your book until I laid it down I was convulsed with laughter. Someday I intend reading it.

Groucho Marx on Dawn Ginsberg's Revenge *by Sidney J. Perelman*

To see him fumbling with our rich and delicate language is to experience all the horror of seeing a Sèvres vase in the hands of a chimpanzee.

Evelyn Waugh on Sir Stephen Spender

The long experience of the book, personally speaking, was like a long hike home in wet socks and gym shoes, uncomfortable and unnecessary.

Out *on May Sarton*

I think her lack of greater popularity is due to her habit of dissecting her bowels and displaying for public observation.

Maine Life *on May Sarton*

Insects sting, not from malice, but because they want to live. It is the same with critics – they desire our blood, not our pain.

Friedrich Nietzsche

Show me a critic without prejudices, and I'll show you an arrested cretin.

George Jean Nathan

A reviewer is obligated to point out typographical errors, no matter how trivial. In the 'About the Author' note at the end of the book, we are told 'Roy Blount, Jr is a novelist. Now.' This makes sense only if the errant 'w' at the end of the last word is omitted. Apart from this bit of inadvertent humour, First Hubby is flawlessly lame.

L.S. Klepp on First Hubby *by Roy Blount, Jr, in* Entertainment Weekly

The covers of this book are too far apart.
Ambrose Bierce, review

Book reviewers can be divided into batchers (who review
several books at a time), bethcers ('bethcer I could have
written it better'), bitchers, botchers and butchers.
Paul Jennings

Asking a working writer what he thinks about critics is like
asking a lamppost what he feels about dogs.
Christopher Hampton

They point to an elephant and say that 'that is a terrible
rhinoceros'.
Ford Maddox Ford on literary critics

Any reviewer who expresses rage and loathing for a novel is
preposterous. He or she is like a person who has put on full
armour and attacked a hot fudge Sunday.
Kurt Vonnegut

Heath does not mention the Sahara. Anyone familiar with that
desert will know about the Erg. The Erg is a high inland plateau,
intensely dry, hot and shingly, more or less inimical to any form
of life. The fact that the author's initials are E.R.G. proved fatally
intrusive on my powers of free association, and the analogy ...
offered irresistible proof that *le style c'est l'homme*. That this
wretched, drivelling affair, its impressions fuzzy with jet lag and
neutral-flavoured as an airline meal, should have been made into
a best seller, with all the attendant flimflam of the hired train and
8.2 autographed copies per minute, is a signpost towards the gap
between those who buy books and those who read them.
Jonathan Keates on Travels *by Edward Heath in the New Statesman*

Critics are like eunuchs in a harem: they know how it's done, they've seen it done every day, but they're unable to do it themselves.

Brendan Behan

Unless the bastards have the courage to give you unqualified praise, I say ignore them.

John Steinbeck on critics

The ratio of literacy to illiteracy is constant, but nowadays the illiterates can read and write.

Alberto Moravia

Read over your compositions, and wherever you meet with a passage which you think is particularly fine, strike it out.

Samuel Johnson, recalling the advice of a college tutor

Donkeyosities, egotistical earthworms, hogwashing hooligans, critic cads, random hacks of illiteration, talent wipers of wormy order, the gas-bag section, poking hounds, poisonous apes, maggotty numbskulls, evil-minded snapshots of spleen and, worst of all, the mushroom class of idiots.

Amanda Malvina Fitzalan Anna Margaret McLelland McKittrick Ros, an unsuccessful writer, on her critics

A vain, silly transparent coxcomb without either solid talents or a solid nature.

J.G. Lockhart on Samuel Pepys

There is a certain race of men that either imagine it their duty, or make it their amusement, to hinder the reception of every work of learning or genius, who stand as sentinels in the avenues of fame, and value themselves upon giving Ignorance and Envy the first notice of a prey.
    Samuel Johnson, Rambler

It is only fair to Allen Ginsberg to remark on the utter lack of decorum of any kind in his dreadful little volume. Howl is meant to be a noun, but I can't help taking it as an imperative.
    John Hollander on Howl *by Allen Ginsberg, in the* Partisan Review

Our American professors like their literature clear and cold and pure and very dead.
    Sinclair Lewis on receiving the Nobel Prize

The face to launch a thousand dredgers.
    Jack de Manio on Glenda Jackson in Women in Love

That face that lunched a thousand shits.
    Anonymous, on the conviviality of the (Greek-born) Arianna Stassinopoulos (now Huffington)

So boring you fall asleep halfway through her name.
    Alan Bennett on Arianna Stassinopoulos, in the Observer

I fell asleep reading a dull book, and I dreamed that I was reading one, so I awoke from sheer boredom.
    Heinrich Heine

He is not really a writer, but a non-stop talker to whom someone has given a typewriter.
    Gerald Brenan on Henry Miller, Thoughts in a Dry Season

That's not writing, it's typing.
  Truman Capote on James Michener

You can type this shit George, but you can't say it.
  Harrison Ford to George Lucas after reading the script for Star Wars.

Having to read a footnote resembles having to go downstairs to answer the doorbell while in the middle of making love.
  Noel Coward

A collection of short stories is generally thought to be a horrendous clinker; an enforced courtesy for the elderly writer who wants to display the trophies of his youth, along with his trout flies.
  John Cheever on short stories

Then there is my noble and biographical friend who has added a new terror to death.
  Sir Charles Wetherell, lawyer and judge, on Lord Campbell's Lives of the Lord Chancellors. *The quote is also attributed to John Lyndhurst, who was excluded from the book because he was still alive*

Beckett was early commandeered by Enthusiasts whose object is always to quarantine their heroes. Under their influence, critics dwindle into a priesthood, readers vanish into a congregation, and art freezes into a sacrament that can never be questioned.
  Robert Robinson on Samuel Beckett's enthusiasts

I love it when you talk like that. It reminds me of how much we lost when the grammar schools went comprehensive.
  Ann Leslie to Robert Robinson, who had been talking for some time

Sir Walter Scott, when all is said and done, is an inspired butler.
  William Hazlitt

He could not think up to the height of his own towering style.
  G.K. Chesterton on Tennyson

Hardy became a sort of village atheist brooding and blaspheming over the village idiot.
  G.K. Chesterton on Thomas Hardy

A village explainer. Excellent if you were a village, but if you were not, not.
  Gertrude Stein on Ezra Pound

Chesterton is like a vile scum on a pond ... All his slop – it is really modern Catholicism to a great extent, the never taking a hedge straight, the mumbo-jumbo of superstition dodging behind clumsy fun and paradox ... I believe he creates a milieu in which art is impossible. He and his kind.
  Ezra Pound on G.K. Chesterton

Where were you fellows when the paper was blank?
  Fred Allen to editors who heavily edited one of his scripts

My Lord
February 1755
I have been lately informed by the proprietor of The World that two papers in which my dictionary is recommended to the Public were written by your Lordship. To be so distinguished is an honour which, being very little accustomed to favours from the Great, I know not well how to receive, or in what terms to acknowledge.

When upon some slight encouragement I first visited your Lordship I was overpowered like the rest of Mankind by the enchantment of your address, and could not forbear to wish that I might boast myself Le Vainqueur du Vainqueur de la Terre, that I might obtain that regard for which I saw the world contending, but I found my attendance so little encouraged, that neither pride nor modesty would suffer me to continue it. When I had once addressed your Lordship in public, I had exhausted all the art of pleasing which a retired and uncourtly Scholar can possess. I had done all that I could, and no Man is well pleased to have his all neglected, be it ever so little.

Seven years, My Lord, have now passed since I waited in your outward Rooms or was repulsed from your Door, during which time I have been pushing on my work through difficulties of which it is useless to complain, and have brought it at last to the verge of Publication without one Act of assistance, one word of encouragement, or one smile of favour. Such treatment I did not expect, or I never had a Patron before ...

Is not a Patron, My Lord, one who looks with unconcern on a Man struggling for Life in the water and when he has reached ground encumbers him with help? The notice which you have been pleased to take of my Labours, had it been early, had been kind; but it was delayed till I am indifferent and cannot enjoy it, till I am solitary and cannot impart it, till I am known and do not want it.

I hope it is no very cynical asperity not to confess obligation where no benefit has been received, or to be unwilling that the Public should consider me as owing that to a Patron, which Providence has enabled me to do for myself.

Having carried on my work thus far with so little

obligation to any Favourer of Learning I shall not be disappointed though I should conclude it, if less be possible, with less, for I have been long wakened from that Dream of hope, in which I once boasted myself with so much exaltation, My lord, Your Lordship's Most humble Obedient Servant, Sam: Johnson

Samuel Johnson to Lord Chesterfield

PATRON: *n.s.* One who countenances, supports or protects. Commonly a wretch who supports with insolence, and is paid with flattery.

Samuel Johnson, Dictionary of the English Language

They teach the morals of a whore, and the manners of a dancing master.

Samuel Johnson on Lord Chesterfield's letters

An Egyptian King, buried and forgotten in the pyramid of his fame.

American preacher Henry Ward Beecher on Dr Johnson

Very nice, though there are dull stretches.

Antoine de Rivarol on a two-line poem

Mentula conatur Pipleium scandere montem:
Musae furcillis praecipitem eiciunt.
[Mr Prick is trying to climb up the mount of poetry; the Muses push him out head first with their pitchforks.]

Catullus, cv, on Mamurra's literary efforts, tr. Amy Richlin

Chaucer, notwithstanding the praises bestowed upon him, I think obscene and contemptible; he owes his celebrity merely to his antiquity.

Lord Byron on Geoffrey Chaucer. Attrib.

A hyena that wrote poetry in tombs.

Friedrich Nietzsche on Dante

A Methodist parson in Bedlam.

Horace Walpole on Dante

Dr Donne's verses are like the Peace of God, for they pass all understanding.

James I on John Donne

His verse … is the beads without the string.

Gerard Manley Hopkins on Robert Browning

Malt does more than Milton can
To justify God's ways to man.

A.E. Housman, A Shropshire Lad, 'The Welsh Marches'

Our language sunk under him.

Joseph Addison on John Milton

This obscure, eccentric and disgusting poem.

Voltaire on Milton's Paradise Lost

The whole of Milton's poem, *Paradise Lost*, is such barbarous trash, so outrageously offensive to reason and to common sense that one is naturally led to wonder how it can have been tolerated by a people amongst whom astronomy, navigation and chemistry are understood.

William Cobbett on John Milton

Paradise Lost is one of those books which the reader admires, lays down and forgets to take up again. Its perusal is a duty rather than a pleasure.

> Samuel Johnson

Having never had any mental vision, he has now lost his bodily sight; a silly coxcomb, fancifying himself a beauty; an unclean beast, with nothing more human about him than his guttering eyelids; the fittest doom for him would be to hang him on the highest gallows, and set his head on the Tower of London.

> Salmasius [Claude de Saumaise] on John Milton

He was dull in a new way that made people think him great.

> Samuel Johnson on Thomas Gray, poet

Thomas Gray walks as if he had fouled his small-clothes and looks as if he smelt it.

> Christopher Smart

There are two ways of disliking poetry. One is to dislike it. The other is to read Pope.

> Oscar Wilde on Alexander Pope

Great Wits are sure to Madness near alli'd
And thin Partitions do their Bounds divide ...

> John Dryden on the Earl of Shaftesbury, Absalom and Achitophel

His imagination resembled the wings of an ostrich. It enabled him to run, though not to soar.

> Thomas Babington Macaulay on John Dryden

A Cherub's face, a reptile all the rest;
Beauty that shocks you, parts that none will trust,
Wit that can creep, and pride that licks the dust.
Alexander Pope on John Hervey, An Epistle to Dr. Arbuthnot

The great honour of that boast is such
That hornets and mad dogs may boast as much.
Lord Hervey on Alexander Pope

Who is this Pope I hear so much about? I cannot discover
what is his merit. Why will my subjects not write in prose?
George II on Alexander Pope

He hardly drank tea without a stratagem.
Samuel Johnson on Alexander Pope

Damn with faint praise, assent with civil leer,
And without sneering, teach the rest to sneer;
Willing to wound, and yet afraid to strike,
Just hint a fault, and hesitate dislike;
Alike reserved to blame, or to commend,
A tim'rous foe, and a suspicious friend...
Alexander Pope on Joseph Addison, An Epistle to Dr Arbuthnot

Hi Grace! impossible! what dead!
Of old age too, and in his bed!
And could that Mighty Warrior fall?
And so inglorious after all!
... Come hither, all ye empty things,
Ye bubbles rais'd by breath of Kings;
Who float upon the tide of state,
Come hither, and behold your fate.
Let pride be taught by this rebuke,

How very mean a thing's a Duke;
From all his ill-got honours flung,
Turn'd to that dirt from whence he sprung.
Jonathan Swift on John Churchill, Duke of Marlborough, A Satirical
Elegy on the Death of a late Famous General

Had it not been for the good nature of these very mortals
they contemn, these two superior beings were entitled, by
their birth and hereditary fortune, to be only a couple of link-
boys. I am of opinion their friendship would have continued,
though they had remained in the same kingdom: it had a very
strong foundation – the love of flattery on one side, and the
love of money on the other.
*Lady Mary Wortley Montagu on Jonathan Swift and Alexander Pope, letter
to the countess of Bute*

The Phrenzy of the 'Poems' was bad enough in its way; but it
did not alarm us half so seriously as the calm, settled, imper-
turbable drivelling idiocy of *'Endymion'* ... Mr Hunt is a small
poet, but he is a clever man. Mr Keats is a still smaller poet,
and he is only a boy of pretty abilities, which he has done
everything in his power to spoil ... We venture to make one
small prophecy, that his bookseller will not a second time
venture £50 upon any thing he can write. It is a better and a
wiser thing to be a starved apothecary than a starved poet; so
back to the shop, Mr John, back to 'plasters, pills, and
ointment boxes', etc. But for Heaven's sake, young Sangrado,
be a little more sparing of extenuatives and soporifics in your
practice than you have been with your poetry.
Blackwood's review of Endymion *by John Keats, probably written by John
Gibson Lockhart with help from Christopher North*

Here are Jonny Keats' piss-a-bed poetry, and three novels by God knows whom ... No more Keats, I entreat: flay him alive; if some of you don't I must skin him myself: there is no bearing the drivelling idiotism of the Mankin.

Lord Byron on John Keats

Fricassee of dead dog ... A truly unwise little book. The kind of man that Keats was gets ever more horrible to me. Force of hunger for pleasure of every kind, and want of all other force — such a soul, it would once have been very evident, was a chosen 'vessel of Hell'; and truly, for ever there is justice in that feeling.

Thomas Carlyle on Monckton Milnes's Life of Keats

The same old sausage, fizzing and sputtering in its own grease.

Henry James on Thomas Carlyle

Such writing is a sort of mental masturbation ... a bedlam vision produced by raw pork and opium.

Lord Byron on John Keats, letter to John Murray

The world is rid of Lord Byron, but the deadly slime of his touch still remains.

John Constable (the artist) on news of Byron's death

A tadpole of the Lakes.

Lord Byron on John Keats

A denaturalized being who, having exhausted every species of sensual gratification, and drained the cup of sin to its bitterest dregs, is resolved to show that he is no longer human, even in his frailties, but a cool, unconcerned fiend.

John Styles on Lord Byron

Mad, bad, and dangerous to know.
Lady Caroline Lamb on Lord Byron

A man must serve his time to every trade
Save censure – critics all are ready made.
Lord Byron, English Bards and Scotch Reviewers

Byron! – he would be all forgotten today if he had lived to be a
florid old gentleman with iron-grey whiskers, writing very long,
very able letters to *The Times* about the Repeal of the Corn Laws.
Max Beerbohm on Lord Byron

It was to me offensive, and I can never make out his great power,
which his admirers talk of. Why, a line of Wordsworth's is a lever
to lift the immortal spirit! Byron can only bore the spleen.
Charles Lamb on Lord Byron

Charles Lamb I sincerely believe to be in some considerable
degree insane. A more pitiful, rickety, gasping, staggering,
stammering tomfool I do not know.
Thomas Carlyle. Attrib.

Here is Miss Seward with six tomes of the most disgusting
trash, sailing over Styx with a Foolscap over her periwig as
complacent as can be – Of all Bitches dead or alive a
scribbling woman is the most canine.
Lord Byron on Anna Seward

From the poetry of Lord Byron they drew a system of ethics
compounded of misanthropy and voluptuousness – a system
in which the two greatest commandments were to hate your
neighbour and to love your neighbour's wife.
Thomas Babington Macaulay

His writing bears the same relation to poetry which a Turkey carpet bears to a picture. There are colours in the Turkey carpet out of which a picture might be made. There are words in Mr Montgomery's writing which, when disposed in certain orders and combinations, have made, and will make again, good poetry. But, as they now stand, they seem to be put together on principle in such a manner as to give no image of anything 'in the heavens above, or in the earth beneath, or in the waters under the earth'.

Thomas Babington Macaulay on Robert Montgomery

I spent a horrid, horrid night. I dreamt I was chained to a rock and being talked to death by Harriet Martineau and Macaulay.

Reverend Sydney Smith on Thomas Babington Macaulay, historian, and Harriet Martineau, philanthropist

Shelley is a poor creature, who has said or done nothing worth a serious man being at the trouble of remembering ... Poor soul, he has always seemed to me an extremely weak creature; a poor, thin, spasmodic, hectic, shrill and pallid being ... The very voice of him, shrill, shrieky, to my ear has too much of the ghost.

Thomas Carlyle on Percy Bysshe Shelley

A lewd vegetarian.

Charles Kingsley on Percy Bysshe Shelley

A mere sodomite and a perfect leper.

Ralph Waldo Emerson on Algernon Swinburne

A foul mouth is so ill-matched with a white beard that I would gladly believe the newspaper-scribes alone responsible for the bestial utterances which they declare to have dropped from a teacher whom such disciples as these exhibit to our disgust and compassion as performing on their obscene platform the last tricks of tongue now possible to a gap-toothed and hoary ape, carried at first notice on the shoulder of [Thomas] Carlyle, and who now in his dotage spits and chatters from a dirtier perch of his finding and fouling: coryphaeus or choragus of his Bulgarian tribe of auto-coprophagous baboons, who make the filth they feed on.

Algernon Swinburne on Ralph Waldo Emerson

Walt Whitman is as unacquainted with art as a hog with mathematics.

London Critic on Walt Whitman

Longfellow is to poetry what the barrel-organ is to music.

Van Wyck Brooks on Henry Wadsworth Longfellow

The gentleman was a sweet, beautiful soul, but I have entirely forgotten his name.

Ralph Waldo Emerson, attending Henry Wadsworth Longfellow's funeral

The word 'honor' in the mouth of Mr Webster is like the word 'love' in the mouth of a whore.

Ralph Waldo Emerson on Daniel Webster

Waldo is one of those people who would be enormously improved by death.

Saki, The Feast of Nemesis

A bell with a wooden tongue.
Ralph Waldo Emerson on William Wordsworth

Two voices there are: one is of the deep;
It learns the storm-cloud's thunderous melody …
And one is of an old half-witted sheep
Which bleats articulate monotony …
And, Wordsworth, both are thine.
James Kenneth Stephen on William Wordsworth

He keeps one eye on a daffodil and the other on a
canalshare.
Walter Savage Landor on William Wordsworth

Wordsworth went to the Lakes, but he never was a lake poet.
He found in stones the sermons he had already put there.
Oscar Wilde on William Wordsworth

Dark, limber verses stuft with lakeside sedges,
And propt with rotten stakes from rotten hedges.
William Savage Landor on William Wordsworth

Mr Wordsworth, a stupid man, with a decided gift for
portraying nature in vignettes, never ruined anyone's morals,
unless, perhaps, he has driven some susceptible persons to
crime in a very fury of boredom.
Ezra Pound on William Wordsworth

It is no more than moderately good. I put by its side the
poems of Matthew Arnold and think what a delightfully loud
splash the two would make if I dropped them into a river.
Dylan Thomas on the Immortality Ode *by William Wordsworth*

A weak, diffusive, weltering, ineffectual man ... a great possibility that has not realized itself. Never did I see such apparatus got ready for thinking, and so little thought. He mounts scaffolding, pulleys, and tackle, gathers all the tools in the neighbourhood with labour, with noise, demonstration, precept, abuse, and sets – three bricks.
Thomas Carlyle on Samuel Taylor Coleridge

Carlyle is a poet to whom nature has denied the faculty of verse.
Alfred Lord Tennyson on Thomas Carlyle, letter to Gladstone

A dirty man with opium-glazed eyes and rat-taily hair.
Lady Frederick Cavendish on Alfred Lord Tennyson

English Literature's performing flea.
Sean O'Casey on P.G.Wodehouse

There is no setting the point of precedency between a louse and a flea.
Samuel Johnson on Christopher Smart, comparing him to Samuel Derrick

Reading him is like wading through glue.
Alfred Lord Tennyson on Ben Jonson

There was little about melancholia that he didn't know; there was little else that he did.
W.H. Auden on Alfred Lord Tennyson

A fly would break its legs walking across his face.
Anonymous on W.H. Auden

My face looks like a wedding cake that has been left out
in the rain.
  W.H. Auden on himself

No poet or novelist wishes he were the only one who ever
lived, but most of them wish they were the only one alive,
and quite a number fondly believe their wish has been
granted.
  W.H. Auden

An unmanly sort of man whose love-life seems to have been
largely confined to crying in laps and playing mouse.
  W.H. Auden on Edgar Allan Poe

The higher water mark, so to speak, of Socialist literature is
W.H. Auden, a sort of gutless Kipling.
  George Orwell The Road to Wigan Pier

He is all ice and wooden-faced acrobatics.
  Wyndham Lewis on W.H. Auden

He is all blood, dirt and sucked sugar stick.
  W. B. Yeats on Wilfred Owen

By appointment: Teddy Bear to the Nation.
  Alan Bell on John Betjeman, in The Times

The Rabbie Burns of England.
  James Knox on John Betjeman

All right, then, I'll say it: Dante makes me sick.
  Lope Felix de Vega Carpio after being told he was about to die

The finest collection of frames I ever saw.
> *Sir Humphrey Davy, when asked what he thought of the Paris art galleries.*
> *Attrib.*

If people only knew as much about painting as I do, they would never buy my pictures.
> *Sir Edwin Henry Landseer to W. P. Frith*

If the old masters had labelled their fruit, one wouldn't be so likely to mistake pears for turnips.
> *Mark Twain*

If Botticelli were alive today he'd be working for *Vogue*.
> *Peter Ustinov*

Tracey Emin's bed is art because it's made by an artist, and yours isn't, because it isn't.
> *AA Gill*

Cold, mechanical, conceptual bullshit.
> *Kim Howells MP, Culture Minister, on the Turner Prize*

Pretentious, self-indulgent, craftless tat.
> *Ivan Massow giving his opinion on conceptual art while Chairman of the*
> *Institute of Contemporary Arts*

Skill without imagination is craftsmanship and gives us many useful objects such as wickerwork picnic baskets. Imagination without skill gives us modern art.
> *Tom Stoppard*

Art today is institutionalised narcissism, a conspiracy between creators and curators to make poor people feel stupid.
> *Stephen Bayley*

He bores me. He ought to have stuck to his flying machines.
Auguste Renoir on Leonardo da Vinci

Degas is nothing but a peeping Tom, behind the coulisses, and among the dressing-rooms of the ballet dancers, noting only the travesties on fallen debased womanhood.
Pamphlet published by the Churchman

He will never be anything but a dauber.
Titian on Tintoretto

Daubaway Weirdsley.
Punch *on Aubrey Beardsley, British artist*

Rembrandt is not to be compared in the painting of character with our extraordinarily gifted English artist, Mr Rippingille.
John Hunt, 19th-century art critic, on Rembrandt

The English public takes no interest in a work of art until it is told that the work in question is immoral.
Oscar Wilde

I never saw anything so impudent on the walls of any exhibition, in any country, as last year in London. It was a daub professing to be a 'harmony in pink and white' (or some such nonsense); absolute rubbish, and which had taken about a quarter of an hour to scrawl or daub – it had no pretence to be called a painting. The price asked for it was two hundred and fifty guineas.
John Ruskin on James Whistler's Symphony in Grey and Green

I doubt that art needed Ruskin any more than a moving train needs one of its passengers to shove it.

Tom Stoppard on John Ruskin, in The Times Literary Supplement

A life passed among pictures does not make a painter – else the policeman in the National Gallery might assert himself, as well allege, that he who lives in a library must needs die a poet. Let not Mr Ruskin flatter himself that more education makes the difference between himself and the policeman when both stand gazing in the Gallery. There they might remain till the end of time; the one decently silent, the other saying, in good English, many high-sounding empty things, like the crackling of thorns under a pot – undismayed by the presence of the Masters with whose names he is sacrilegiously familiar; whose intentions he interprets, whose vices he discovers with the facility of the incapable, and whose virtues he descants upon with a verbosity and flow of language that would, could we hear it, give Titian the same shock of surprise that was Balaam's when the first great critic proffered his opinion.

James Whistler on John Ruskin, The Gentle Art of Making Enemies

That he is indeed one of the very greatest masters of painting is my opinion. And I may add that in this opinion Mr Whistler himself entirely concurs.

Oscar Wilde on James Whistler

A LADY: I only know of two painters in the world: yourself and Velasquez.
WHISTLER: Why drag in Velasquez?

James Whistler

I don't mind. I have gloves on.
> *Mark Twain after running his hand over a Whistler painting, which caused the artist to exclaim: 'Don't touch that, Can't you see, it isn't dry yet'*

Well, not bad, but there are decidedly too many of them, and they are not very well arranged. I would have done it differently.
> *James Whistler when asked if he agreed that the stars were especially beautiful one night*

Perhaps not, but then you can't call yourself a great work of nature.
> *James Whistler after a sitter complained that his portrait was not a great work of art*

Maybe, my dear, but the shock will come when you see what you paint.
> *James Whistler to a student who told him that she only painted what she saw*

The explanation is quite simple. I wished to be near my mother.
> *James Whistler after a snob asked him why he had been born in such an unfashionable place as Lowell, Massachusetts*

I cannot tell you that, madam. Heaven has granted me no offspring.
> *James Whistler when asked if he thought genius hereditary*

Mr Whistler has always spelt art with a capital 'I'.
> *Oscar Wilde on James Whistler*

GENTLEMEN –
... What has Oscar in common with Art? except that he dines at our tables and picks from our platters the plums for the pudding he peddles in the provinces. Oscar – the amiable, irresponsible, esurient Oscar – with no more sense of a picture than of the fit of a coat, has the courage of the opinions ... of others! With ... Oscar you have avenged the Academy. I am, Gentlemen, yours obediently. JAMES McNEILL WHISTLER.

> *James Whistler on Oscar Wilde, letter to the committee of the National Art Exhibition in the World*

With our James vulgarity begins at home, and should be allowed to stay there.

> *Oscar Wilde on James Whistler, letter to the* World

A poor thing, Oscar! – but, for once, I suppose you own.

> *James Whistler on Oscar Wilde*

As for borrowing Mr Whistler's ideas about art, the only thoroughly original ideas I have ever heard him express have had reference to his own superiority as a painter over painters greater than himself.

> *Oscar Wilde on James Whistler, letter, in* Truth

...I am awe-stricken and tremble, for truly, 'the rage of the sheep is terrible!'

> *James Whistler on Oscar Wilde, letter, in* Truth

My dear Whistler, you leave your pictures in such a sketchy, unfinished state. Why don't you ever finish them?

> *Frederic Leighton, British painter, on James Whistler*

My dear Leighton, why do you ever begin yours?
James Whistler's riposte to Frederic Leighton

Rossetti is not a painter. Rossetti is a ladies maid.
James Whistler on Rossetti

I have been to it and am pleased to find it more odious than I even dared to hope.
Samuel Butler on the Rossetti Exhibition

Like a carbuncle on the face of an old and valued friend.
Charles, Prince of Wales, 1986, on a proposed extension to the National Gallery

A pot of paint has been thrown in the public's face.
Variously believed to have been said by John Ruskin about Whistler's painting Nocturne in Black and Gold: The Falling Rocker, *or by Camille Mauclair about Jean Puy's* Stroll under the Pines

Mr Lewis' pictures appeared to have been painted by a mailed fist in a cotton glove.
Dame Edith Sitwell on Wyndham Lewis

It resembles a tortoise-shell cat having a fit in a plate of tomatoes.
Mark Twain on J. M. W. Turner's The Slave Ship

It makes me look as if I were straining at a stool.
Winston Churchill on his portrait by Graham Sutherland

If my husband would ever meet a woman on the street who looked like the woman in his paintings, he would fall over in a dead faint.
Mrs Pablo Picasso on her husband's paintings

His pictures seem to resemble, not pictures, but a sample book of patterns of linoleum.
> *Cyril Asquith on Paul Klee*

A decorator tainted with insanity.
> *Kenyon Cox on Paul Gauguin*

The only genius with an IQ of 60.
> *Gore Vidal on Andy Warhol*

Epstein is a great sculptor. I wish he would wash.
> *Ezra Pound on Jacob Epstein*

How can I take an interest in my work when I don't like it?
> *Francis Bacon*

I stick to my business, which is art. Suggest you stick to yours, which is butchery.
> *Jacob Epstein, telegram to Nikita Khrushchev after he visited Britain in the 1950s and made what was described as a 'vigorous' observation about the Epstein sculpture in New College Chapel*

The immoral profession of musical criticism must be abolished.
> *Richard Wagner*

Of all the bulls that live, this hath the greatest ass's ears.
> *Elizabeth I on the musician John Bull*

Those people on the stage are making such a noise I can't hear a word you're saying.
> *Henry Taylor Parker, American music critic, rebuking some members of an audience who were talking near him*

I like Wagner's music better than any other music. It is so loud that one can talk the whole time without people hearing what one says. That is a great advantage.
Oscar Wilde on Richard Wagner

I love Wagner, but the music I prefer is that of a cat hung up by its tail outside a window and trying to stick to the panes of glass with its claws.
Charles Baudelaire on Richard Wagner

Wagner has beautiful moments but awful quarter hours.
Gioacchino Rossini on Richard Wagner

The music of Wagner imposes mental tortures that only algebra has a right to inflict.
Paul de Saint-Victor on Richard Wagner, in La Presse

It has no more real pretension to be called music than the jangling and clashing of gongs and other uneuphonious instruments with which the Chinamen, on the brow of a hill, fondly thought to scare away our English blue-jackets.
The Musical World on Richard Wagner's Lohengrin

Wagner's music is better than it sounds.
Mark Twain

Is Wagner a human being at all? Is he not rather a disease?
Friedrich Nietzsche on Richard Wagner

The wild Wagnerian corybantic orgy, this din of brasses, tin pans and kettles, this Chinese or Caribbean clatter with wood sticks and ear-cutting scalping knives ... Heartless sterility, obliteration of all melody, all tonal charm, all music ... This revelling in the destruction of all tonal essence, raging satanic fury in the orchestra, this diabolic, lewd caterwauling, scandal-mongering, gun-toting music, with an orchestral accompaniment slapping you in the face...

> *J. L. Klein on Richard Wagner*

I like your Opera. One day I think I'll set it to music.

> *Richard Wagner to a young composer, also attributed to Ludwig van Beethoven*

At nine o'clock (the Opera began at eight) a lady came in and sat down very conspicuously in my line of sight. She remained there until the beginning of the last act. I do not complain of her coming late and going earlier. For this lady, who had very black hair, had stuck over her right ear the pitiable corpse of a large white bird, which looked exactly as if someone had killed it by stamping on its breast, and then nailed it to the lady's temple, which was presumably of sufficient solidity to bear the operation. I am not, I hope, a morbidly squeamish person, but the spectacle sickened me. I presume that if I had presented myself at the doors with a dead snake round my neck, a collection of black beetles pinned to my shirtfront, and a grouse in my hair, I should have been refused admission. Why, then, is a woman to be allowed to commit such a public outrage?

    ... I once, in Drury Lane Theatre, sat behind a matinee hat decorated with the two wings of a seagull artificially reddened at the joints so as to produce an illusion of being freshly plucked from a live bird. But even that lady stopped short of the whole seagull.

… I suggest to the Covent Garden authorities that, if they feel bound to protect their subscribers against the danger of my shocking them with a blue tie, they are at least equally bound to protect me against the danger of a woman shocking me with a dead bird.

George Bernard Shaw, letter to The Times, *1905. Shaw had been instructed to wear a black tie at Covent Garden*

After Rossini dies, who will there be to promote his music?

Richard Wagner on Gioacchino Rossini

Don't trouble yourself to play further. I much prefer the second.

Gioacchino Rossini to a would-be composer who had just played the first of two works from which he wished Rossini to choose the better

Rossini would have been a great composer if his teacher had spanked him enough on the backside.

Ludwig van Beethoven on Gioacchino Rossini

What can you do with it? It's like a lot of yaks jumping about.

Sir Thomas Beecham on the Seventh Symphony by Ludwig van Beethoven

When I composed that, I was conscious of being inspired by God Almighty. Do you think I can consider your puny little fiddle when He speaks to me?

Ludwig van Beethoven in reply to a complaint by a violinist that a passage was unplayable

All Bach's last movements are like the running of a sewing-machine.

Arnold Bax on Johann Sebastian Bach

The audience seemed rather disappointed; they expected the ocean, something big, something colossal, but they were served instead with some agitated water in a saucer.
Louis Schneider on La Mer *by Claude Debussy*

Little pink bonbons stuffed with snow.
Claude Debussy on Edvard Grieg

I like the bit about quarter to eleven.
Erik Satie on From Dawn to Noon on the Sea *from* La Mer *by Claude Debussy*

Too many pieces of music finish too long after the end.
Igor Stravinsky

Very vile – a catarrhal or sternutatory concerto. One frequently recurring phrase is a graphic instrumentation of a fortissimo sneeze, and a long passage is evidently meant to suggest a protracted, agonized bravura on the pocket handkerchief.
George Templeton Strong on a concerto by Franz Liszt, Diary

Liszt's orchestral music is an insult to art. It is gaudy musical harlotry, savage and incoherent bellowings.
Boston Gazette on Franz Liszt

Composition indeed! Decomposition is the proper word for such hateful fungi!
The Dramatic and Musical World *on Franz Liszt, 1855*

The leader of cacophonists … is Arnold Schoenberg … He
learned a lesson from militant suffragettes. He was ignored till
he began to smash the parlor furniture, throw bombs, and hitch
together ten pianolas, all playing different tunes, whereupon
everybody began to talk about him. In Schoenberg's later
works, all the laws of construction, observed by the masters,
from Bach to Wagner, are ignored, insulted, trampled upon. The
statue of Venus, the Goddess of Beauty, is knocked from its
pedestal and replaced by the stone image of the Goddess of
Ugliness, with the features of a Hottentot hag.

Henry T. Finck, Musical Progress

Shostakovich is without doubt the foremost composer of
pornographic music in the history of art. He has accomplished the feat of penning passages which, in their faithful
portrayal of what is going on, become obscene …The whole
scene is little better than a glorification of the sort of stuff
that filthy pencils write on lavatory walls.

W. J. Henderson on Dmitri Shostakovich, in the New York Sun

I had another dream the other day about music critics. They
were small and rodent-like with padlocked ears, as if they had
stepped out of a painting by Goya.

Igor Stravinsky, in the Evening Standard

Rachmaninov's immortalizing totality was his scowl. He was a
six-and-a-half-foot-tall scowl.

Igor Stravinsky on Sergei Rachmaninov

I can compare *Le Carnaval Romain* by Berlioz to nothing but
the caperings and gibberings of a big baboon, over-excited by
a dose of alcoholic stimulus.

George Templeton Strong on Hector Berlioz, Diary

The opening Allegro took me straight back to childhood and gave me in turn the rusty windlass of a well, the interlinking noises of a goods train that is being shunted, then the belly-rumblings of a little boy acutely ill after a raid on an orchard, and finally the singular alarmed noise of poultry being worried to death by a Scotch terrier. The second movement gave me continuously and throughout its short length the noise of a November wind in telegraph poles on a lonely country road. The third movement began with a dog howling at midnight, proceeded to imitate the regurgitations of the less-refined or lower-middle-class type of water-closet cistern, modulating thence into the mass snoring of a naval dormitory around dawn – and concluded inconsequentially with the cello reproducing the screech of an ungreased wheelbarrow. The fourth movement reminded me immediately and persistently and vividly of something I have never thought of since the only time I heard it: the noise of a Zulu village in the Glasgow Exhibition – a hubbub all the more singular, because it had a background of skirling Highland bagpipes. Both noises emerged in this final movement of this Fourth Quartet of Béla Bartók.

Alan Dent on Béla Bartók, quoted in The Later Ego, *by James Agate*

A Tub of Pork and Beer.

Hector Berlioz on George Frideric Handel

In the first movement alone I took notice of six pregnancies and at least four miscarriages.

Sir Thomas Beecham on the Seventh Symphony by Anton Bruckner

To me it seems quite obvious that the real Brahms is nothing more than a sentimental voluptuary ... He is the most wanton of composers ... Only his wantonness is not vicious; it is that of a great baby ... rather tiresomely addicted to dressing himself up as Handel or Beethoven and making a prolonged and intolerable noise.

George Bernard Shaw on Johannes Brahms, in the World

If there is anyone here whom I have not insulted, I beg his pardon.

Johannes Brahms on leaving a gathering of friends

Brahms is just like Tennyson, an extraordinary musician with the brains of a third-rate village policeman.

George Bernard Shaw on Johannes Brahms

I played over the music of the scoundrel Brahms. What a giftless bastard! It annoys me that this self-inflated mediocrity is hailed as a genius. Why, in comparison with him, Raff is a giant, not to speak of Rubinstein, who is after all a live and important human being, while Brahms is chaotic and absolutely empty dried-up stuff.

Peter Tchaikovsky on Johannes Brahms, Diary

Music that stinks to the ear.

Eduard Hanslick on Peter Tchaikovsky

Dramatized stench.

A review of George Bernard Shaw's Mrs Warren's Profession

I nearly trod in some once.

Sir Thomas Beecham on Stockhausen

Splitting the convulsively inflated larynx of the Muse, Berg utters tortured mistuned cackling, a pandemonium of chopped-up orchestral sounds, mishandled men's throats, bestial outcries, bellowing, rattling, and all other evil noises ... Berg is the poisoner of the well of German music.

Berlin Germania *on Alban Berg*

Here love has nothing in it but filth, dirt, cold cruelty and sticky frog-like sexuality, combined with the dry rationalism of a biped calculating machine.

V. Gorodinsky on Ernst Krenek, Music of Spiritual Poverty

It sounded like as though a pack of rats were being slowly tortured to death, while, from time to time, a dying cow moaned.

Berlin Signale *on* Dichotomy *by Wallingford Riegger*

The musical equivalent of blancmange.

Bernard Levin on Frederick Delius

A provincial Debussy.

A. J. P. Taylor on Frederick Delius

Listening to the Fifth Symphony of Ralph Vaughan Williams is like staring at a cow for forty-five minutes.

Aaron Copland

Critics are misbegotten abortions.

Ralph Vaughan Williams on music critics

I can say nothing for the music of *Madame Butterfly*. Western music is too complicated for a Japanese. Even Caruso's celebrated singing does not appeal very much more than the barking of a dog in faraway woods.

> *Jihei Hashigushi after attending the New York premiere of* Madame Butterfly *by Puccini*

You know whatta you do when you shit? Singing, it's the same thing, only up!

> *Enrico Caruso*

The only time you want to see 100 gypsies on your doorstep.

> *Publicity by Mole Valley District Council, for a Romany orchestra's visit to Surrey*

It is quite untrue that the English people don't appreciate music. They may not understand it but they absolutely love the noise it makes.

> *Sir Thomas Beecham*

I had not realized that the Arabs were so musical.

> *Sir Thomas Beecham on hearing that a concert by Malcolm Sargent in Tel Aviv had been interrupted by the sound of gunfire directed at the concert hall*

A kind of musical Malcolm Sargent.

> *Sir Thomas Beecham on Herbert von Karajan*

The musical equivalent of St Pancras station.

> *Sir Thomas Beecham on Edward Elgar's* Symphony in A Flat

Like playing a birdcage with a toasting fork.

> *Sir Thomas Beecham on the harpsichord*

A glorified bandmaster.
>   *Sir Thomas Beecham on Arturo Toscanini*

Madame, there you sit with that magnificent instrument between your legs, and all you can do is scratch it!
>   *Arturo Toscanini to a woman cellist; also attributed to Sir Thomas Beecham*

CELLIST: What shall I do next?
SIR THOMAS BEECHAM: Get married.
>   *Sir Thomas Beecham to a young female cellist at an audition, after she had completed the first movement of a concerto*

If you will make a point of singing 'All we, like sheep, have gone astray' with a little less satisfaction, we shall meet the aesthetical as well as the theological requirements.
>   *Sir Thomas Beecham to a choir*

Brass bands are all very well in their place – outdoors and several miles away.
>   *Sir Thomas Beecham. Attrib.*

Thank you, and now would you pull the chain.
>   *Sir Thomas Beecham to an incompetent tuba player*

There are two golden rules for an orchestra: start together and finish together. The public doesn't give a damn what goes on in between.
>   *Sir Thomas Beecham*

A musicologist is a man who can read music but can't hear it.
>   *Sir Thomas Beecham*

Dominoes.

George Bernard Shaw to the conductor of a palm-court orchestra in a
restaurant, who had asked what he would like the orchestra to play

If he'd been making shell cases during the war it might have
been better for music.

Camille Saint-Saëns on Maurice Ravel

One should try everything once, except incest and
folk-dancing.

Arnold Bax

Music written by dead guys.

Nigel Kennedy, violinist, on classical music

When Jack Benny plays the violin it sounds as if the strings
are still in the cat.

Fred Allen

His approach to the microphone is that of an accused man
pleading with a hostile jury.

Kenneth Tynan on Frankie Lane

George Melly you're a repulsive sweaty faced lout singing
love songs. Why your past it. Hang your gun up. And all your
dirty jokes leave them to real comedians. You have a mouth
like a ducks ass. Have you only one suit and shabby at that.
And your dirty suggestive songs. Somebody ought to tell you.
You dirty minded oaf. You're a load of rubbish.

Anonymous letter, as spelt, to George Melly

Miss Truman [sic] is a unique American phenomenon with a pleasant voice, of little size and fair quality ... There are few moments during her recital when one can relax and feel confident she will make her goal, which is the end of the song.

Paul Hume on the singer Margaret Truman, in the Washington Post

I have just read your lousy review buried in the back pages of the paper. You sound like a frustrated old man who never made a success, an eight-ulcer man on a four-ulcer job, and all four ulcers working. I have never met you, but if I do you'll need a new nose and plenty of beefsteak and perhaps a supporter below.

Harry S. Truman replying to a review of Truman's daughter's recital in the Washington Post. *Margaret Truman was a singer*

Sinatra could be terribly nice one minute and, well, not so nice the next. I was not impressed with the creeps and Mafia types he kept around him.

Prince Charles on Frank Sinatra

Frank Sinatra is a singer who comes along once in a lifetime ... why did he have to come along in my lifetime?

Bing Crosby

I always knew Frank would end up with a boy.

Ava Gardner on Sinatra's marriage to Mia Farrow

To hear Tom Jones sing Sinatra's *My Way* is roughly akin to watching Tab Hunter play *King Lear*. Mr Jones is, in the words of his own hit, not unusual ... at least not as a singer; as a sex symbol he is nothing short of inexplicable.

Sheridan Morley, in Punch

Do you gargle with pebbles?
Prince Philip to Tom Jones, after a Royal Variety show

He sang like a hinge.
Ethel Merman on Cole Porter

If white bread could sing it would sing like Olivia Newton-John.
Anonymous review

For years I've been vaguely aware of [pop star] Michael Bolton's existence, just as I'd been vaguely aware that there was an Ebola virus in Africa. Horrible tragedies, yes, but they had nothing to do with me.
Joe Queenan

The Beatles are not merely awful, I would consider it sacrilegious to say anything less than that they are godawful. They are so unbelievably horrible, so appallingly unmusical, so dogmatically insensitive to the magic of the art, that they qualify as crowned heads of anti-music, even as the impostor popes went down in history as 'anti-popes'.
William F. Buckley, Jr.

Their lyrics are unrecognisable as the Queen's English.
Edward Heath on the Beatles

Europe is not just about free trade and single currencies, it's about building a continent fit for Sir Edward Heath to conduct the European Community Youth Orchestra in the *Ode to Joy*.
Mark Steyn, the Daily Telegraph

This man has child-bearing lips.
Joan Rivers on Mick Jagger

Surely nothing could be that funny.
George Melly when told the wrinkles on Mick Jagger's face were laughter lines

You have Van Gogh's ear for music.
Billy Wilder to Cliff Osmond. Attrib.

Wood Green shopping centre has been committed to vinyl.
The New Musical Express *on the pop group Five Star*

Five bowls of muesli looking for a spoon.
The New Musical Express *on the pop group Yes*

The 'Mode' make very dubious puffing noises as though they were blowing up a paddling pool.
Smash Hits on Depeche Mode

Her voice sounded like an eagle being goosed.
Ralph Novak on Yoko Ono, in People

He has an attractive voice and a highly unattractive bottom. In his concert performances he now spends more time wagging the latter than exercising the former, thereby conforming to the established pattern by which popular entertainers fall prey to the delusion that the public loves them for themselves, and not for their work.
Clive James on Rod Stewart

I remember when pop music meant jerking off to pictures of Marc Bolan and duffing up Bay City Roller's fans in lunch breaks. Being 13 was never as vapid as this. If it had been, we would all be traffic wardens by now.

Melody Maker on the pop group Bros

They are the Hollow Men. They are electronic lice.

Anthony Burgess on disc jockeys, in Punch

Bambi with testosterone.

Owen Gleiberman on Prince, in Entertainment Weekly

A vacuum with nipples.

Otto Preminger on Marilyn Monroe

Boy George is all England needs – another queen who can't dress.

Joan Rivers

Malibu is the only place in the world where you can lie on the sand and look at the stars – or vice versa.

Joan Rivers

A walking X-ray.

Oscar Levant on Audrey Hepburn

Diana Rigg is built like a brick mausoleum with insufficient flying buttresses.

John Simon reviewing Abelard and Heloise *by Ronald Miller*

Mummy, what is that lady for?

Child at a matinee performance by Hermione Gingold

A very old 13.
> *Noel Coward, of an actress after the most recent of her many facelifts*

Mr Gielgud has the most meaningless legs imaginable.
> *Ivor Brown on John Gielgud's Romeo*

His ears make him look like a taxi-cab with both doors open.
> *Howard Hughes on Clark Gable*

If you say 'Hiya, Clark, how are you?' he's stuck for an answer.
> *Ava Gardner on Clark Gable*

The shit hits the fan.
> *Headline suggested by Kenneth Tynan after Rex Harrison punched an autograph hunter*

She was good at playing abstract confusion in the same way that a midget is good at being short ... As far as talent goes, Marilyn Monroe was so minimally gifted as to be unemploy-able, and anyone who holds to the opinion that she was a great natural comic identifies himself immediately as a dunce.
> *Clive James*

It's like kissing Hitler.
> *Tony Curtis on kissing Marilyn Monroe*

I watched The Music Lovers. One can't really blame Tchaikovsky for preferring boys. Anyone might become a homosexualist who had once seen Glenda Jackson naked.
> *Auberon Waugh, in* Private Eye

You have obviously spent so much time with your head wedged between your buttocks that your vision has been obscured by reflection of your own putrid entrails. If the art of literacy or dramatic criticism is to remain viable, we must seek to eliminate people like you who degrade the art form by taking cheap shots at performers' physical liabilities and who must darkly illuminate their critiques with pseudo-intellectual name calling. If you must persist in deriding Ms Minnelli's so-called imperfections, at least do so with the stroke of your pen rather than with the excrement of your bowels.

From a letter to John Simon, drama critic of New York *magazine, after he had passed unfavourable comment on the facial appearance and acting ability of Liza Minnelli*

The syphilis and gonorrhoea of the theatre.
David Mamet on Frank Rich and John Simon, critics

As wholesome as a bowl of cornflakes and at least as sexy.
Dwight MacDonald on Doris Day

Maybe it's the hair. Maybe it's the teeth. Maybe it's the intellect. No, it's the hair.
Tom Shales on Farrah Fawcett

A bargain basement Bette Davis, whose lightest touch as a comedienne would stun a horse.
Time on Susan Hayward

He looks as if his idea of fun would be to find a cold damp grave and sit in it.
Richard Winnington on Paul Henreid

She looked as though butter wouldn't melt in her mouth – or anywhere else.

> *Elsa Lanchester on Maureen O'Hara. Attrib.*

A face unclouded by thought.

> *Lillian Hellman on Norma Shearer*

What exactly is on your mind – if you'll excuse the exaggeration?

> *Inquiry by David Letterman*

[A] vamp who destroys families and sucks on husbands like a praying mantis.

> *Il Tempo on Elizabeth Taylor at the time of her affair with Richard Burton during the filming of* Cleopatra

Overweight, overbosomed, overpaid and under-talented, she set the acting profession back a decade.

> *David Susskind on Elizabeth Taylor in* Cleopatra

Miss Taylor is monotony in a slit skirt, a pre-Christian Elizabeth Arden with sequinned eyelids and occasions constantly too large for her.

> New Statesman *on Elizabeth Taylor in* Cleopatra

Elizabeth Taylor looks like two small boys fighting underneath a mink blanket.

> *Blackwell, American designer*

Just how garish her commonplace accent, squeakily shrill voice, and the childish petulance with which she delivers her lines are, my pen is neither scratchy nor leaky enough to convey.

> *John Simon on Elizabeth Taylor's Kate,* The Taming of the Shrew

Elizabeth Taylor has more chins than the Chinese telephone directory.
Joan Rivers

…An incipient double chin, legs too short, and she has a slight pot belly.
Richard Burton on Elizabeth Taylor

I will marry her … Of course, you may be quite certain I shall be at the centre on the stage. Elizabeth will be in the wings – knitting.
Richard Burton on Elizabeth Taylor

Her arms are too fat, her legs are too short, and she is too big in the bust.
Richard Burton on Elizabeth Taylor, his new wife

In general, Mr Burton resembles a stuffed cabbage.
Harry Medved and Randy Dreyfuss on Richard Burton in 'The Assassination of Trotsky,' The Fifty Worst Films of All Time

What is she peddling, anyway? Sex repeal?
Mae West on Twiggy

She cannot change her face, which is that of a worried hamster.
Review of Prunella Scales playing all six female parts in Anatole France *by David Tylden-Wright*

She looks like she combs her hair with an egg-beater.
Louella Parsons on Joan Collins

He looks like an extra in a crowd scene by Hieronymus Bosch.

> *Kenneth Tynan on Don Rickles, in the* New Yorker

Like acting with two and a half tons of condemned veal.

> *Coral Browne on a leading man*

Annette Crosbie played Viola like a Shetland pony.

> *Theatre critic Sarah Davenport on* Twelfth Night

When he mounts into the air it is by means of a chair and a table, and his descents are similarly accomplished.

> *James Agate on Fred Astaire in* The Gay Divorce, *in the* Sunday Times

He has taken to ambling across our stages in a spectral, shell-shocked manner, choosing odd moments to jump and frisk, like a man through whom an electric current is being inter-mittently passed.

> *Kenneth Tynan on Ralph Richardson in* The White Carnation

No man looking like a golliwog can persuade us that he is talking like a god.

> *Harold Hobson on Ralph Richardson as Othello*

Tony Britton's habit of curling his lip villainously and so relentlessly gives one the impression that he had it permanently waved.

> *Plays and Players on Tony Britton in* A Woman of No Importance *by Oscar Wilde*

A bore is starred.

> *Village Voice review of* A Star is Born *starring Barbra Streisand*

She looks like a cross between an aardvark and an albino rat surmounted by a platinum-coated horse bun.
John Simon on Barbra Streisand

A woman whose face looked as if it had been made of sugar and someone had licked it.
George Bernard Shaw on Isadora Duncan

She not only worships the Golden Calf, she barbecues it for lunch.
Oscar Levant on Zsa Zsa Gabor

I've just spent an hour talking to Tallulah for a few minutes.
Fred Keating on Tallulah Bankhead

I thought I told you to wait in the car.
Tallulah Bankhead, when greeted by a former admirer whom she had not seen for many years. Attrib.

She was always a star, but only intermittently a good actress.
Brendan Gill on Tallulah Bankhead, in The Times

She was an open, wayward, free, cosmopolitan, liberated, sensuous human being. In thus systematically invading her own privacy she was the first of the modern personalities.
Lee Israel on Tallulah Bankhead

I'm as pure as the driven slush.
Tallulah Bankhead

The T is silent, as in Harlow.
Lady Margot Asquith, explaining that her name should not be pronounced 'Margot'. The reference is to Jean Harlow

Dorothy [Tutin] played St Joan like a beatnik in a coffee-bar.
Alan Drury, in the Listener

Like a toastmaster celebrating his golden wedding.
James Agate on Henry Ainley as Prospero in The Tempest, *in the* Sunday Times

Julian Glover's Anthony ... enters red, sweaty and with his bow-tie askew, like some raddled, over-used deb's delight.
Review of Anthony and Cleopatra

Millamant must be the empress of her sex, and her words, whether tinkling like a fountain or cascading like Niagara, must always flow from a great height. From Miss Brown's mouth they do not flow at all; they leak ...
Kenneth Tynan on Pamela Brown in The Way of the World *by William Congreve*

Miss Moira Lister speaks all her lines as if they are written in very faint ink on a tele-printer slightly too far away to be read with comfort.
Bernard Levin reviewing The Gazebo *by Alec Coppel*

Denis Quilley played the role with all the charm and animation of the leg of a billiard table.
Bernard Levin on Denis Quilley as Charles Condamine in High Spirits *(a musical version of Noel Coward's* Blithe Spirit*)*

As swashbuckling Cyrano, Mr Woodward's performance buckles more than it swashes.
Kenneth Tynan on Edward Woodward in Cyrano, *in the* Spectator

We are privileged to see Mr Samuel Goldwyn's latest 'discovery'. All we can say about this actor is that he is tall, dark and not the slightest bit handsome.

Detroit Free Press on David Niven in Dodsworth

This was Doris Day's first picture; before she became a virgin.

Oscar Levant on Doris Day in Romance on the High Seas

Guido Nadzo was Nadzo Guido.

Brooks Atkinson on Valentino look-alike Guido Nadzo

Mr Creston Clarke played King Lear at the Tabor Grand last night. All through five acts of the Shakespearean tragedy he played the king as though under the premonition that someone was about to play the ace.

Eugene Field, Denver Post

[Jay] Robinson was all right. But what is gameness in a man who is suffering delusions of adequacy

Walter Kerr on Buy Me Blue

Not content to stop the show, she merely slowed it down.

Anonymous, on Elaine Paige

It is a generous role for womanly and impassioned actresses, and many performers have essayed it. I can think of four, however, who have not: Totie Fields, W. C. Fields, Tutankhamen's mummy, and a trained monkey. Not until now, that is. Miss Gordon's performance combines elements of all four.

John Simon on Ruth Gordon in the title role of Mrs Warren's Profession *by George Bernard Shaw*

Very believably playing an English secretary, Julie fell for Omar, who had been cast as a Russian spy because there was no role available as a date-picker.

> Clive James on Omar Sharif in The Tamarind Seed co-starring Julie Andrews, in the Observer

You thought Dirk Benedict had problems in TV's *Battlestar Galactica*? In *Scavenger Hunt* he really had problems – in one mercifully brief scene he was out-acted by a jock-strap.

> Rona Barrett on Dirk Benedict

It is greatly to Mrs Patrick Campbell's credit that, bad as the play was, her acting was worse. It was a masterpiece of failure.

> George Bernard Shaw on Mrs Patrick Campbell

When you were a little boy, somebody ought to have said 'hush' just once.

> Mrs Patrick Campbell to George Bernard Shaw

She was a sinking ship firing upon her rescuers.

> Alexander Woollcott on Mrs Patrick Campbell

Oh, to be in England, now that June's here.

> Robert Garland about Lady June Inverclyde, who had just arrived in America

In real life, Keaton believes in God. But she also believes that the radio works because there are tiny people inside it.

> Woody Allen on Diane Keaton

An acting style that's really a nervous breakdown in slow-motion.

> John Simon on Diane Keaton

She was so dramatic she stabbed the potatoes at dinner.

The Reverend Sydney Smith, Dean of St Paul's on Sarah Siddons, a melo-dramatic actress

Do you know how they are going to decide the Shakespeare-Bacon dispute? They are going to dig up Shakespeare and dig up Bacon; they are going to set their coffins side by side, and they are going to get Tree to recite Hamlet to them. And the one who turns in his coffin will be the author of the play.

W. S. Gilbert on Herbert Beerbohm Tree

At the end, when the whale has lured Harris north with a come-hither flick of its tail, Miss Rampling is caught in the ice floes, leaping from one to t'other and clad in thigh boots, homespun poncho *and a turban*, as if she expected David Bailey to surface and photograph her for *Vogue*'s Arctic number.

Alexander Walker on Charlotte Rampling in Orca the Killer Whale, *in the* Evening Standard

Dame Anna Neagle was game enough to have a little stab at the Charleston, and was wildly and sympathetically applauded by admirers who plainly felt any gesture more extravagant than holding a hand above her head – as though hailing a cab, or conceivably signalling for help – was a grave imposition upon a Lady of her advanced years.

Kenneth Hurren reviewing No, No, Nanette, *in the* Spectator

Tallulah Bankhead barged down the Nile last night as Cleopatra – and sank.

John Mason Brown

A plumber's idea of Cleopatra.

W. C. Fields on Mae West

She has a face that belongs to the sea and the wind, with large rocking-horse nostrils and teeth that you just know bite an apple every day.
  Cecil Beaton on Katharine Hepburn

Katherine Hepburn ran the whole gamut of emotions from A to B.
  Dorothy Parker reviewing The Lake *by Dorothy Massingham and Murray MacDonald*

He is mostly required to be controlling, staid and dull – demands well within his range.
  Benedict Nightingale on Charlton Heston's performance in Love Letters

I think they have made a slight mistake. They've left the show in Detroit, or wherever it was warming up, and brought in the publicity stills.
  Walter Kerr on the musical Ilya Darling

I have knocked everything but the knees of the chorus girls, and nature has anticipated me there.
  Percy Hammond, critic, on a musical

It's like getting a prize from the snipers because they have missed you.
  Michael Caine on winning an award from the London Film Critics Circle

Critics are ink-stained wretches.
  Alexander Woollcott

Actors? They're poor, abject, disagreeable, perverse, ill-minded slightly malicious creatures. They must have the centre of the stage or at least the second-centre. They'd like to stop, but they can't. And of that august company of idiots, I'm afraid I'm a member.
Richard Burton

Insecurity, commonly regarded as a weakness in normal people, is the basic tool of an actor's trade.
Miranda Richardson

This is a good day for lying, drug-abusing prima donnas who want to have their cake with the media and the right to then shamelessly guzzle it with their Cristal champagne.
Piers Morgan on Naomi Campbell

The definition of countryside is the murder of Piers Morgan.
Stephen Fry

When I read the lives of celebrities in our newspapers I sometimes wish we had a Freedom *From* Information Act.
Theodore Dalrymple

A guy who, if you ain't talking about him, ain't listening.
Marlon Brando on actors

You can pick out actors by the glazed look that comes into their eyes when the conversation wanders away from themselves.
Michael Wilding

Actors should be treated like cattle.
Alfred Hitchcock

He was once Slightly in Peter Pan, and has been wholly in Peter Pan ever since.
> Kenneth Tynan on Noel Coward. Attrib.

He was his own greatest invention.
> John Osborne on Noel Coward

Television? Television is for being on, dear boy not for watching.
> Noel Coward

Two things should be cut – the second act and the child's throat.
> Noel Coward on a dull play with an annoying child star

If they'd stuffed the child's head up the horse's arse, they would have solved two problems at once.
> Noel Coward, referring to a performance starring child actress Bonnie Langford and a horse, after the latter defecated on stage

Not just an artist, but a critic, too!
> Sir Thomas Beecham, during a performance when a horse on stage defecated

He's the kind of man who thinks Mea Culpa is an Italian starlet.
> Brian Viner on the impresario Lord Grade

The reason why so many people turned up at Louis Mayer's funeral was because they wanted to make sure he was dead.
> Sam Goldwyn

NEWMAN: Don't forget I pulled you up from the gutter
DIRECTOR: From the gutter to you – this is up?
Sydney Newman, Canadian film producer to a director

It proves what they always say: give the public what they want to see and they'll come out for it.
Anonymous on the crowds at the funeral of Hollywood mogul Harry Cohn

Hollywood films either want to tell us a truth we already know or a falsehood we want to believe in.
William Goldman

What critics call dirty in our movies they call lusty in foreign films.
Billy Wilder

I'm sure pictures like this give people pimples.
Pauline Kael on Sweet November

Television? No good will come of this device. The word is half Greek and half Latin.
C.P. Scott

Television is a medium of entertainment which permits millions of people to listen to the same joke at the same time, and yet remain lonesome.
T. S. Eliot, in the New York Post

TV is an invention that permits you to be entertained in your living-room by people you wouldn't have in your home.
Sir David Frost

I once saved David Frost from drowning.
Peter Cook asked if he had any regrets in his life

The bubonic plagiarist.
Jonathan Miller on Sir David Frost

He rose without trace.
Kitty Muggeridge on the career of David Frost

I'm afraid I'm watching television that night.
Peter Cook, upon receiving a telephone call from Sir David Frost inviting him to dinner with Prince Andrew and Sarah Ferguson

There are days when any electrical appliance in the house, including the vacuum cleaner, seems to offer more entertainment possibilities than the TV set.
Harriet Van Horne

People say there's nothing good on TV, but there's not supposed to be. I mean, Christ, people are watching it eight hours a day now. Can you imagine if it was actually good? This nation would come to a standstill.
David Letterman

Looking at the past by digging holes in the ground is like making a cookery programme exclusively by examining the washing up.
AA Gill on Archaeology programmes

I don't wish to cause unrest but, statistically speaking, several people will have died in the night before tomorrow's issue hits the streets. A macabre thought, but it's not all bad news. At least you'll be spared the indignity of having to watch Wednesday's edition of *Pebble Mill*. It's with Ross King.
Victor Lewis-Smith, television critic, in the Evening Standard

We are drowning our youngsters in violence, cynicism and sadism piped into the living-room and even the nursery. The grandchildren of the kids who used to weep because the Little Match Girl froze to death now feel cheated if she isn't slugged, raped and thrown into a Bessemer converter.
Jenkin Lloyd Jones

I have beside me, as I write, two tubes of glutinous liquid, which, I am told, when mixed, will form an adhesive powerful enough to weld together two elephants who would rather part company, and hold up the Clifton Suspension Bridge should it ever run out of suspenders. I would prefer, however, to put this admirable concoction to a different use. I would like, in fact, to spoon out great dollops of it into your beard.
Letter to Elkan Allan, TV critic and compiler of Critical Viewer's Guide to the Week's Television *in the* Sunday Times

I sometimes wonder which would be nicer – an opera without an interval, or an interval without an opera.
Ernest Newman

You know, I go to the theatre to be entertained ... I don't want to see plays about rape, sodomy and drug addiction ... I can get all that at home.
Peter Cook, caption to cartoon in the Observer

Popular Stage-playes ... are sinfull, heathenish, lewde, ungodly Spectacles, and most pernicious Corruptions; condemned in all ages, as intolerable Mischiefes to Churches, to Republickes, to the manners, mindes and soules of men. And that the Profession of Play-poets, of Stage-players; together with the penning, acting, and frequenting of Stage-players, are unlawful, infamous, and misbeseeming Christians.

William Prynne, 17th-century critic

A good many inconveniences attend play-going in any large city, but the greatest of them is usually the play itself.

Kenneth Tynan

It had only one fault. It was kind of lousy.

James Thurber on a play

I saw it at a disadvantage – the curtain was up.

Walter Winchell on a show starring Earl Carroll

I've had a perfectly wonderful evening. But this wasn't it.

Groucho Marx

The play was a great success, but the audience was a disaster.

Oscar Wilde

What a tiresome affected sod.

Noel Coward on Oscar Wilde

Long experience has taught me that in England nobody goes to the theatre unless he or she has bronchitis.

James Agate

Busy yourselves with that, you damned walruses, while the rest of us proceed with the play.
John Barrymore, throwing a fish into the stalls of a coughing audience

I would just like to mention Robert Houdini who in the eighteenth century invented the vanishing bird-cage trick and the theatre matinee. May he rot and perish. Good afternoon.
Orson Welles, addressing the audience at the end of a matinee performance

It has taken 33 years for Jean-Paul Sartre's *The Devil and the Good Lord* to reach London, but our luck was bound to run out sooner or later.
Kenneth Hurren, in the Mail on Sunday

I've seen more excitement at the opening of an umbrella.
Earl Wilson, reviewing a play

The touring production of *Five Guys Named Moe* ... performed a bluesey, doleful number with so little feeling that I suspect the only cotton their ancestors ever picked was out of an Anadin bottle.
Victor Lewis-Smith, newspaper critic, 1994

All the joy of standing by at an autopsy.
Variety magazine on the film Divorce His, Divorce Hers

Watching my plays performed in London is like seeing them in translation.
Lillian Hellman

There was laughter at the back of the theatre, leading to the belief that someone was telling jokes back there.
George S. Kaufman on a Broadway comedy

Remarkable economy of means, and of effect.
Henry James on a Punch and Judy show

When Mr. Wilbur calls his play *Halfway to Hell* he under-
estimates the distance.
Brooks Atkinson

Darling, they've absolutely ruined your perfectly dreadful
play.
Tallulah Bankhead to Tennessee Williams after seeing the film version of
Orpheus Descending, *entitled* The Fugitive Kind

A mishmash of Stalinism with New Dealism with
Hollywoodism with opportunism with shaky experimental-
ism with mesmerism with onanism, all mosaicked into a
remarkable portrait of what the makers of the film think the
Soviet Union is like – a great glad two-million-dollar bowl of
canned borscht, eminently approvable by the Institute of
Good Housekeeping.
James Agee on Mission to Moscow

There is enough Irish comedy to make us wish Cromwell had
done a more thorough job.
James Agee on Fort Apache

They only got two things right – the camels and the sand.
Lowell Thomas on Lawrence of Arabia

If Peter O'Toole was any prettier they'd have to call it
Florence of Arabia.
Noel Coward on O'Toole's T.E. Lawrence in the film Lawrence of Arabia

To sit through this film is something like holding an elephant on your lap for two hours and fifteen minutes.

Time *on* Circus World

As synthetic and padded as the transvestite's cleavage.

Frank Rich, 'The Butcher of Broadway', on La Cage aux Folles, *in the* New York Times

An American musical so bad that at times I longed for the boy-meets-tractor theme of Soviet drama.

Bernard Levin on Rodgers and Hammerstein's Flower Drum Song, *in the* Daily Express

It is not true that Andrew Lloyd Webber and I are no longer speaking to each other. I saw his last show. At least I hope it was his last show.

Sir Tim Rice

There is less in this than meets the eye.

Tallulah Bankhead on the revival of a play by Maeterlinck

He displayed a sneaky knack for extending the life of a production beyond the reasonable expectations of the playwright's mother.

Walter Kerr on David Merrick

Very well then: I say Never.

George Jean Nathan on Tonight or Never

A crazy fanatic ... a crazy cranky being ... not only consistently dirty but deplorably dull ... A gloomy sort of ghoul ... blinking like a stupid old owl.

Newspaper review of Hedda Gabler *by Henrik Ibsen*

It can probably be said that Pinter raised to a new level of acceptability the kind of play in which the audience not only has no precise idea of what is going on, but seriously doubts whether the author has, either.

> *Kenneth Hurren on* The Birthday Party *by Harold Pinter, in the* Mail on Sunday

A theatrical whore of the first quality.

> *Peter Hall on Bertolt Brecht*

Shakespeare, Madam, is obscene, and, thank God, we are sufficiently advanced to have found it out.

> *Frances Trollope on William Shakespeare*

Crude, immoral, vulgar and senseless.

> *Leo Tolstoy on William Shakespeare*

One of the greatest geniuses that ever existed, Shakespeare undoubtedly wanted taste.

> *Horace Walpole on William Shakespeare*

This enormous dunghill.

> *Voltaire on William Shakespeare*

We can say of Shakespeare that never has a man turned so little knowledge to such great account.

> *T. S. Eliot on William Shakespeare*

Pale, marmoreal Eliot was there last week, like a chapped office boy on a high stool, with a cold in his head.

> *Virginia Woolf on T. S. Eliot*

When I read Shakespeare
I am struck with wonder
that such trivial people
should muse and thunder
in such lovely language.
> *D. H. Lawrence*

I have tried lately to read Shakespeare, and found it so
intolerably dull that it nauseated me.
> *Charles Darwin on William Shakespeare*

Not a single one [of the sonnets] is very admirable ... They
are hot and pothery: there is much condensation, little
delicacy; like raspberry jam without cream, without crust,
without bread.
> *Walter Savage Landor on William Shakespeare's sonnets*

A sycophant, a flatterer, a breaker of marriage vows, a
whining and inconstant person.
> *Elizabeth Forsyth on William Shakespeare*

Shakespeare never had six lines together without a fault.
Perhaps you may find seven, but this does not refute my
general assertion.
> *Samuel Johnson on William Shakespeare*

To the King's theatre, where we saw *A Midsummer Night's
Dream* which I had never seen before nor shall ever again for
it is the most insipid, ridiculous play that I ever saw in my
life.
> *Entry in Samuel Pepys' Diary*

A strange, horrible business, but I suppose good enough for
Shakespeare's day.
Queen Victoria giving her opinion of King Lear

The intensity of my impatience with him occasionally reaches
such a pitch, that it would positively be a relief to me to dig
him up and throw stones at him.
George Bernard Shaw on William Shakespeare, Dramatic Opinions and
Essays

The way Bernard Shaw believes in himself is very refreshing
in these atheistic days when so many people believe in no
God at all.
Israel Zangwill on George Bernard Shaw

He is an old bore; even the grave yawns for him.
Herbert Beerbohm Tree on Israel Zangwill

George too Shaw to be good.
Dylan Thomas on George Bernard Shaw

He is the true Elizabethan blank-verse beast, itching to
frighten other people with the superstitious terrors and
cruelties in which he does not himself believe, and wallowing
in blood, violence, muscularity of expression and strenuous
animal passion as only literary men do when they become
thoroughly depraved by solitary work, sedentary cowardice,
and starvation of the sympathetic centres. It is not surprising
to learn that Marlowe was stabbed in a tavern brawl: what
would be utterly unbelievable would be his having succeeded
in stabbing anyone else.
George Bernard Shaw on Christopher Marlowe, Dramatic Opinions
and Essays

The first man to have cut a swathe through the theatre and left it strewn with virgins.

Frank Harris on George Bernard Shaw

If I take the trouble to criticize the Covent Garden performance of *Hamlet* ... my object must be understood to be vindictive rather than artistic.

George Bernard Shaw

He hasn't an enemy in the world, and none of his friends like him.

Oscar Wilde on George Bernard Shaw

Oscar Wilde's talent seems to me to be essentially rootless, something growing in a glass on a little water.

George Moore, novelist

He was over-dressed, pompous, snobbish, sentimental and vain. But he had an undeniable flair for the possibilities of commercial theatre.

Evelyn Waugh on Oscar Wilde

I really enjoy only his stage directions ... He uses the English language like a truncheon.

Max Beerbohm on George Bernard Shaw

Politics in a work of art is like a pistol-shot at a concert.

Henri Stendhal

Mr Shaw is (I suspect) the only man on earth who has never written any poetry.

G. K. Chesterton on George Bernard Shaw

He writes like a Pakistani who has learned English when he was twelve years old in order to become a chartered accountant.

John Osborne on George Bernard Shaw in the Manchester Guardian

There are no human beings in Major Barbara; only animated points of view.

William Archer on Major Barbara *by George Bernard Shaw,* World

A good man fallen among Fabians.

Vladimir Ilich Lenin on George Bernard Shaw. Attrib.

An Irish smut dealer.

Anthony Comstock on George Bernard Shaw

A desiccated bourgeois ... a fossilized chauvinist, a self-satisfied Englishman.

Pravda *on George Bernard Shaw, 1924*

I object to publishers: the one service they have done me is to teach me to do without them. They combine commercial rascality with artistic touchiness and pettiness, without being either good businessmen or fine judges of literature. All that is necessary in the production of a book is an author and a bookseller, without any intermediate parasite.

George Bernard Shaw

Thank you for the manuscript; I shall lose no time in reading it.

Benjamin Disraeli's standard reply to authors who sent him unsolicited copies of their books

Against Locke's philosophy I think it an unanswerable objection that, although he carried his throat about with him in this world for seventy-two years, no man ever condescended to cut it.
Thomas de Quincey on John Locke

Great editors do not discover nor produce great authors; great authors create and produce great publishers.
John Farrar

When I split an infinitive, god damn it, I split it so it stays split.
Raymond Chandler, letter to his British publisher

As repressed sadists are supposed to become policemen or butchers, so those with irrational fear of life become publishers.
Cyril Connolly

Books seem to me to be pestilent things, and infect all that trade in them ... with something very perverse and brutal. Printers, binders, sellers and others that make a trade and gain out of them, have universally so odd a turn and corruption of mind that they, have a way of dealing peculiar to themselves and not conform to the good of society and that general fairness which cements mankind.
John Locke

Authors are easy to get on with – if you're fond of children.
Michael Joseph, publisher

Every author, however modest, keeps an outrageous vanity chained like a madman within the padded cell of his breast.
Logan Pearsall Smith

Times are bad. Children no longer obey their parents, and everyone is writing a book.
Marcus Tullius Cicero

A more horrible offence against Art than what you have put ... on the cover of the Essays, has never been perpetrated even in Newcastle. I reject your handbill with disdain, with rage, with contumelious epithets ... Of the hellish ugliness of the block of letterpress headed 'What the Press says', I cannot trust myself to write, lest I be betrayed into intemperance of language ... Some time ago you mentioned something about changing the cover ... This is to give you formal notice that if you do anything of the sort ... I will have your heart's blood.
George Bernard Shaw, letter to his publisher

NORTHCLIFFE: The trouble with you, Shaw, is that you look as if there were a famine in the land.
SHAW: The trouble with you, Northcliffe, is that you look as you were the cause of it.
George Bernard Shaw to Lord Northcliffe

I will not eat oysters. I want my food dead, not sick and wounded.
Woody Allen

Cheese – milk's leap towards immortality.
Clifton Fadiman

Only the dull are brilliant at breakfast.
Oscar Wilde

By all means, let's start now.

Alfred Hitchcock, after eating an inadequate meal and being told by the host 'I do hope you will dine with us again soon'

Custard is a detestable substance produced by a malevolent conspiracy of the hen, the cow and the cook.

Ambrose Bierce

Cauliflower is nothing but cabbage with a college education.

Mark Twain

Avoid any restaurant where a waiter arrives with a handful of knives and forks just as you reach the punchline of your best story and says: 'which of you is having the fish?'

John Mortimer

The cold truth is that family dinners are more often than not an ordeal of nervous indigestion, preceded by hidden resentment and ennui and accompanied by psychosomatic jitters.

M.F.K. Fisher

We are living in a world today where lemonade is made from artificial flavors and furniture polish is made from real lemons.

Alfred E. Newman

Fish is the only food considered spoiled once it smells like what it is.

P.J. O'Rourke

You needn't tell me that a man who doesn't love oysters and asparagus and good wines has got a soul, or a stomach either. He's simply got the instinct for being unhappy.
  'Saki', pen name of Scottish writer Hector Hugh Munro

One of the disadvantages of wine is that it makes a man mistake thoughts for words.
  Samuel Johnson

The trouble with the world is that everybody in it is three drinks behind.
  Humphrey Bogart

If they do no other good they do at least this, that they prepare their patients early for death, undermining little by little and cutting off their enjoyment of life.
  Michel de Montaigne on physicans who prescribe diets

The art of medicine consists in amusing the patient while nature cures the disease.
  Voltaire

Throw physic to the dogs; I'll none of it.
  William Shakespeare

I find medicine is the best of all trades because whether you do any good or not you still get your money.
  Jean Baptiste Molière

When a lot of remedies are suggested for a disease, that means it cannot be cured.
  Anton Chekhov, The Cherry Orchard

Despite all our toils and progress, the art of medicine still falls somewhere between trout casting and spook writing.
Ben Hecht

Nobody can read Freud without realizing he was the scientific equivalent of another nuisance, George Bernard Shaw.
Robert M. Hutchins on Sigmund Freud

Anyone who pays to see a psychiatrist needs their head looking at.
Woody Allen

If the human brain were simple enough to understand, we'd be too simple to understand it.
Emerson Pugh

I've frequently observed that people who believe in a sixth sense are usually deficient in the other five.
Victor Lewis-Smith

He was meddling too much in my private life.
Tennessee Williams on why he had given up visiting his psychoanalyst

Actually I loathed the Viennese quack.
Vladimir Nabokov on Sigmund Freud

The trouble with Freud is that he never played the Glasgow Empire Saturday night.
Ken Dodd

Man is the only animal for whom his existence is a problem he has to solve.
Erich Fromm, US psychologist

The English are not a very spiritual people, so they invented cricket to give them some idea of eternity.
George Bernard Shaw

They came to see me bat, not to see you bowl.
W. G. Grace, refusing to leave the crease after being bowled first ball. Attrib.

Look, Nastase, we used to have a famous cricket match in this country called Gentlemen versus Players. The Gentlemen were put down on the scorecard as 'Mister' because they were gentlemen. By no stretch of the imagination can anybody call you a gentleman.
Trader Horn, Wimbledon umpire, on being asked by Ilie Nastase to address him as 'Mr Nastase'

A man whose chief ambition is to show his bravery in hunting foxes. A term of reproach used of country gentlemen.
Dr Johnson's dictionary entry for 'Foxhunter'

Golf is the only sport where a white man can dress like a black pimp and get away with it.
Robin Williams

There are three kinds of man you must never trust; a man who hunts south of the Thames, a man who has soup for lunch; and a man who waxes his moustache.
Sir James Richards, quoting his father

A little mutant monstrosity that was born in the toxic dump of somebody's imagination.
The Los Angeles Times *on Atlanta's 1996 Olympic mascot, Whatizit*

You can't see as well as these fucking flowers – and they're fucking plastic.
John McEnroe to a line judge at the US Open, 1980

Advertising is the rattling of a stick inside a swill bucket.
George Orwell

Ours is the age of substitutes: instead of language we have jargons; instead of principles, slogans; and instead of genuine ideas, bright suggestions.
Eric Bentley

People of the same trade seldom meet together but the conversation ends in a conspiracy against the public, or in some diversion to raise prices.
Adam Smith, The Wealth of Nations

An economist is someone who can't see something working in practice without asking whether it would work in theory.
Wolfgang Walter Heller, advisor to President Kennedy

Economic forecasters were invented to make weather forecasters look good.
Irwin Stelzer

An entrepreneur is a person who makes decisions and is sometimes right.
William Heinecke

A fool and his money get a lot of publicity.
Al Bernstein

If you would know what the Lord God thinks of money, you only have to look at those to whom He gives it.
Maurice Baring

There is plenty of affordable housing. It is simply occupied by the wrong people. The problem in New York is not high rents but low income.
John Gilbert III, President, New York Landlords' Association

It is a social experience for most people. They want to meet the people in the queue.
David Mills, Chief Executive of the Post Office, defending Post Office queues, 2004

Overseas aid is a transfer of money from poor people in rich countries to rich people in poor countries.
Peter Bauer

Nothing links man to man like the frequent passage from hand to hand of cash.
Walter Richard Sickert

A bank is a place that will lend you money if you can prove that you don't need it.
Bob Hope

The salary of the chief executive of the large corporation is not a market award for achievement. It is frequently in the nature of a warm personal gesture by the individual to himself.
John Kenneth Galbraith, Annals of an Abiding Liberal

In any successful enterprise there must be an uneven number of directors and three is too many
Giovanni Agnelli, founder of Fiat

Use advisors carefully … above all don't ask them for advice
Businessman Hugh Osmond

The only way to run a small business in Brown's Britain is to start with a large one.
Alex Salmond, Scottish Nationalist Party leader

The worst imaginable world would be one in which the leading expert in each field had total control over it.
Friedrich Hayek

The louder he talked of his honour the faster we counted our spoons.
Ralph Waldo Emerson, The Conduct of Life, 'Worship'

Finding a businessman interested in the arts is like finding chicken shit in the chicken salad.
Alice Neel

In studying the science of yesteryear one comes upon such interesting notions as gravity, electricity, and the roundness of the earth – while an examination of more recent phenomena shows a strong trend towards spray cheese, stretch denim, and the Moog synthesizer.
Fran Lebowitz

The first thing we do, let's kill all lawyers.
William Shakespeare, Henry VI, part 2

Ninety-nine per cent of lawyers give the rest a bad name.
  Steven Wright

This is a British murder inquiry and some degree of justice must be seen to be more or less done.
  Tom Stoppard, Jumpers

In one respect, at least, [Tony Blair's] claim to have 'set the people free' was entirely valid. Unfortunately those people are all convicted terrorists.
  Dominic Lawson

The majestic egalitarianism of the law, which forbids rich and poor people alike to sleep under bridges, to beg in the streets, and to steal bread.
  Anatole France, The Red Lily

The law-courts of England are open to all men, like the doors of the Ritz Hotel.
  Charles, Lord Darling

The one great principle of English law is to make business for itself.
  Charles Dickens

Lawyers, not poets, are the unacknowledged legislators of mankind.
  Columnist Simon Carr

I have come to regard the law-courts not as a cathedral but rather as a casino.
  Richard Ingrams, in the Guardian

A jury consists of 12 persons chosen to decide who has the better lawyer.
Robert Maxwell

The jury system puts a ban upon intelligence and honesty, and a premium upon ignorance, stupidity and perjury.
Mark Twain

Laws are generally found to be nets of such a texture, as the little creep through, the great break through, and the middle-sizes are alone entangled in.
William Shenstone

Laws are like cobwebs, which may catch small flies, but let wasps and hornets break through.
Jonathan Swift

Laws are like spiders' webs: if some poor weak creature comes up against them it is caught; but a bigger one can break through and get away.
Solon, an Athenian statesman

When I hear any man talk of an unalterable law the only effect it produces on me is to convince me that he is an unalterable fool.
Sydney Smith

No brilliance is needed in the law. Nothing but common sense, and relatively clean fingernails.
John Mortimer, A Voyage Round My Father

I do not care to speak ill of any man behind his back, but I believe the gentleman is an attorney.

Samuel Johnson

Like an ostrich he put his head in the sand, thereby exposing his thinking parts.

George Carman QC on David Mellor

A qadi [judge] who, when two parties part in peace,
Rekindles their dispute with binding words.
Indifferent to this world and its luxuries, he seems,
But in secret, he wouldn't say no to camel dung.
Oh, people, pause and hark
To the charming qualities of our qadi,
A homosexual, drunkard, fornicator, and takes bribes,
A tell-tale liar whose judgements follow his whims.

Ibn Ayas on Ibn al-Naqib, the Egyptian Chief Justice, Mameluke era (1250 – 1517)

My definition of utter waste is a coachload of lawyers going over a cliff, with three empty seats.

Lamar Hunt on the increasing problems of litigation in the National Football League

George Jeffreys pointed his stick at one of the rebels hauled before him in the famous 'bloody assizes' saying: 'There is a rogue at the end of my cane.' 'At which end. My Lord?' retorted the man.

Anonymous

He lied like an eye-witness.

Russian proverb

PRISONER (*in the dock before being sentenced to be hanged*): My Lord, spare me: I am a product of my upbringing.
JUDGE: So am I! Send him down.

YOUNG BARRISTER: My lord, my unfortunate client ... my lord, my unfortunate client ... my lord, my ... my ...
LORD ELLENBOROUGH: Go on, sir, go on. As far as you have proceeded hitherto, the court is entirely in agreement with you.
> Lord Ellenborough

JUDGE: Counselor, are you trying to show contempt for this court?
LAWYER: No, your Honour, I'm trying to conceal it.

Possibly not, m'Lud, but you are much better informed.
> F.E. Smith to a judge who had failed to understand one of the barrister's lengthy legal speeches. The judge told Smith: 'I have listened to you, Mr Smith, but I am none the wiser'

It is not for me, m'Lud, to attempt to fathom the inscrutable workings of Providence.
> F. E. Smith to Judge Willis after the judge had interrupted his lengthy discourse, asking: 'What do you suppose I am on the bench for, Mr Smith?

LORD SANDWICH: You will die either on the gallows, or of the pox.
WILKES: That must depend on whether I embrace your lordship's principles or your mistress.
> John Wilkes; sometimes attributed to Samuel Foote. Quoted in Portrait of a Patriot by Chenevix-Trench

I have forgotten more law than you ever knew, but allow me to say, I have not forgotten much.

Judge John Maynard, replying to Judge Jeffrey's assertion that he was so old he had forgotten the law

One could drive a schooner through any part of his argument and never scrape against a fact.

David Houston, American politician, on William Jennings Bryan, American lawyer and politician

I can't take my chauffeur everywhere.

Derek Laud, Conservative Candidate, explaining a drink-driving charge

CONVICTED CRIMINAL: As God is my judge – I am innocent.
MR JUSTICE BIRKETT: He isn't; I am, and you're not!

Sir Norman Birkett

[It is reported that] after a ten year stand off, Lord Longford is again visiting the Moors murderer Ian Brady. Thank goodness, a nation will sleep more soundly for knowing that, at last, this revolting psychopath is being properly punished.

Simon Heffer

The difference is that we Europeans accept we've all got to die of something or other. Americans think death is a calamity for which you can sue somebody.

Jonathan Miller

You are a low-down, depraved son-of-a-bitch. There were only seven Democrats in Hinsdale County, and you ate five of them.

US trial judge sentencing Alferd [sic] Packer for cannibalism, 1874

From every treetop some wild woods songster will carol his mating song, butterflies will sport in the sunshine, the busy bee will hum happy as it pursues its accustomed vocation. The gentle breeze will tease the tassels of the wild grasses, and all nature, José Manuel Miguel Xavier Gonzales, will be glad but you. You won't be here to enjoy it because I command the sheriff or some other officer of this country to lead you out to some remote spot, swing you by the neck from the knotting bough of a sturdy oak, and let you hang until you are dead. And then, José Manuel Miguel Xavier Gonzales, I further command that such officer or officers retire quickly from your dangling corpse, that vultures may descend from the heavens upon your filthy body until nothing shall remain but the bare, bleached bones of a cold-blooded, copper-coloured, blood-thirsty, throat-cutting, chilli-eating, sheep-herding, murdering son-of-a-bitch.

Transcript from US District Court, New Mexico Territory, 1881, in the case of USA v. Gonzales

Here comes counsel for the other side.

Sydney Smith on the arrival of the lawyer Lord Brougham at a performance of The Messiah

Prisoner, God has given you good abilities, instead of which you go about the country stealing ducks.

William Arabin, judge

Anger is just and love is just but justice is not just.

D.H. Lawrence

One day, you'll do something nice.

Mrs Prosser, to her son David (who assisted with this book)

In the history of the world no one has ever washed a rented car.

Lawrence Summers, Harvard President

Conscience is the inner voice that warns us somebody may be looking.

H.L. Mencken

Common sense is the deposits of prejudice laid down in the mind before the age of 18.

Albert Einstein

Moral indignation is in most cases two per cent moral, 48 per cent indignation and 50 per cent envy.

Vittorio De Sica

We know of no spectacle so ridiculous as the British public in one of its periodical fits of morality.

Thomas Babington Macaulay

You see, I always divide people into two groups. Those who live by what they know to be a lie, and those who live by what they believe, falsely, to be the truth.

Christopher Hampton, The Philanthropist

I wonder what he meant by that.

Talleyrand on the death of the scheming Prince Metternich

Truth is like sunlight: people used to think it was good for you.

From King of the Hill, *US cartoon*

Some men love truth so much that they seem to be in continual fear lest she should catch a cold on overexposure.
Samuel Butler

Such truth as crosses no man's pleasure nor profit is to all men welcome.
Thomas Hobbes

He that shall follow truth too close at the heels – it shall happily kick out his teeth.
Thomas Hobbes

Self-interest speaks all sorts of tongues, and plays all sorts of roles, even that of disinterestedness.
François, Duc de La Rochefoucauld

And whoever walks a mile full of false sympathy walks to the funeral of the whole human race and whoever forces himself to love anybody begets a murderer in his own body.
D.H. Lawrence: reply to Jesus

An orgy looks particularly alluring seen through the mists of righteous indignation.
Malcolm Muggeridge

Dost thou think, because thou art virtuous, there shall be no more cakes and ale?
William Shakespeare, Twelfth Night

Frivolity is the privilege of the secure, or the refuge of the desperate.
Matthew d'Ancona, British journalist

A very old political monk shuffling around in Gucci shoes.
Rupert Murdoch on the Dalai Lama

Religion is the venereal disease of mankind.
Henri de Montherlant

I shudder at the thought of religion, I flee the Bible as a viper, and revolt at the touch of a Christian, for their tender mercies may next fall upon my head.
G.J. Holyoake at a lecture in Cheltenham (see page 340)

Nothing returns one quicker to God than the sight of a scientist with no imagination, no vocabulary, no sympathy, no comprehension of metaphor, and no wit, looking soulless amid the wonders of nature.
Howard Jacobson on Richard Dawkins

Oysters are more beautiful than any religion ... There's nothing in Christianity or Buddhism that quite matches the sympathetic unselfishness of an oyster.
Andrei Dimitrievich Sakharov

Men never do evil so completely and cheerfully as when they do it from religious conviction.
Blaise Pascal

Religion is the source of all imaginable follies and disturbances; it is the parent of fanaticism and civil discord; it is the enemy of mankind.
Voltaire

The godless arch scoundrel Voltaire is dead – dead like a dog, like a beast.
Wolfgang Amadeus Mozart

My prayer to God is a very short one: 'Oh Lord, make my enemies ridiculous.' God has granted it.
Voltaire

Anything too stupid to be said should be sung.
Voltaire

When I'm sitting on the woolsack in the House of Lords I amuse myself by saying 'bollocks', *sotto voce*, to the bishops.
Lord Hailsham, Lord Chancellor

MR IRSHAD, *(a Muslim, writing to Bertrand Russell):* In your book you have used the word 'Flight' for the migration of the Holy Prophet from Mecca to Medina … 'Hijrat' (migration) was a strategic withdrawal to a friendly place made according to plan, under Divine guidance. You will not like to use the word 'flight' when the British armies took to their heels at Dunkirk in World War II. How do you account for using the word 'flight' for an event that has a religious sanctity for the Muslim world?

BERTRAND RUSSELL, *(replying to Mr Irshad): September 16, 1963.*
Dear Mr Irshad, Thank you for your letter. 1. The British armies did flee from Dunkirk just as Mohammed fled from Mecca to Medina. 2. I do not believe that Mohammed or anyone else was impelled by 'divine inspiration'. 3. To call flight 'strategic withdrawal' is ludicrous. 4. The picture of the prophet should be displayed as a matter of interest to

students and scholars. 5. Chauvinism is harmful and also accompanies the absence of any humour or humility.
Yours sincerely BERTRAND RUSSELL
P.S. I am opposed to all superstition: Muslim, Christian, Jewish or Buddhist.

The next time anyone asks you: 'What is Bertrand Russell's Philosophy?' the correct answer is: 'What year please?'
Sydney Hook, on Bertrand Russell

Religion is the sign of the oppressed creature, the feeling of a heartless world and the spirit of conditions which are unspiritual. It is the opium of the people.
Karl Marx

Many people think they have religion when they are troubled with dyspepsia.
Robert G. Ingersoll, Liberty of Man, Woman and Child

Many people believe that they are attracted by God, or by Nature, when they are only repelled by man.
William Ralph Inge, More Lay thoughts of a Dean

As you, Sir, have introduced religion into this meeting, which I have carefully avoided in my lecture, I will answer your question frankly and sincerely ... Home colonization is an economic scheme, and as we can ill bear the burden of God here, he may lie rather heavy on our hands there. Our national debt and our national taxes hang like millstones round the neck of the poor man's prosperity, saying nothing of the enormous gatherings of capitalists in addition to all this; and in the face of our misery and want we are charged twenty millions more for the worship of God ... I appeal to your heads and your pockets if we are not too poor to have a God. If poor men cost the state so much, they would be put like officers on half-pay. I think that while our distress lasts it would be wise to do the same thing with the Deity.

> *G.J. Holyoake at a lecture in Cheltenham, 1842, on home colonization, when asked by a clergyman in the audience what provision should be made for God in the new colonies. For these statements Holyoake was prosecuted for blasphemy and sentenced to six months' imprisonment during which time his daughter died of starvation*

The whole religious complexion of the modern world is due to the absence from Jerusalem of a lunatic asylum.

> *Havelock Ellis*

Illness is a consequence of sin.

> *Archbishop Paul Cordes, head of the Vatican Agency for Humanitarian Relief, presenting the Papal Message for Lent, 2002*

Heaven, as conventionally conceived, is a place so inane, so dull, so useless, so miserable, that nobody has ever ventured to describe a whole day in heaven. Though plenty of people have described a day at the seaside.

> *George Bernard Shaw*

Probably no invention came more easily to man than Heaven.

> *Georg Christoph Lichtenberg, Aphorisms*

There is a very good saying that if triangles invented a god, they would make him three-sided.

> *Baron de Montesquieu, Lettres persanes*

An honest god is the noblest work of man.

> *Robert G. Ingersoll, The Gods*

God can stand being told by Professor Ayer and Marghanita Laski that He doesn't exist.

> *J.B. Priestley, in the Listener*

If it turns out that there is a God, I don't think that he's evil.
But the worst that you can say about him is that basically he's
an underachiever.
Woody Allen

I don't know if God exists, but it would be better for his
reputation if he didn't.
Jules Renard

Man is quite insane. He wouldn't know how to create a
maggot and he creates Gods by the dozen.
Michel de Montaigne, Essais

God is the immemorial refuge of the incompetent, the
helpless, the miserable. They find not only sanctuary in His
arms, but also a kind of superiority, soothing to their
macerated egos; He will set them above their betters.
H.L. Mencken

An inordinate fondness for beetles.
*J.B.S. Haldane, when asked what inferences could be drawn about the
nature of God from a study of his works*

If God were suddenly condemned to live the life which He
has inflicted on men, He would kill Himself.
Alexandre Dumas fils, Pensées d'album

God made everything out of nothing. But the nothingness still
shows through.
Paul Valery

Forgive, O Lord, my little jokes on Thee
And I'll forgive Thy great big one on me.
Robert Frost

... a nice, arid, savage, pathetic, old chap.
  I.A. Richards on Robert Frost

[God] invented the giraffe, the elephant, and the cat. He has no real style, He just goes on trying other things.
  Pablo Picasso

Her conception of God was certainly not orthodox. She felt towards Him as she might have felt towards a glorified sanitary engineer; and in some of her speculations she seems hardly to distinguish between the Deity and the Drains.
  Lytton Strachey on Florence Nightingale

My dear child, you must believe in God in spite of what the clergy tell you.
  Benjamin Jowett, theologian and classicist, quoted in Margot Asquith's
  Autobiography

I asserted — and I repeat — that a man has no reason to be ashamed of having an ape for his grandfather. If there were an ancestor whom I should feel shame in recalling it would rather be a man — a man of restless and versatile intellect — who, not content with an equivocal success in his own sphere of activity, plunges into scientific questions with which he has no real acquaintance, only to obscure them by an aimless rhetoric, and distract the attention of his hearers from the real point at issue by eloquent digressions and skilled appeal to religious prejudice.
  T.H. Huxley, biologist, replying to Bishop Wilberforce in an Oxford debate
  on Darwin's theory of evolution

Operationally, God is beginning to resemble not a ruler but the last fading smile of a Cheshire Cat.
  Julian Huxley, biologist and first director-general of UNESCO, Religion
  without Revelation

... the sort of atheist who does not so much disbelieve God as personally dislike Him.
> *George Orwell,* Down and Out in Paris and London

I have no need of that hypothesis.
> *Pierre-Simon, Marquis de Laplace, on being asked by Napoleon why he had not mentioned God in his book on the universe*

A local cult called Christianity.
> *Thomas Hardy*

For a priest to turn a man when he lies a-dying, is just like one that has a long time solicited a woman, and cannot obtain his end; at length makes her drunk, and so lies with her.
> *John Selden*

Every day people are straying away from the church and going back to God. Really.
> *Lenny Bruce*

While I cannot be regarded as a pillar, I must be regarded as a buttress of the church, because I support it from the outside.
> *Lord Melbourne. Attrib.*

We must preserve the Church of England. It's our only defence against real religion.
> *British Elder Statesman, unknown*

It is hard to tell where MCC ends and the Church of England begins.
> *J.B. Priestley, in the* New Statesman

It is no accident that the symbol of a bishop is a crook and the sign of an archbishop is a double-cross.
Dom Gregory Dix

When the last trumpet shall sound, a commission will be set up on the significance of the trumpet, the financial implication of the trumpet, and for a report to come back in three years' time.
John Sentanu, Archbishop of York, on The Church of England

He had tried the knightly way and failed, ignominiously. In his misery he turned to religion, and there, in religion, discovered a new field for achieving the personal distinction for which his soul so ardently and incessantly longed. The world refused to recognize him as Assisi's greatest soldier. Very well. It should recognize him as Assisi's greatest man of God.
Aldous Huxley on St Francis of Assisi

All raw, uncooked and protesting.
Virginia Woolf on Aldous Huxley

The numerous vermin of mendicant friars, Franciscans, Dominicans, Augustins, Carmelites, who swarmed in this century [the 13th], with habits and institutions variously ridiculous, disgraced religion, learning, and common sense. They seized on scholastic philosophy as a science particularly suited to their minds; and, excepting only Friar Bacon, they all preferred words to things. The subtle, the profound, the irrefragable, the angelic, and the seraphic Doctor acquired those pompous titles by filling ponderous volumes with a small number of technical terms, and a much smaller number of ideas. Universities arose in every part of Europe, and thousands of students employed their lives upon these grave follies.
Edward Gibbon on medieval Christendom

Show me just what Muhammed brought that was new, and there you will find things only evil and inhuman ...

Pope Benedict XVI, quoting the Byzantine Emperor Manuel II Paleologus

With this I am at the end and I pronounce my judgement. I condemn Christianity. I raise against the Christian church the most terrible of all accusations that any accuser ever uttered. It is to me the highest of all conceivable corruptions. It has had the will to the last corruption that is even possible. The Christian church has left nothing untouchable by its corruption; it has turned ever value into a vileness of the soul. Let anyone dare to speak to me of its 'humanitarian' blessings! To abolish any distress ran counter to its deepest advantages: it lived on distress, it created distress to eternalize *itself*.

The worm of sin, for example: with this distress the church first enriched mankind. The 'equality of all souls before God', this falsehood, this pretext for the rancour of all the base-minded, this explosive of a concept which eventually became a revolution, modern idea, and the principle of decline of the whole order of society – is Christian dynamite. 'Humanitarian' blessings of Christianity! To breed out of *humanitas* a self-contra-diction, an art of self-violation, a will to lie at any price, a repugnance, a contempt for all good and honest instincts! Those are some of the blessings of Christianity!

Parasitism is the *only* practice of the church; with its ideal of anaemia, its 'holiness', draining all blood, all love, all hope for life; the beyond as the will to negate every reality; the cross as the mark of recognition for the most subter-ranean conspiracy that ever existed – against health, beauty, whatever has turned out well, courage, spirit, graciousness of the soul, against life itself.

This eternal indictment of Christianity I will write on all walls, wherever there are walls – I have letters to make even the blind see. I call Christianity the one great curse, the one great innermost corruption, the one great instinct of revenge, for which no means is poisonous, stealthy, subterranean, small enough – I call it the one immortal blemish of mankind.

Friedrich Nietzsche, The Antichrist

If we take in our hand any volume; of divinity or school metaphysics, for instance; let us ask, Does it contain any experimental reasoning, concerning matter of fact and existence? No. Commit it then to the flames; for it can contain nothing but sophistry and illusion.

David Hume, An Enquiry Concerning Human Understanding, *1748*

I have to believe in the Apostolic Succession. There is no other way of explaining the descent of the Bishop of Exeter from Judas Iscariot.

Sydney Smith

Frankly I'm amazed it survived the invention of the tambourine.

Jack Dee on Christianity

The Christian religion not only was at first attended with miracles, but even at this day cannot be believed by any reasonable person without one.

David Hume, Essays, 'Of Miracles'

I am a Catholic. As far as possible I go to Mass every day. As far as possible I kneel down and tell these beads every day. If you reject me on account of my religion, I shall thank God that he has spared me the indignity of being your representative.

Hilaire Belloc, MP for Salford (1906-10), in his first election campaign

Hearing nuns' confessions is like being pecked to death by ducks.
Catholic chaplain quoted by Chris Patten

Bad weather is God's way of telling us to burn more
Catholics.
Rowan Atkinson, Blackadder

We know these new English Catholics. They are the last word
in Protest. They are Protestants protesting against
Protestantism.
D.H. Lawrence, letter to Lady Cynthia Asquith

I don't feel the attraction of the Kennedys at all ... I don't
think they are Christians; they may be Catholics but they are
not Christians.
Mary McCarthy

A single friar who goes counter to all Christianity for a
thousand years must be wrong.
Charles V, Holy Roman Emperor, on Martin Luther, at the Diet of Worms

A Lutheran's foot has six toes.
Polish insult

Puritanism – the haunting fear that someone, somewhere,
may be happy.
H.L. Mencken

Mencken, with his filthy verbal haemorrhages, is so low down
in the moral scale, so damnable dirty, so vile and degenerate,
that when his time comes to die it will take a special dispensa-
tion from Heaven to get him into the bottommost pit of Hell.
Letter to H.L. Mencken, in the Jackson News

Faith may be defined briefly as an illogical belief in the occurrence of the improbable.
H.L. Mencken

Mr Mencken did not degenerate from an ape, but an ass. And in the process of 'evolution' the tail was eliminated, the ears became shorter, and the hind parts smaller; but the ability to bray was increased, intensified, amplified, and otherwise assified about one million times.
J.D. Tedder on H.L. Mencken

The chief contribution of Protestantism to human thought is its massive proof that God is a bore.
H.L. Mencken

The Puritan hated bear-baiting, not because it gave pain to the bear, but because it gave pleasure to the spectators.
Thomas Babington Macaulay, History of England

Sir, the pretending of extraordinary revelations and gifts of the Holy Ghost is an horrid thing, a very horrid thing.
Bishop Joseph Butler to one of the Wesleys, quoted in Wesley, Works, *XIII*

No visit to Dove Cottage, Grasmere, is complete without examining the outhouse where Hazlitt's father, a Unitarian minister of strong liberal views, attempted to put his hand up Dorothy Wordsworth's skirt.
Alan Coren

He boils his eggs in widow's tears.
Bishop Montgomery Campbell, Bishop of London on the Archbishop of Canterbury, Geoffrey Fisher

Tell my clergy when I've gone to weep no tears —
I'll be no deader than they have been for years.
Bishop Henry Montgomery Campbell

I've heard of the milk of human kindness but I've never met
the cow before.
Bishop Henry Montgomery Campbell, after staying the night at a vicarage

I'm taking steps to have the Thames widened.
Bishop Montgomery Campbell on the news of Mervin Stockwood's
appointment as Bishop of Southwark, over the river

A base impudent brazen-faced villain, a spiteful ignorant pedant,
a gross idolater, a great liar, a mere slanderer, an evil man,
hardened against all shame [while his book is] full of insolence
and abuse, chicanery and nonsense, detestable, misty, erroneous,
wicked, vile, pernicious, terrible, and horrid doctrines, tending
to corrupt the mind and stupefy the conscience, with gross
iniquity, audacious hostility, pitiful evasion, base, palpable,
shocking, and solemn deceit, clouds of gross, abominable, and
absolute falsehoods, foul, artful, base, with wicked and horrid
reproaches, malicious invectives, low quibbles, unmeaning puffs,
unbounded rancour, scurrilous, gross, and virulent abuse,
monstrous, stupid, and intolerable absurdity, poor and palpable
sophistry, idiotical construction, blasphemous comparisons,
foppish insolence, senseless jargon, the style of a bully, rude
imputations, profane banter and burlesque, perfect downright
barefaced and impudent forgery, abusive rage, base dealing,
violent and shameful opposition, high and poetical rant, solemn
juggling with God and man, chimerical notions, virulent
invective, mock sorrow, nauseous repetition, horrid extrava-
gance, treacherous disingenuity, scurrilous reason, base

intendment, injurious dealing, [and finally] dreadful language.

The Reverend Adam Gibb, anti-Burgher leader, ed. Tertius Gaudens, reviewing a pamphlet by the Burgher minister, the Revd Archibald Hill, 1782. Quoted in Scottish Pageant 1707-1802, *ed. Agnes Mure Mackenzie*

No kingdom has ever had as many civil wars as the kingdom of Christ.

Baron de Montesquieu, Lettres persanes

No one ever made more trouble than 'Gentle Jesus, meek and mild.'

James M. Gillis

HECKLER: Christianity has been on the earth for 2,000 years, and look at the state of the world today.
DONALD SOPER: Water has been on the earth longer than that, and look at the colour of your neck.

Next time someone offers a penny for your thoughts – sell.

Peter Kay putdown to heckler

It was just one of those parties which got out of hand.

Lenny Bruce on the Crucifixion

If Jesus Christ were to come today, people would not even crucify him. They would ask him to dinner, and hear what he had to say, and make fun of it.

Thomas Carlyle

Things have come to a pretty pass when religion is allowed to invade the sphere of private life.

Lord Melbourne. Attrib.

Damn it all, another bishop dead. I verily believe they die to vex me.

Lord Melbourne. Attrib.

There can hardly be a town in the South of England where you could throw a brick without hitting the niece of a bishop.

George Orwell, The Road to Wigan Pier

CLERGYMAN: How did you like my sermon, Mr Canning?
GEORGE CANNING: You were brief.
CLERGYMAN: Yes, you know I avoid being tedious.
CANNING: But you were tedious.

Yes, about ten minutes.

Duke of Wellington, asked by a vicar whether there was anything he would like his sermon to be about

A clergyman had nothing to do but to be slovenly and selfish – read the newspaper, watch the weather, and quarrel with his wife. His curate does all the work and the business of his own life is to dine.

Jane Austen, Mansfield Park

Parson, I have, during my life, detested many men; but never anyone so much as you ... Priests have, in all ages, been remarkable for cool and deliberate and unrelenting cruelty; but it seems to be reserved for the Church of England to produce one who has a just claim to the atrocious pre-eminence. No assemblage of words can give an appropriate designation of you; and therefore, as being the single word which best suits the character of such a man, I call you Parson...

William Cobbett to Thomas Malthus

A crafty and lecherous old hypocrite whose very statue seems to gloat on the wenches as they walk the States House yard.
William Cobbett on Benjamin Franklin

When the white man came we had the land and they had the Bibles; now they have the land and we have the Bibles.
Dan George, Canadian Indian Chief, who acted in a number of films, including Little Big Man

Whenever we read the obscene stories, the voluptuous debaucheries, the cruel and torturous executions, the unrelenting vindictiveness, with which more than half the Bible is filled, it would be more consistent that we called it the word of a demon than the Word of God. It is a history of wickedness, that has served to corrupt and brutalize mankind; and for my own part, I sincerely detest it, as I detest everything that is cruel … As to the Christian system of faith, it appears to me as a species of atheism – a sort of religious denial of God. It professes to believe in a man rather than in God. It is as near to atheism as twilight is to darkness. It introduces between man and his Maker an opaque body, which it calls a Redeemer, as the moon introduces her opaque self between the earth and the sun, and it produces by this means a religious or irreligious eclipse of the light. It has put the whole orbit of reason into shade.
Tom Paine, The Age of Reason

That revolting odious Jew production, called Bible, has been for ages the idol of all sorts of blockheads, the glory of knaves, and the disgust of wise men. It is a history of lust, sodomies, wholesale slaughtering, and horrible depravity, that the vilest parts of all other histories, collected into one book, could not parallel. Priests tell us that this concentration of abominations was written by a god; all the world believe priests, or they would rather have thought it the outpourings of some devil.

Charles Southwell in the Oracle of Reason, *an openly atheistic weekly newspaper, 1841. Southwell was fined £100 and imprisoned for a year*

Jesus was a crackpot.

Bhagwan Shree Rajneesh

A parish demagogue.

Percy Bysshe Shelley on Jesus

It is so stupid of modern civilization to have given up believing in the devil when he is the only explanation of it.

Ronald Knox, Catholic priest and writer, Let Dons Delight

A liar and a father of lies.

Dante on the Devil, Inferno, XXIII

Even in the valley of the shadow of death, two and two do not make six.

Leo Tolstoy on his deathbed, refusing to reconcile himself with the Russian Orthodox Church

There is no fate that cannot be surmounted by scorn.

Albert Camus

Imanis metula es. [You're a big prick.]

Pompeii graffiti

Your arsehole is filled with blue mud.

South-east Salish (North American Indian) insult

Commictae spurca saliva lupae
[The foul saliva of a pissed-over whore.]

Catullus, XCIX,10, tr. Amy Richlin

Your blistered crotch!
Insult from the Marquesas Islands

Lahis felat a.II. [Lahis gives blow jobs for $2.]
Pompeii graffiti

Your mouth and your arsehole smell the same, Theodorus.

So much so that it would be a good trick for doctors to tell them apart.

You should certainly have made a sign saying which was your mouth, which your arsehole.

Just now when you were gabbing, I thought you'd farted.
Nicharchus, from the Greek

Cosmus Equitiaes magnus cinaedus et fellator est suris apertis.
[Equitias' slave Cosmus is a big queer and a cocksucker with his legs wide open.]
Pompeii graffiti

I thought (so help me Gods!) it made no difference
Whether I smelt Aemilius' mouth or arsehole,
One being no cleaner, the other no filthier.
But in fact the arsehole's cleaner and kinder.
It has no teeth. The mouth has teeth half a yard long
And gums like an ancient wagon-chassis.
Moreover, when it opens up it's like the cunt
Of a pissing mule gaping in a heat wave.
Catullus, XCVII, tr. Guy Lee

Zoile, quid solium subluto podice perdis? Spurcius ut fiat, Zoile,
merge caput. [Zoilus, if you want to pollute the public bathing
place, Don't stick in your arse first, stick in your face.]
Martial, II.42, tr. Richard O'Connell

Vibennius and son – believed
The public baths' best pair of thieves.
(Father's filthy hands go roving
Through some hapless bather's clothing
Whilst, elsewhere, the son has got 'em
Wedged up his voracious bottom.)
Why don't you both just go to hell!
For Father's crimes are known too well,
And few among the punters crave
A boy whose buttocks need a shave.
Catullus, XXXIII, tr. Simon Christmas

If you were as narrow-arsed as you are narrow-minded, or
broad-minded as your anus is broad, you would be the most
perfect of people walking the earth.
Di'bil, from the Arabic

Sabina felas, no belle faces.
[Sabina, you give blow-jobs, you don't do good.]
*Pompeii graffiti. The original Latin, as in many of these examples from
Pompeii, is misspelt. Amy Richlin has suggested this freestyle translation*

I am the Roman Emperor, and am above grammar.
Sigismund, when his Latin was criticized

You assumed the '*toga virilis*', which you at once turned into a
woman's toga. First you were a public whore, and the price
of your shame was fixed, nor was it small; but soon Curio
intervened, who led you away from the prostitution business
and, as if he had given you a bridal gown, established you in a
steady and fixed marriage. No boy bought for the sake of lust
was ever so much in the power of his master as you were in
Curio's. How many times his father threw you out of his own

house, how many times he posted guards to keep you from crossing the threshold! But you, with night as your ally, your lust urging you on, and your payment compelling you, were let down through the roof-tiles. These shames that house could bear no longer. Don't you know I'm talking about things well known to me? Recall that time, when Curio the father was grieving, lying in bed, and his son flinging himself at my feet weeping entrusted you to me ... He himself, moreover, burning with love, affirmed that he could not bear the longing caused by your separation and would go into exile ... But now let us pass over your sex crimes and shameful acts; there are certain things which I cannot pronounce with decency; you, however, are that much freer, since you have allowed things to your discredit which you could not hear named by an enemy who had any sense of shame.

Cicero on Anthony, Philippics, II.44-7, tr. Amy Richlin

Your stinking foreskin filth.
Polynesian insult

Their teeth, because of their foul food, are like the nails of a female circumciser whose knives are too blunt.
Hassan Ibn Thabit, a contemporary of Muhammad, on the Hawazin

A waste of skin.
Lancashire expression

When you rise up from a chair, Lesbia,
(I've seen it happen frequently)
You get butt-fucked by your skirt.
The damned thing catches in the narrow crack
Between those massive buns of yours,
Those ship-crunching pillars of Hercules.

You pull with your left hand, you pull with your right,
Wincing and grunting till it comes loose.
An unladylike *faux pas*, to say the least.
Want a tip on etiquette, Lesbia?
Don't get up, and don't sit down.
  Martial, XI.99, tr. Joseph Salemi

He waddles like an Armenian bride.
  Osmanli insult

As flash as a rat with a gold tooth.
  Australian expression

Villainous and loathsome screamer! Your audacity
fills the whole earth, the whole Assembly,
all taxes, all indictments, all law-courts,
you mud-churner, you who have thrown
our whole city into chaos and confusion,
you who have defeated our Athens with your shouting,
watching like the tunny-fishers from the rocks above for
shoals of tribute.
  Aristophanes on the Athenian general Cleon, The Knights. *The words are*
  spoken by the chorus. Tr. Alan H. Sommerstein

The language of Aristophanes reeks of his miserable quackery:
it is made up of the lowest and most miserable puns; he
doesn't even please the people, and to men of judgement and
honour he is intolerable; his arrogance is insufferable, and all
honest men detest his malice.
  Plutarch on Aristophanes

Plato is a bore.
  Friedrich Nietzsche

You're happy to get fucked, Saufeia,
But not to share a bath with me.
That something's very wrong is clear;
But not so clear what it might be.
Perhaps you know that from your chest
There hangs a pair of scraggy tits,
Or worry that, when you're undressed,
You've stretch marks round your nether bits.
Perhaps your groin is torn and mangled,
Gaping wide from back to front.
Perhaps an unknown something dangles
Tongue-like from your fleshy cunt.
But not at all, quite the reverse –
There's nothing wrong with what you've got.
The truth is that your fault is worse.
The truth is: you're an idiot.
  Martial, III.72, tr. Simon Christmas

The more I read him, the less I wonder that they poisoned him.
  Thomas Babington Macaulay on Socrates

A crawling and disgusting parasite, a base scoundrel, and pander to unnatural passions.
  William Cobbett on Virgil

Every man with a belly full of the classics is an enemy of the human race.
  Henry Miller

A gentleman need not know Latin, but he should at least have forgotten it.
  Brander Matthews. Attrib.

The classics are only primitive literature. They belong in the same class as primitive machinery and primitive music and primitive medicine.

Stephen Leacock, Homer and Humbug

His heart shall not be content in life, he shall receive no water in the necropolis and his soul shall be destroyed for eternity.

Egyptian curse, inscription aimed at 'anyone who desecrates the tomb-chapel'

May you get fucked by a donkey! May your wife get fucked by a donkey! May your child fuck your wife!

Egyptian legal curse, c. 950 BC

After this opened Job his mouth, and cursed his day. And Job spake, and said, Let the day perish wherein I was born, and the night in which it was said, There is a man child conceived. Let that day be darkness; let not God regard it from above, neither let the light shine upon it; ... let the blackness of the day terrify it. As for that night, let darkness seize upon it; let it not be joined unto the days of the year, let it not come into the number of months. Lo, let that night be solitary, let no joyful voice come therein. Let them curse it that curse the day, who are ready to raise up their mourning. Let the stars of the twilight thereof be dark; let it look for light, but have none; neither let it see the dawning of the day: Because it shut not up the doors of my mother's womb, nor hid sorrow from mine eyes. Why died I not from the womb? Why did I not give up the ghost when I came out of the belly? Why did the knees prevent me? Or why the breasts that I should suck? ... Wherefore is light given to him that is in misery, and life unto the bitter in soul; Which long for death, but it cometh

not; and dig for it more than for hid treasures; Which rejoice
exceedingly, and are glad, when they can find the grave?
   Job cursing the day he was born, Job 3: 1-22

Cursed shalt thou be in the city, and cursed shalt thou be in
field. Cursed shall be thy basket and thy store. Cursed shall
be the fruit of thy body, and the fruit of thy land, the increase
of thy kine, and the flocks of thy sheep. Cursed shalt thou be
when thou comest in, and cursed shalt thou be when thou
goest out...
   Moses' curse in Deuteronomy 28: 16-19

May the earth refuse thee her fruits and the river his waters,
may wind and breeze deny their breath. May the sun not be
warm for thee, nor Phoebe bright, may the clear stars fail thy
vision. May neither Vulcan nor the air lend thee their aid, nor
earth nor sea afford thee any path. Mayst thou wander an
exile and destitute, and haunt the doors of others, and beg a
little food with trembling mouth. May neither thy body nor
thy sick mind be free from querulous pain, may night be to
thee more grievous than day, and day than night. Mayst thou
ever be piteous, but have none to pity thee; may men and
women rejoice at thy adversity. May hatred crown thy tears,
and mayst thou be thought worthy, having borne many ills, to
bear yet more. And (what is rare) may the aspect of thy
fortune, though its wonted favour be lost, bring thee but ill-
will. Mayst thou have cause enough for death, but no means
of dying; may thy life be compelled to shun the death it prays
for. May thy spirit struggle long ere it leave thy tortured
limbs, and rack thee first with long delaying.
   Ovid, Ibis, *tr. J.H. Mozley*

But the Jews will not be pleased with thee, neither the Christians, until thou follow their religion; say, The Direction of God is the true direction. And verily if thou follow their desires, after the knowledge which hath been given thee, thou shalt find no patron or protector against God. They to whom we have given the book of the Koran, and who read it with its true reading, they believe therein; and whoever believeth not therein, they shall perish.

Koran, *II*

O pour out thy wrath upon the heathen who know thee not, and upon the kingdoms who invoke not thy name; for they have devoured Jacob and laid waste his beautiful dwelling. Pour out thy indignation upon them and cause thy fierce anger to overtake them. Pursue them in wrath and destroy them from under the heavens of the Lord.

Judaic curse ritually invoked at the Passover between the third and fourth cups of wine. The door to the outside must be opened for its pronouncement. Leo Abse, who referred the editor of this book to this curse, said he had been told that, at times of danger, isolation and persecution, the pronouncement of this curse upon their persecutors was a source of great comfort to Jews assembled for the Passover

The Lord strike him with madness and blindness. May the heavens empty upon him thunderbolts and the wrath of the Omnipotent burn itself unto him in the present and future world. May the Universe light against him and the earth open to swallow him up.

Pope Clement on a now-forgotten subject

May you croak in the faith of the Poles!

Ukrainian, regarded as an outrageous curse

May the fleas of a thousand camels infest your armpits.
Arab curse

Cursed by your mother's anus. Cursed by your father's testicles.
Yoruba verbal duelling, quoted by Chief Oludare Olajuba, References to
Sex in Yoruba Oral Literature

Careful: my knife drills your soul
listen, [name victim]
One of the wolf people
listen I'll grind your saliva into the earth
listen I'll cover your bones with black flint
listen I'll cover your bones with black feathers
listen I'll cover your bones with black rocks
Because you're going where it's empty
Black coffin out on the hill
listen the black earth will hide you, will
find you a black hut
Out where it's dark, in that country
listen I'm bringing a box for your bones
A black box
A grave with black pebbles
listen your soul's spilling out
listen it's blue.
*Cherokee Indian chant designed to bring about the death of a victim,
adapted by Jerome Rothenberg,* Sacred Formulas of the Cherokees

May you dig up your Father by moonlight and make soup of
his bones.
Fiji Islands curse

Go in your Mother's cunt.
Serbian insult

Go to holy shit!
Cuban insult

I shit on the balls of your dead ones.
Spanish gypsy insult

Go to the prick's house!
Cuban insult

Copulate with my Father who is dead!
Admiralty Islands' most unpardonable insult

I shit in your Mother's milk.
Spanish insult

Copulate with your wife.
Trobriand Islands' most unpardonable insult

I hope that your piles hang like a bunch of grapes.
Greek insult directed at homosexuals

I shit on your Father's nose.
Farsi (Iranian) insult

I shit on God, on the cross, and on the carpenter who made it (and on the son of the whore who planted the pine)!
Catalan insult

May shit be on your hair.
Farsi (Iranian) insult for women

I shit on the cock of Passion!
Catalan insult

May a fart be on your beard.
Farsi (Iranian) insult for men

Christ is a bastard ... Christ is a whoremaster ... God damn and confound all Gods.
John Taylor, fined and imprisoned for blasphemy in the 18th Century

May the devil damn you to the stone of dirges, or to the well of ashes seven miles below hell; and may the devil break your bones! And all my calamity and harm and misfortune for a year on you!
Curse from the Cois Fharraige, west of Galway City, in Connemara

I will tear your crotch apart.
Farsi (Iranian) insult between women

I'll stick a pig's leg up your cunt until your back-teeth rattle.
Japanese insult

A donkey's head in your cunt.
Farsi (Iranian) insult used by a woman to call another stupid

Your Grandmother on roller-skates.
Central American curse

Your Grandmother skating around the sink.
Central American curse

Your Grandmother in trousers.
Central American curse

Woe unto bloody Lichfield!
George Fox, founder of the Quakers

May hound-wounding, heart-ache, and vultures gouging her
eyes,
Derangement and madness on her mind come soon!
May the entrails and mansion of pleasure out of this worm
fall out!
But may she still be alive till everyone's sick of the sight!
Peadar Ó Doirnín, An Guairne

A plague o' both your houses!
William Shakespeare, Romeo and Juliet

You common cry of curs! whose breath I hate
As reek o' the rotten fens, whose loves I prize
As the dead carcases of unburied men
That do corrupt my air, I banish you;
And here remain with your uncertainty!
Let every feeble rumour shake your hearts!
Your enemies, with nodding of their plumes,
Fan you into despair! Have the power still
To banish your defenders; till at length
Your ignorance – which finds not till it feels,
Making but reservation of yourselves,
Still your own foes – deliver you as most
Abated captives to some nation
That won you without blows!
William Shakespeare, Coriolanus's farewell to his fellow-citizens

Thou cursed cock, with thy perpetual noise,
May'st thou be capon made, and lose thy voice,
Or on a dunghill may'st thou spend thy blood,
And vermin prey upon thy craven brood;
May rivals tread thy hens before thy face
Then with redoubled courage give thee chase;

May'st thou be punished for St Peter's crime,
And on Shrove Tuesday perish in thy prime;
May thy bruised carcass be some beggar's feast —
Thou first and worst disturber of man's rest.
    Sir Charles Sedley, On a cock at Rochester

May you be cursed with chronic anxiety about the weather.
    John Burroughs
you are the dumbest thing
on the earth the slimiest
most rotten thing in the universe
you motherfuckin germ
you konk-haired blood suckin punks
you serpents of pestilence you
samboes you green witches gnawing the heads of infants
you rodents you whores you sodomites you fat
slimy cockroaches crawling to your holes
with bits of malcolm's flesh
i hope you are smothered
in the fall of a huge yellow moon.
    Welton Smith on black people who failed to support Malcolm X, The
    Nigga Section

I charm thy life
From the weapons of strife,
From stone and from wood,
From fire and from flood,
From the serpent's tooth,
And the beasts of blood:
From Sickness I charm thee,
And Time shall not harm thee;
But Earth which is mine,
Its fruits shall deny thee;

And Water shall hear me, And know thee and fly thee;
And the Winds shall not touch thee
When they pass by thee,
And the Dews shall not wet thee,
When they fall nigh thee:
And thou shalt seek Death
To release thee, in vain;
Thou shalt live in thy pain
While Kehama shall reign,
With a fire in thy heart,
And a fire in thy brain;
And Sleep shall obey me,
And visit thee never,
And the Curse shall be on thee
For ever and ever.
    Robert Southey, The Curse of Kehama

May you wander over the face of the earth forever, never
sleep twice in the same bed, never drink water twice from
the same well, and never cross the same river twice in a year.
    Gypsy curse

Saddam, oh Saddam
Thou flesh-knotter you
Claim not to be Muslim
For you are truly a Jew
Your deeds have proved ugly
Your face is darkest black
And we will set fire
To your bottom and your back
    Poem on Saddam Hussein, broadcast on Saudi television during the Gulf
    War

Son of a Scots manse though you were
I've take the rare scunner against you,
You who thieve the golden hours of bairns,
You who bitch up the world's peoples
With crystal images, pitch-black lies,
You who have ended civilized conversation
And dished out licenses to print banknotes,
May your soul shrink to the size of a midge
And never rest in a couthie kirkyard
But dart across a million wee screens
And be harassed by TV jingles for ever and ever,
For thine's the kingdom of the televisor,
You goddam bloody genius, John Logie Baird!
Robert Greacen, Curse

Fuck you.
*Ed Koch, in response to a reporter's allegations of war criminality. And
countless others*

I hope you will pray too that the Lord will smite him hip and
thigh, bone and marrow, heart and lungs and all there is to
him; that he shall destroy him quickly and utterly.
*Bob Jones III, a Christian fundamentalist, on Alexander Haig, after the
latter refused Ian Paisley a visa to visit the USA*

For him that stealeth a Book from this Library, let it change into a serpent in his hand and rend him. Let him be struck with Palsy, and all his Members blasted. Let him languish in Pain crying aloud for Mercy and let there be no sur-cease to his Agony till he sink in Dissolution. Let Bookworms gnaw his Entrails in token of the Worm that dieth not, and when at last he goeth to his final Punishment, let the flames of Hell consume him for ever and aye.

Curse Against Book Stealers, Monastery of San Pedro, Barcelona. Tr.

Fuck off, Norway.

Paul Gascoigne, when asked by live Norwegian television if he had a message for the Norwegian people before the England-Norway World Cup qualifier

Die, may he; Tiger, catch him, snake bite him; Steep hill, fall down on him; Wild boar, bite him.

Curse of Todas tribe in southern India

I fart in your general direction.

Monty Python and the Holy Grail

Now I can finally say what a diplomat normally cannot to those he comes into contact with: I hope you encounter every curse imaginable!

Koji Haneda, First Secretary, Embassy of Japan (London), closing a letter to the Editor of this book

INDEX

INDEX

INDEX

INDEX

INDEX

INDEX

Mirabeau, Honorë Gabriel
Riquetti, Comte de 211
Mirror, Daily 186
Mitchell, Austin 156
Mitford, Mary Russell 235
Mitford, Nancy 10, 61, 236
Mitterand, Francois 169
Muhammed 338, 345
Mole Valley District Council
288
Moliére (John-Baptiste
Poquelin) 323
Molotov, Vyacheslav 123
Monroe, Marilyn 294, 295
Montagu, Lady Mary
Wortley 265,
Montaigne, Michel de 25,
27, 323, 341
Montesquieu, Charles de
Secondat, Baron de 340,
350
Montgomery, Bernard Law,
Viscount 24, 214
Montgomery, Robert 268
Montherlant, Henri de 337
Monty Python 369
Mooney, Paul 69
Moore, George 233, 318
Moore, John 175
Moore, Suzanne 19, 20
Moore, Thomas 148
Moravia, Alberto 256
More, Sir Thomas 83
Morgan, Elaine 22
Morgan, Piers 226, 306
Morley, Sheridan 291
Morris, Desmond 44
Morris, William 238
Mortimer, John 322, 330
Moses 360
Mountbatten, Louis, Earl 60,
217
Mozart, Wolfgang Amadeus
338
Mugabe, Robert 176
Muggeridge, Kitty 309

Muggeridge, Malcolm 85,
127, 164, 165, 336
Muggins, Peter 196
Muldoon, Robert 93
Murdoch, Rupert 227-228,
337
Murphy, Maureen 190
Murry, J. Middleton 245
Music World, The 280
Mussolini, Benito 110, 252

Nabokov, Vladimir 237, 239,
324
Nadzo, Guido 302
National Lampoon 87
Napoleon Bonaparte 3, 73,
74, 88, 214, 343
Nash, Ogden 10, 43, 98
Nashe, Thomas 231
Nastase, Ilie 325
Nathan, George Jean 253,
254, 314
Nation, Carry 15
Neagle, Anna 304
Needham, Richard 170
Neel, Alice 328
Neil, Andrew 230
Nelson, Horatio, Lord 88
Newman, Alfred E. 322
Newman, Ernest 310
Newman, Sydney 308
New Musical Express 293
New Statesman 297
Newton-John, Olivia 292
New York Herald 196
Nicharchus 354
Nicholas II, Tsar 157
Nicholls, Jill 11
Nicholson, Harold 55, 217
Nietzche, Fredrich
Women and Men 1, 3, 19, 25
The English 85
Germans 87
Government 108
Critics 254
Dante 262

Wagner 280
Religion 346
Plato 357
Nightingale, Benedict 305
Nightingale, Florence 22,
342
Niven, David 302
Nixon, Richard 93, 106,
201, 202, 221
Norbury, Lord 51
Norman, Matthew 34
Normanby, Lord 64
Norris, Steven 128, 174
North, Christopher 265
Northcliffe, Alfred
Harmsworth, Lord 217,
218, 321
Novak, Ralph 293,

Obama, Barack 94, 205, 206
Observer, The 246
O'Brien, Conor Cruise 124
O'Casey, Sean 271
O'Connell, Daniel 150, 151
O'Conner, Flannery 252
O'Doirín, Peadar 365
O'Faolain, Sean 84
O'Hara, Maureen 297
Olajuba, Oludare 362
Onassis, Aristotle 32, 167
Ono, Yoko 11, 293
O'Rourke, P. J. 97, 206, 322
Orton, Joe 13
Orwell, George
Kipling 15
England 90, 95
Politics 159, 189
Socialism 207
Writers 237, 272
Advertising 326
Religion 343, 351
Osborne, George 178
Osborne, John 13, 43, 214,
307, 319
Osmond, Cliff 293
Osmond, Hugh 328

INDEX

INDEX

INDEX

INDEX